ACCESSORY TO *Murder*

Written From A Prison Work Camp

ACCESSORY TO *Murder*

The Enemies, Allies, And Accomplices To The Death of Our Culture

Randall A. Terry

Library of Congress Cataloging-in-Publication Data

Terry, Randall A.
    Accessory to murder : the enemies, allies, and accomplices to the death of our culture / Randall A. Terry. — 1st ed.
        p. cm.
    ISBN 1-931600-80-5
    1. Abortion—United States. I. Title.
HQ767.5.U5T48 1990
363.4'6—dc20   90-39507
                                                                    CIP

To the Victims
of lies and tyranny

This reprint is sponsored in part by:
Miss Velia Menzi and Diana Ronald-Szabo,
Who share the following:

In memory of our precious mother, Enrica Menzi, two brothers, Eugene and Richard Menzi; their wives, Beatrice and Gida; our sister, Valda Ryan and her husband, Don; and Diana's husband, Steve Szabo.

We honor Randall Terry, a general in God's army, who has given so unselfishly of himself through much suffering in the cause of saving babies from the brutality of abortion, America's holocaust.

We pray for a spiritual and moral revolution. We have strayed far from God's moral teachings and we must work to get back on the road He prepared for us, which will give us true freedom of conscience.

J.H. Newman, the English Statesman, put it succinctly: "We Christians are cast into a certain mold. So far as we keep within it, we are not sensible that it is a mold or has an outline. It is when our hearts would overflow in some evil direction, then we discover that we are confined and consider ourselves in prison. It is the law in our members warring against the law of the spirit which brings us into a distressing bondage."

May America Return to God's moral Laws.

Miss Velia Menzi (96 years old)
Diana Ronald-Szabo (81 years old)

CONTENTS

AUTHOR'S NOTE

I t has been fifteen years since I wrote Accessory to Murder in a State Prison work camp (a modern-day chain gang) in Alpharetta, Georgia. Tragically, the belligerents of the "culture wars" I expose in this book are the same players that existed fifteen years ago.

The essence of this book is as critical today as it was in the 1990's — with this caveat; the wicked this book confronts are more corrupt, more vile, and more arrogant in their atrocities than they were a decade ago; and the media is more jaundiced with this exception: Talk radio and certain cable news outlets, as well as the Internet, have broken the stranglehold that the major networks and newspapers had on information and editorial slant. Thank God. The challenge before us is to now use all the means at our disposal to convey the Truth.

This I believe: Truth has within it the seeds of its own victory; lies have within them the seeds of their own destruction.

We must courageously herald the Truth, proclaim the Truth, and lionize the Truth while exposing the lies of those who hate Truth and Justice. In time, the Truth shall prevail — and we who have stood with the Truth will prevail against the dark forces of our times.

I believe the day will come — in my lifetime, when many of the villainous organizations and movements exposed in this book are lying on the ash heap of history, where their ideological predecessors (like Nazism and Communism) can welcome them with open arms.

Their defeat will not happen in a vacuum. It will come because the servants of Truth took the fight to the enemy, and prevailed.

So, my challenge to you is this: Know the Truth, and then expose and confront her enemies. The contest may be long and arduous, but victory will be ours.

ACKNOWLEDGMENTS

As stated on the cover, almost all of this book was written behind bars.

Timothy Duffy's research (and chasing of quotes I thought I heard . . . somewhere) was a veritable bedrock to this project. He miraculously deciphered my chicken scratch and loaded the manuscript into the computer; and his editorial changes were fabulous.

Bob Jewitt brought materials in, manuscripts out, and was a constant friend (as well as paralegal) to me throughout my imprisonment.

Jay Sekulow, Esq., Rev. Larry Baker, Rev. Buddy Roberts, Rev. Howard Creecy, Rev. Bob Dawkins, Rev. Bob Lake, and Michael Hirsh (soon to be esquire), all visited me several times. Your welcomed faces brought much needed fellowship and brightness during dark hours.

The entire staff of Operation Rescue (who are among my dearest friends) have hung tough through incredibly difficult ordeals. Their sacrifices over the past two years, often known only to God, fill my heart with deep respect and gratitude to God.

Many kind people (too many to be named!) have given their good ideas and criticisms to this book. You know who you are! Thank You!

And many, many precious saints around the country have stood with me in ways too countless to be recalled but all of which have helped us beyond measure.

At the time of this printing, scores of godly, courageous men and women are behind bars all over America for daring to try to stop the murder of innocent babies. You are in our prayers.

God save this country.

PART ONE

THE ANGER

1

A LETTER FROM JAIL

D ear Beloved,
  Greetings in the name of Jesus from the Parker Center Jail in Los Angeles, California.

It is now Monday, March 27, 1989, 1:30 P.M. I am presently being held behind bars, sharing a cell with three other pro-lifers. This has been a most challenging, exciting, and at times fearful week.

I knew we were in for a battle when, upon our arrival in Los Angeles, the Ramada Inn canceled the room reservations for all Operation Rescue participants. However, due to the hard work and quick efforts of our local staffers, we were able to secure alternative facilities immediately. Thank God.

On Wednesday afternoon, we held our first press conference. The room was filled with numerous radio, newspaper, and television media. I approached the microphones with seven or eight cameras rolling and said, "I appreciate your coming today. This story is not about Randall Terry nor is it about Operation Rescue. It is about little children brutally murdered. I believe many of you want to report this story with integrity. All I ask is that you show the American public the truth and let them decide how they feel." At that point Gary Leber brought up Baby Choice in a white coffin and, placing her on a table to my left, opened the lid. I continued, "This is Baby Choice. She was murdered by a salt solution at nineteen weeks. She will answer all your questions." The rest of the staff and I then walked out of the room.

The media's reaction was not what I expected. As I proceeded into the parking lot, they ran after me, yelling questions, demanding answers, and accusing us of staging a media stunt. Many were enraged. Just before I reached the van, one reporter screamed, "Why won't you answer our questions?" "My question is," I responded, stopping dead in my tracks, "will you show the American public this murdered baby girl?"

The media then returned to the conference room, and they did photograph and film Baby Choice. To my knowledge, however, no television station or newspaper had the integrity to show these pictures of truth to the American people. This reaffirmed my belief that the print and picture media are the greatest perpetrators of the holocaust. They are willfully deceiving the American people. They showed our men being killed in Vietnam; they show bloodied accident victims and murdered born victims; but they refuse to show murdered unborn children.

Holy Week Persecution

That week, I experienced the most hostile and vicious criticism of my entire life. One local television station ran two nights of venom-filled editorials railing against me personally. During the next three days of rescues, I refused to talk with any media except to say, "Stop hiding the truth from the American public. Show the murdered baby boys and girls." We understand that two television stations did show footage of our pictures of murdered babies. For this we are grateful, but there remains much more to be shown.

Wednesday. On Wednesday night, March 22, our first rally was attended by over seventeen hundred people. For many of those present, this was their first exposure to the Rescue Movement. About four hundred and fifty of these committed to rescue the following morning.

Thursday. As we gathered at a local church early Thursday, we were greeted by the proaborts. These death activists proceeded to block off both ends of the street and thus prohibited us from departing for the abortion mill. When the police warned them that if they failed to move their cars they would be subject to arrest and their cars would be towed, they backed down and removed their vehicles. (Had they not, we were ready to move them ourselves with over forty husky volunteers.)

We then traveled to one of the most notorious abortion mills in the country—owned by one of the most notorious murderers[1] in the country, Edwin Allred. This death merchant operates over thirty abortion mills, has murdered thousands of children, and reportedly has killed three mothers in the process. We were determined to rescue there.

We were able to block access to the doors for several hours. Our sidewalk counselors turned away at least two women. By noon, however, the authorities had removed all our people. Thirty children a day are scheduled to be killed at this mill. We had hoped to stop all killings here today; but tragically, nine mothers were determined to have their children murdered and did enter the mill. We thank God for the children who were rescued and the mothers who were spared exploitation. We mourn for those children who died.

At this rescue site in Cypress, the police acted professionally. Our people were issued a citation and released Thursday afternoon. That evening, over eight hundred people attended the rally. Of these, six hundred affirmed that they were willing to risk arrest to rescue children the following day.

Good Friday. On Good Friday in Long Beach, these six hundred were joined by two hundred and fifty screaming proaborts. We were still able to close the mill for the entire day without any arrests. The proaborts told bold-faced lies (as usual), stating that this wasn't an abortion facility and that no abortions were scheduled. Then a pro-abortion activist attorney tried to force the police to open a path through the rescuers by claiming that he had two women who wished to enter the mill for abortions. Unfortunately, the media continued to parrot the pro-abortion rhetoric. Despite the proabort deception, one woman who was scheduled to have her child killed did change her mind and chose life for her baby.

Friday's rally was attended by over two thousand people. We held a memorial service for "Baby Choice." This was one of the most moving services we've ever held. Each individual was asked to come forward to view her body, and all were touched by the reality that we were responsible for her murder.

Following the service, as I began to preach, three proaborts in the back of the church ignited a smoke grenade. Fortunately, our people didn't panic; and a courageous pastor grabbed the grenade and rushed outside. A few pro-lifers then chased the three proaborts. They were able to apprehend them and hold them until the police arrived to make the arrests. Fortunately, the grenade had not emitted enough smoke to force an evacuation of the building; and the rally continued with over eight hundred committing to rescue the next day.

Saturday. Saturday's rescue was the most intense rescue I have ever participated in. There were nearly four hundred proaborts intermingled with the rescuers. They screamed, yelled, chanted, and howled each time we led in song or issued instructions. A few members of the Communist Revolutionary Party were pushing or shoving rescuers. The hatred (perhaps born of desperation?) on the faces and in the words of the proaborts startled many rescuers.

The police arrived slowly over a two-hour period. Eventually, there were two dozen mounted police and over two hundred uniformed officers on the scene. All were wearing riot gear. The warning of imminent arrest cleared the area of all proaborts.

I was shocked at what occurred next. An officer on the scene ordered his men to employ indiscriminate pain compliance on all rescuers regardless of sex or age. Our women and elderly had their arms twisted, their fingers bent, their backs stepped upon. The police literally stopped at nothing in their efforts to force the rescuers to walk.

One woman's arm was broken. Another man blacked out from the pain and was removed from the scene in an ambulance. Many had fingers shoved up their nostrils as policemen lifted them up by their noses. Others had knuckles pressed into their eye sockets. I've never seen anything like it.

The police waded through the crowd almost immediately, dragging me out and dropping me on my face in the street. I have neither prayed so fervently nor felt so much pain in a long time. These sentiments were echoed by hundreds of others who also suffered at the hands of this unprofessional police force.

One elderly woman in her sixties was among the first arrested. The police twisted her arms and employed many other pain compliances upon her, but she refused to move. Her spirit prevailed. She would not walk. As the rescuers watched her courage in the face of the brutality, more were determined not to walk away from the murder scene. As the policemen looked on, many were moved to tears.

The police then carried me to the bus where I sat and waited, separated from the other rescuers. It was here that I had the most heart-wrenching experience I have had in many years. As I sat, I heard a fellow rescuer ask a simple question of one police officer, "Why are you doing this?" The officer responded, "I'm just doing my job." These words were a dagger in my heart. In a moment of time, I imagined police officers, not unlike these, in the not-too-distant future, dragging away my children from their home for God knows what reason and hearing the policeman echo, "I'm just doing my job." I began to sob as I realized how much was at stake for my children's future, for your children's future. I felt that those were the most damning words of all time, "I'm just doing my job." Roman soldiers said it. German policemen said it. I wept and wept as I thought of what a fearful time we live in. God help us.

Once in custody, I was again separated from the other rescuers and not allowed to communicate with the rescue leadership. The authorities charged me and three others with felony conspiracies to commit misdemeanor trespass. Absurd, isn't it?

That day nearly eight hundred rescuers were arrested, handcuffed, and taken to a local gymnasium. Because several of us had extra charges and several more had been taken down to the city jail, over 420 rescuers stood in solidarity and refused to give their names. As of right now, there are four hundred still in custody. Their spirits are high; the worship and preaching have been anointed. I trust that these seeds of sacrifice will bring forth fruits of fresh courage across this country. These things have not occurred in a corner.

The Heat Is Rising

My hope is that all of us will be freed within the next twenty-four hours—on our own recognizance and with all felony charges dropped. This is our goal.

This has been one of the most intense weeks in my life. Our enemies now take us very, very seriously. A proabort spokesperson has declared on the evening news that they intend to pursue me with Racketeering Influenced and Corrupt Organizations Act (RICO) charges and to prosecute me for the transportation of "fetal parts" across state lines. Planned Parenthood reportedly bragged that they will crush us within one year. The National Abortion Rights Action

League (NARAL) has now launched a two-million-dollar advertising campaign designed to mask the reality of baby-killing. The American Civil Liberties Union (ACLU) has joined the fray and filed suit against us here in California. The NOW has added me to their RICO suit against Joe Scheidler in Chicago.

Our enemies now realize the impact of the Rescue Movement; thus, their efforts to thwart us are growing more and more desperate.

But, by the grace of God, as we keep our faces low and continue in obedience to Him, the gates of hell shall not prevail against us. We will continue to mobilize the church and other pro-life Americans, bringing thousands of pastors and tens of thousands of new rescuers into the Rescue Movement until we have crushed legalized child-killing. Planned Parenthood, the NOW, the ACLU, NARAL, and their allies, in their arrogance, are no match for the living God.

Please pray for us. The heat of this battle has risen beyond our expectations, and it only promises to get hotter.

With Christ in the battle for life,
Randall A. Terry
National Director

P.S. I'm out of jail. Everyone was released without paying bail. Again, please pray for us as you stand for the children and with us. God bless you.

2

THE BLESSING OF ANGER

In the late heat of an arid Middle Eastern day, a young man followed three yoke of oxen in from the field, another hard day's work near an end. As he approached the village, he heard the din of noise fading in and out. The closer he came, the more discernible the sounds: lamenting, crying, wailing, howling. He quickened his pace, spurring his oxen to do the same. Once in the village, he saw the source of the commotion. Dozens of men and women in the street were moaning and crying out with great sobs of anguish. "Certainly someone has died," the young man thought. "Maybe many have died. I have never witnessed such heartache."

Some of his friends saw him and ran over, tears filling their eyes. He asked, "What is the matter with the people? Why are they weeping?"

"The men of Jabesh sent messengers throughout Judah to send for help!" one blurted.

"But why?" Saul responded.

"King Nahash of Ammon has laid siege to the city. All the men of the city begged King Nahash to make a covenant with them—that they would serve him rather than fight."

"Yes," another said, still crying, "So Nahash offered them terms of peace. He demands to gouge out the right eye of every man, woman, and child in Jabesh in order to bring shame and disgrace on all Israel!" The others began weeping again, lifting their voices in a gut-wrenching lament. "The elders of Jabesh have agreed to accept the

offer in seven days, unless someone arises to defend the city and engage Nahash in battle."

"King Nahash is strong," Joab continued through his tears. "We
are weak. We could never prevail against such a mighty army!" His
voice became still louder and more shrill, "God has abandoned us
into the hands of these uncircumcised heathen!"

They all expected Saul to join in their lamentation. No one expected what followed.

Saul stood for a moment, absorbing all he had heard, looking
over the weeping congregation. Then, in a way that only God understands, the Spirit of the Almighty came upon him and enveloped
him, literally filling his very being. Saul felt a strength and determination he had never known in his life—and one other thing—*rage*. He
was so outraged that his body began to tremble. He was never more
aware of God's presence, and he had never felt such rage. He was
furious that the Ammorites would dare such an atrocity against the
people of God; he was outraged that the elders of Jabesh would accept such an offer—surrendering themselves, their wives, and children to one-eyed blindness. He was furious with all these people for
their cowardly response. He was seething with holy anger in a hereto-
fore unknown experience with the Almighty. In that moment of inspired fury, he shouted out at the top of his lungs, "What? Is there no
God in Israel?"

The volume of his voice and the fierceness in his eyes shocked his
friends to attention and gripped those standing by with terror. Anyone within earshot turned to see the new commotion. The noise died
down immediately. "And this is our response to such treachery!" he
stormed, waving his hands about. "Can you do no more than weep
and wail!" Suddenly, he grabbed a friend standing there with a sword
at his side. "Give me that!" he demanded, pulling the sword from his
sheath. The frightened people quietly retreated a few steps.

He strode angrily back toward his oxen, shouting as he went,
"Our brothers are in danger, and *this* is your response? Unbelievable!" He reached his oxen, unhooked the first two, and moved them
a few feet into the center of the large crowd that had gathered.

"Now is not a time to weep!" he shouted at the crowd, as he lifted
the sword above his head, clenching the handle with both fists, "It is a
time to fight." In that moment he swung the sword with all his might,
slicing deep into the neck of one of his oxen and severing its spinal

chord. The animal quietly moaned and fell to the ground. Blood splattered everywhere. Women screamed. The terrified crowd surged backward.

"Are you mad?" someone yelled.

"Stop him!" another shouted.

It was too late. Another fatal blow had been delivered to the second oxen. The stunned crowd watched in disbelief as one mighty blow after another was delivered to the carcasses. In a few short minutes they were reduced to bloodied hunks of flesh, bone, hair, and innards.

Puffing and perspiring, Saul picked up a mangled hunk of meat in each hand and turned his attention to the crowd.

"Now," he gasped, shoving the flesh into the hands of two young men, "I want all of you to take a piece of this oxen to every village in Israel. Tell the men that if they don't come and follow Samuel and Saul into battle against Nahash, this shall be done to their oxen. Tell them they have six days to report here. Now go!"

One at a time, the men in the crowd did as they were ordered, picking up bloodied hunks of oxen flesh, running through the gate. Everywhere they went, they recounted the dilemma of Jabesh-Gilead, recited Saul's outrage and his orders, and showed the bloodied hunks of oxen flesh. Saul meant business. The fear of God gripped men's hearts throughout Israel. Over the next six days, they came out as one man to Saul, determined to rescue Jabesh-Gilead.

The citizens of Jabesh learned of their imminent deliverance, and on the seventh day feigned surrender to Nahash. While Nahash was preoccupied with the people of Jabesh, Saul and the Israelite army came in from three sides, swiftly shattering the enemy's army. No two enemy survivors were left together. Jabesh was delivered.

God anointed Saul with a holy anger to lead the way in a great victory for the people of God. Where are the angry Sauls today?

My Hope for You

If you are a Christian, I sincerely hope that, among other things, this book enrages you. I hope that as you see a glimpse of the death industry and its murderous agenda, the lying prophets who undergird it and the compromise with death in the church, you will feel a righteous anger like you haven't felt in years or perhaps in your whole life. And for those who seek to suppress a proper anger, I hope that you get set free from the false constraints with which our religious culture has shackled you. If you are not a Christian, I hope you become one. If you are a death activist, I hope you too get outraged as you see the hatred, violence, and deception of the movement you so fervently believe in. Then I hope you repent before you face God at the judgment seat.

Tragically, American Christianity (which is quite often radically different from Biblical Christianity) has forgotten or even suppressed one of the most powerfully motivating forces for righteous change—godly anger. An idolatrous desire to be respectable or to not rock the boat has caused some to bury angry feelings and to compromise with the enemy rather than to let godly anger take its course—a course that might involve them in uncomfortable confrontation.

Others, in a sincere desire to do the will of God, have been sold a bill of goods in a package called *mush-love*. We don't get angry; we don't confront; we don't act. Why? Because we're supposed to love all mankind. This dangerously false concept of love enables us to spiritualize our fear, laziness, or apathy under the banner of love. Mush-love paves the way for the demonic and human enemies of God to run rough-shod over righteousness and justice. It opens the gate for the wicked to oppress the poor and the fatherless, while we tell ourselves we can't get angry and rebuke the godless because, after all, "they don't know Jesus" and we have to be loving.

Before you say, "But . . . ," let me quickly agree that not all anger is godly or helpful. James said, "The wrath of man does not produce the righteousness of God" (James 1:20, NKJV). Paul wrote that one of the works of the flesh was "outbursts of wrath" (Galatians 5:20, NKJV), and Proverbs says, "A soft answer turns away wrath, but a harsh word stirs up anger" (Proverbs 15:1, NKJV).

But do these Scriptures mean that Christians should never be angry? Do they mean that if we are truly godly, our minds and lives will never be disrupted or motivated by godly anger; that we'll just go on our way, calmly tolerating any and all injustice that we encounter and turning our eyes from the unrighteousness that fills our society?

Too many Christians think, "We can't 'make a scene' because of what sinners do. Jesus would have us just keep loving them" (translated, Jesus would just have us look the other way). "We have to be like Jesus," they insist.

In Christ's Image

We do need to be like Jesus. It should be the desire of every Christian to be conformed into the image of Christ (see Romans 8:29). But what was Jesus like? More to the point, did Jesus ever get angry? If so, what motivated Him to anger?

Unfortunately, many of our concepts and mental images of the Lord proceed more from Renaissance art than the Scriptures. We envision the Lord as a man with sandy blond hair, mystic (almost spacy) blue eyes, who walks around with a lamb in His arms. The message? Why, this man wouldn't hurt a flea! Jesus, get angry? Outraged? No way!

But this is not the man the Bible portrays. Yes, Jesus was a kind, gentle man, who bound up the hurting (see Isaiah 61:1–3), who touched the untouchable, who loved the unlovable (see Romans 5:8–10), who forgave the unforgivable (see John 8:7). (It is possible, however, that, being Jewish, he had dark hair and dark eyes!) These aspects of Christ's character and actions we are all well aware of and very comfortable with. And rightly so—knowing how hurt, untouchable, unlovable, and unforgivable we have been in our lives!

But we have much difficulty envisioning the whole Jesus—a Jesus who got indignant at times, a Jesus who said things that were not "nice" and in fact extemely harsh, and a Jesus who did things that were quite radical and quite unbecoming for a religious leader. Simply put, we forget that Jesus got *mad.*

The Lord Felt Anger

One Sabbath, Jesus was worshipping in a synagogue in Capernaum. There was also present a man with a withered hand. The Pharisees were watching Jesus closely, seeing whether He would heal the man on the Sabbath so they might accuse Him of violating the Law. Jesus asked these Pharisees, "Is it lawful on the Sabbath to do good or to do harm, to save a life or to kill?" When they gave no answer, Scripture says He "look[ed] around at them with anger, grieved at their hardness of heart" and healed the man (see Mark 3:1–6). The Greek word for anger means violent passion, ire, or justifiable abhorrence.[1] Jesus wasn't a little upset; He was infuriated.

On another occasion, some young mothers were trying to bring their babies to Jesus so that He might bless them. The disciples thought that they were doing the Lord a favor and rebuked the mothers, trying to keep them and their children away. "Hey, the Lord's too busy to deal with unimportant things like children! Bug off!" (It's sad that such an attitude still prevails in the church.) Scripture continues, "But when Jesus saw this, He was indignant . . ." (Mark 10:14). The New King James Version says that Jesus was "greatly displeased." The Greek word means to be greatly afflicted (with grief). This is the kind of anger you feel when you see both the injustice and the victim of the injustice. It produces an anger mixed with grief.

The Lord Said Harsh and Unkind Words

In our hollow remaking of the Lord Jesus, we envision a man who never raised His voice and never said an unkind word. In another episode with children, the Lord did say, "And whoever receives a little child like this in My name receives Me. But whoever causes one of these little ones who believes in Me to sin, it would be better for him if a millstone were hung around his neck and he were drowned in the depth of the sea" (Matthew 18:5–6, NKJV). These words hardly fit the unbalanced, gentle Jesus we've created. Here is the Lord speaking of drowning someone who harms children! (I wonder what he thinks of abortionists. I'm sure the lake of fire will reveal it.)

On another occasion, the Lord Jesus severely rebuked the scribes and Pharisees. I'm sure the common folk who listened could hardly believe their ears as Jesus exclaimed,

> Woe to you, scribes and Pharisees, hypocrites! For you travel land and sea to win one proselyte, and when he is won, you make him twice as much a son of hell as yourselves. . . . Blind guides, who strain out a gnat and swallow a camel! . . . Woe to you, scribes and Pharisees, hypocrites! For you are like whitewashed tombs which indeed appear beautiful outwardly, but inside are full of dead men's bones and all uncleanness. Even so you also outwardly appear righteous to men, but inside you are full of hypocrisy and lawlessness. . . . Serpents, brood of vipers! How can you escape the condemnation of hell? (Matthew 23:15, 24, 27–28, 33, NKJV)

To the lawyers he said, "Woe to you lawyers as well! For you weigh men down with burdens hard to bear, while you yourselves will not even touch the burdens with one of your fingers" (Luke 11:46).

These are harsh words, not kind words. What compounds the insult of these fiery condemnations is that they were spoken to the religious leaders of the day—the men who were supposedly the most holy. For the Lord to call them "serpents" and "vipers" and to accuse them of being like "whitewashed tombs . . . full of dead man's bones and all uncleanness" was the depth of degradation to a Jewish mind. Jesus was referring to these Pharisees in the absolute worst possible terms.

Can you imagine publicly rebuking compromised religious and political leaders of our day using this type of language? Can you see yourself confronting Episcopal Bishop John Spong of Newark, New Jersey, the author of *Living in Sin? A Bishop Rethinks Human Sexuality,* rebuking him for his serious errors concerning sexual activity? This cleric has even ordained practicing homosexuals to the ministry. Here is a man whose espoused views on homosexuality mock the Scriptures, and who has justified perversion in the name of God.[2] If the Lord said what he did to the Pharisees, can you imagine what He would say to this man if He were here? Why then are we so afraid to rock the boat and to call a spade a spade? Don't we desire to be like Christ?

The Lord Did Radical Things

Imagine yourself in the temple on another busy day during the Passover. It was crowded. People were praying. Scribes and Pharisees were teaching. The noise of the people and the bleating of animals filled the air. Suddenly—as if from nowhere—an outraged man erupts on the scene, cracking a whip, chasing people, overturning money tables, and yelling at the top of his lungs, "You have made my father's house a den of robbers!" (See John 2:13–25.) Imagine the women and children crying out; the stunned temple guards shocked into inaction; the corrupt religious leaders looking on in rage; the religious moneymakers scrambling to pick up their filthy lucre. It was surely a raucous scene. I honestly cannot envision little Jewish ladies in the corner, clapping their hands, saying of Jesus, "He's such a nice Jewish boy!"

Imagine that scene being duplicated today in America. "Arrest Him!" the faithful would cry. "Charge Him with disturbing the peace, harassment, disorderly conduct, reckless endangerment, and trespass! Never mind that He claims that this is His Father's house!"

So if we are indeed interested in being more like Christ, it is inevitable that we are going to feel anger, say confrontational things, and perhaps do some radical deeds. Yes, this truly can be done in love—love for God, love for righteousness, love for justice, and love for people.

Now, lest anybody think these truths are a ticket to let loose unfettered anger or a justification for those with a self-righteous short temper, hold on! We must examine the context of Christ's fury. Better yet, let's look at those situations in which He *didn't* react in anger.

His Anger Was Not Self-Serving

It is critical to understand that the Lord Jesus did not get angry over personal insult or injury. When He was reviled, blasphemed, beaten, and finally killed, He did not respond in anger. "He was oppressed and He was afflicted, yet He opened not His mouth; He was led as a lamb to the slaughter, And as a sheep before its shearers is silent, so He opened not His mouth" (Isaiah 53:7, NKJV). Jesus was He, "who, when He was reviled, did not revile in return; when He suffered, He did not threaten, but committed Himself to Him who judges righteously" (1 Peter 2:23, NKJV). Prophetically, He said of Himself, "I gave My back to those who struck Me, and My cheeks to those who plucked out the beard; I did not hide My face from shame and spitting" (Isaiah 50:6, NKJV). And when He was dying, He prayed this incredible prayer, "Father, forgive them, for they do not know what they do" (Luke 23:34, NKJV). Jesus bore patiently the injustice against Himself. This can be incredibly difficult, but it must be our goal.

The Lord Jesus, however, was angry with those who hindered children or would harm them. He was angered by hard-hearted religious leaders who loved the letter of their distorted law more than the life, health, and well-being of a fellow human being. He was angered with and spoke harshly to lay and religious leaders alike who misled unsuspecting, truth-seeking people. He was angry with those who dishonored God, those who defiled the sacred sanctuary with corruption, and those who exploited the name and glorious service of our God for a big-dollar business. He reacted quickly and severely to those who so polluted God's service.

Bridling the Flame

Anger is like a flame. Bridled, contained, and directed, it can be a tremendous force for righteousness and change. Out of control, it can be a dangerous, deadly force. The emotion of anger must not be taken lightly. Proverbs says, "A quick-tempered man acts foolishly" (14:17), and "An angry man stirs up strife, and a furious man abounds in transgression" (29:22, NKJV).

On one hand we see the Lord (as well as Saul and others) expressing anger and, on the other, certain Scriptures warning against anger. Is there a contradiction here? No.

Paul wrote to the Ephesians, "Be angry, and do not sin" (Ephesians 4:26, NKJV). We can experience righteous anger that can be a tremendous blessing.

Which Is Which?

When we feel anger rising within us (as we all do from time to time), how can we know if it's good anger or bad anger? One quick way to tell is to look at the source. Why are you angry? Because of an injury done to yourself or one done to someone else?

> For this finds favor, if for the sake of conscience toward God a man bears up under sorrows when suffering unjustly. For what credit is there if, when you sin and are harshly treated, you endure it with patience? But if when you do what is right and suffer for it you patiently endure it, this finds favor with God. (1 Peter 2:19–21)

> [Peter followed,] and who is there to harm you if you prove zealous for what is good? But even if you should suffer for the sake of righteousness, you are blessed. And do not fear their intimidation, and do not be troubled, but sanctify Christ as Lord in your hearts, always being ready to make a defense to everyone who asks you to give an account for the hope that is in you, yet with gentleness and reverence; and keep a good conscience so that in the thing in which you are slandered, those who revile your good behavior in Christ may be put to shame. For it is better, if God should will it so, that you suffer for doing what is right rather than for doing what is wrong. (1 Peter 3:13–17)

The Lord told me to turn the other cheek when I am wronged. However, He did not tell me to look the other way when *you* are wronged. If you are the victim of injustice, I have an obligation to try to help you. This is the example of our Lord. He was not angry at injustices suffered against Himself but was outraged by injustices against others and the dishonoring of God, the Father. We are commanded throughout the Scriptures to defend the defenseless (Psalm 82:3, 4), to speak up for those who cannot speak for themselves (Proverbs 31:8, 9), to rescue those unjustly sentenced to death (Proverbs 24:10–12), to help the widow and fatherless in their distress (James 1:27), to seek justice, to rebuke the ruthless, and to defend the fatherless (Isaiah 1:17). In short, God's Word mandates that we intervene on behalf of the oppressed.

Nehemiah's Example

Nehemiah serves as an excellent example of one who was motivated by anger to seek justice on behalf of others. While the Israelites were rebuilding the wall of Jerusalem, Nehemiah learned that many of his co-laborers were forced to borrow money from their rich Jewish countrymen to buy grain to pay as taxes. Subsequently, when they could not repay the loans, their lands were being repossessed; and some were literally selling their children into slavery.

These downcast Israelites came and cried out to Nehemiah, "And now our flesh is like the flesh of our brothers, our children like their children. Yet behold, we are forcing our sons and our daughters to be slaves, and some of our daughters are forced into bondage already, and we are helpless because our fields and vineyards belong to others" (Nehemiah 5:5).

Nehemiah responded, "Then I was very angry when I had heard their outcry and these words" (Nehemiah 5:6). He then vigorously contended with the rulers and nobles and convinced them to end the practice of usury.

Friend, what got Nehemiah so angry couldn't hold a candle to some of the atrocities we face in our nation. For that matter, some of what angered the Lord doesn't hold a candle to what we're doing in America. He was indignant when they hindered children; we've murdered twenty-five million in ways so barbaric that it defies logic. How do you think He feels now? America's cup is overflowing with wickedness. How long before the cup of God's wrath overflows and we receive all that we deserve?

Child-killing in and of itself is enough to damn any nation to hell. The blood of these babies is crying from the ground for vengeance. The cry of that blood must be a haunting chorus in heaven. God will avenge their blood. He has committed Himself to do so.[3]

Frankly, we're in much danger when we see murders, terrible injustices and flaunted vulgarity and don't get angry. Our consciences have been numbed, and our hearts have become calloused. This is what happened to those German Christians who knew about the concentration camps and did nothing to help the hunted. This is what has happened to us.

We have lived in peaceful coexistence with child-killing (and the other vulgarities) for so long that the carnage of bloody and dismembered bodies, decapitated heads, and real-life horror stories no longer outrages us. We're uncomfortable—yes, distressed—a little, sad, yes, but not outraged. We're not angered enough to drop what we're doing and intervene on behalf of the children. Nor are we incensed enough to commit our lives, our fortunes, and our sacred honors to ending this bloodshed and to reforming our nation. We most certainly have grown calloused.

May God wake us up and fill us with His holy anger. May He deliver us from trying to be nicer than Jesus. In an hour when we should be feeling rage, we're trying to get the world to like us. In an hour when we should be rebuking wicked and corrupt leaders, we're trying to peacefully coexist with an enemy bent on destroying us. In an hour when we should be throwing some tables, we're trying to spiritualize our selfish apathy under the banner of love.

We must remember, however, that anger remains a great instigator, but a poor sustainer. God can and does use anger to motivate us to act, but anger alone will not provide the strength for perseverance in the battle. Moreover, if we are strictly motivated by anger rather than love, mercy, and a desire for truth, we will self-destruct; we will burn out. Our commitment to the establishment of righteousness, therefore, must extend beyond our feelings of anger and be fueled in the long run by our commitment to and love for God and His Word.

The Elder Sellout

Probably the biggest tragedy of 1 Samuel 11 is the response of the elders. They were willing to allow their enemy to gouge out the eyes of their wives and children; they would have condemned their own people to a life of slavery.

By gouging out the Israelites' right eyes, the enemy would have insured that they could work but not fight effectively. The Israelites were predominantly right-handed; and, without their right eye, they would have no right-hand field of vision. They could not see effectively to swing a sword or to defend themselves in battle. Hence they would become the slaves of the Ammorites. The elders knew this and yet were willing to submit to it.

They should have said, "We will fight and die before we will be your slaves. In the name of the God of Israel, we will stand and do battle!" But they didn't. They were cowards.

Simply put, the elders would rather submit to one-eyed slavery than fight their enemy.

It sounds like today. Unfortunately, we live in an hour when thousands of pastors and religious leaders would rather sell us into servitude than to stand against the human enemies of God. Every time the enemy draws a line in the dirt, not only do we refuse to cross it, we back up further!

Pornography is legalized—we back up. Prayer and the Bible are made illegal in public schools—we don't fight. Killing children, once a felony, becomes a "fundamental Constitutional right"—we stand by and watch the blood flow. Witchcraft and human sacrifice are growing at an alarming rate—we don't believe or simply ignore it. Homosexuals use our money to pollute public museums with filth—we don't fight. Child molesters and rapists get a slap on the hand, while Jim Bakker gets forty-five years in prison—we are not outraged. My God, what is wrong with us! We don't get angry. We don't fight. We keep backing up. Before long, *there won't be any place to go.*

May God free His people from the constraints of self-preserving religion to get mad, *really* mad, about what we see.

I'm convinced if we don't wake up and get angry very soon, that we will do what the elders of Jabesh would have done—we'll settle for one-eyed servitude rather than fighting—forgetting that we are selling our children and our children's children into a cycle of slavery and oppression.

Harnessed and directed, godly anger can be a tremendous motivating force. It is my fervent prayer that as you read about the enemies of righteousness, the Spirit of God will come on you as it did Saul, and you will get very, very angry; and that your anger will motivate *you* to action and cause you to motivate *others* to action. Get mad and fight.

PART TWO

THE ARMY

PLANNED PARENTHOOD

D reams often come true. History, in fact, is replete with visionaries who changed the course of nations. But one man's (or woman's) dream is often another's nightmare. Thomas Jefferson and George Washington dreamed of a free America; their dream was King George III's nightmare. William Lloyd Garrison dreamed of an America without slavery; his dream was the slaveowner's nightmare. Adolf Hitler dreamed of eliminating the Jewish race; his dream was a hellish nightmare for millions of European Jews. Josef Stalin dreamed of leading a Soviet state in its domination of the entire world with its Marxist-Leninist ideology; his dream became a living nightmare for the peasants and priests of Russia and remains so for the millions of people still living under faltering communist regimes.

Margaret Sanger, the founder of Planned Parenthood, was such a visionary. She dreamed of a society free from all sexual mores. She envisioned a "race of thoroughbreds"[1] and the utter extinction of those deemed "human weeds."[2] She desired for there to be sterilization of the poor and licensing requirements for couples to have babies. With religious imagery and fervor, she challenged the women of her day to break the current birth control laws.

Her dreams—the joy of hell—have become the horrific nightmare for millions of murdered children and godly parents. They are now an insidious poison infecting the souls and minds of tens of millions of teenagers.

Much of the material in this chapter comes from George Grant's book, *Grand Illusions* (Wolgemuth & Hyatt, 1989), and is used by permission. I am deeply indebted to Mr. Grant for his very clear and precise research of Planned Parenthood and its founder Margaret Sanger.

Planned Parenthood—Born of a Whore

Before we examine what Margaret Sanger believed and worked for, we need to look at who and what she was.

Her Personal Life

Born September 14, 1879, to an Irish immigrant father and Catholic mother, Margaret had ten brothers and sisters.[3] Her family was poor, and this background produced a strong bitterness in her toward large, poor families. In fact, she dedicated much of her life to exterminating them.

The details of her life mirror those on the afternoon soap operas. Although she attended a fashionable boarding school and began nursing studies, Margaret finished neither. She was bored and longed for the life of leisure. She found an answer in marriage.

In 1902, Margaret met and married William Sanger, a promising young architect. She quickly had three children and assumed the role of mother and suburban housewife in their newly purchased, lavish home. Just as quickly, however, she grew tired of the life of a housewife and, following their move to Manhattan, began to associate more and more frequently with her husband's radical and socialist cronies.

Margaret devoted herself completely to her new Bohemian surroundings, failing to properly care for her children or her husband. Her involvement with socialist causes and her insatiable obsession with a newfound interest—sexual freedom—simply monopolized her time. The latter was spurred on by her relationship with revolutionary Emma Goldman and the hours she spent engrossed in her extensive library, which included *Studies in the Psychology of Sex* by Havelock Ellis.

Margaret became the resident expert and promoter of sexual freedom at Mabel Dodge's evening salons. No one championed the cause of sexual liberation as ardently as Margaret; and all were delighted and entertained by her brazen and explicit conversations, that is, all except her husband. William grew tired of her lascivious behavior and whisked her off to Europe.

Margaret and the children, however, didn't remain long on the continent. After only two weeks she begged William to return home. He refused, and she abandoned him. Margaret and the children returned to the Village and her wonderful Bohemian friends. At this time she began distributing *The Woman Rebel*. Unfortunately for Margaret, *The Woman Rebel* violated the Comstock laws which outlawed the publishing of lewd and indecent articles. She was off to Europe again; this time as a fugitive from justice.

She spent most of the next months in England, discoursing with the traditional social radicals as well as two factions new to Margaret, the Malthusians and the Eugenicists. Their philosophies would fundamentally shape the implementation of Margaret's ideas on sexual liberation. Earlier, she had discovered her niche in the social revolution; now she had found the necessary means to change her world and to see her vision come to pass.

Her emphasis would be less on radical rhetoric and more on political expediency. She would employ as authorities to support her philosophy and programs the scientific and mathematical theories of the Malthusians and Eugenicists. She then set out for America with her plan to conquer the world with her religion of sexual liberation.

Upon her return to the States, Margaret was able to secure the dismissal of the charges against her through a massive public relations campaign. She then embarked on a three-and-a-half month speaking tour, addressing throngs of enthusiastic supporters. She also opened the prototype birth control clinic in the Brownsville section of New York City. The clinic was perfectly situated amidst the tenements inhabitated by those whom Margaret despised: Slavs, Jews, and Italians.

If it had not been shortly closed by the authorities, it would have been the ideal location to begin her racial and economic genocide. But it was closed, and Margaret and her sister were sentenced to thirty days for distribution of obscene materials and dangerous medical devices.

Margaret was not deterred. She founded the American Birth Control League and began publishing the *Birth Control Review*. Her professional life was soaring, even though her private life was a wreck.

Her family life was in shambles. Her marriage had ended in divorce; her daughter had caught pneumonia through Margaret's neglect and died; her two boys were likewise forgotten.

She had spent much of her time in Europe romping in bed with radical luminaries of the day—H.G. Wells, Julian Huxley, and Havelock Ellis. The latter, of course, became her mentor and led her even further down the path of perversion. Her sexual escapades continued when she returned to New York City. She continually sought to find happiness in her orgies and endless chain of sexual liaisons.

Eventually, however, she turned again to a marriage of convenience. She managed to marry J. Noah Slee, the president of Three-in-One Oil Company and a millionaire. The rules of the marriage were quite bizarre and reveal Margaret's commitment to fulfill her ungodly lusts. She and her husband lived in separate wings of the home so that she could continue to sleep with whomever she wished at any time. Slee had to actually phone Margaret if he wished a dinner date.

Marriage made little difference in Margaret's life. Only now she had the funds and the connections to implement her dream. She was, however, as committed as ever to her life of infidelity and promiscuity.

Even by today's standards, Margaret Sanger was a very loose woman. By Biblical standards, she was a whore (see Proverbs 7:6–27).

She wasn't, however, just any old floozy. She had class, she had connections, and she had a mission: *to make America's families reflect her own sordid lifestyle.* That was a huge undertaking; but tragically, she and the heirs of her mission have been alarmingly successful in their agenda. Just take a look at today's daytime soap operas.

Margaret was able to use these connections to gain finances, respectability, and success for herself and her organization, the American Birth Control League. This respectability was greatly enhanced in 1942 when she changed its name to Planned Parenthood Federation of America. This success was likewise augmented by her aggressive efforts to bring local affiliates within the Federation.

Margaret's public relations campaigns over the next twenty years served her empire well. She died in 1966, a broken, empty woman; but the organization she had founded and the dream she had fostered had won the respect and admiration of the nation.

What She Believed

Fortunately for those who desire to expose her and, unfortunately for those who wish to paint her as a courageous woman and a bold pioneer, Margaret Sanger littered her path with an abundance of damning quotes, articles, and books. Simply stated, she was a religious bigot, an ardent racist, a eugenicist, and the type of individual who would have loved for Orwell's *1984* to become a reality. She wrote enough to fill volumes; so we will take a general overview of this colorful mother of Planned Parenthood.

Concerning the Poor. One must understand that when Sanger spoke of the unfit, the dysgenic, the feebleminded, human weeds, and defectives, she was not referring to a few poor souls in an insane asylum. Rather, she was speaking of 50 to 80 percent of our population, including blacks, Slavs, Jews, Italians, Poles, poor whites, and the strongly religious. Indeed, she was speaking of the majority of people reading this book. She was probably speaking about you. Listen to what she wrote.

> Everywhere we see poverty and large families going hand in hand. Those least fit to carry on the race are increasing most rapidly. People who cannot support their own off-spring are encouraged by the Church and state to produce large families. Many of the children thus begotten are diseased, or feebleminded: many become criminals. The burden of supporting these unwanted types has to be borne by the healthy elements of the nation. Funds that should be used to raise the standard of our civilization are diverted to maintenance of those who should never have been born.[4]

> [The philanthropists who give free maternity care] encourage the healthier and more normal sections of the world to shoulder the burden of unthinking and indiscriminate fecundity of others; which brings with it, as I think the reader must agree, a dead weight of human waste. Instead of decreasing and aiming to eliminate the stocks that are most detrimental to the future of the race and of the world, it renders them to a menacing degree dominant.[5]

> [Regarding organized charity,] Its very success, its very efficiency, its very necessity to the social order . . . those vast, complex, interrelated organizations aimed to control and diminish the spread of misery, destitution, and all the menacing evils that spring out of this sinisterly fertile soil are the surest sign that our civilization has bred, is breed-

ing, and is perpetuating constantly increasing numbers of defectives, delinquents and dependents. My criticism, therefore, is not directed at the "failure" of philanthropy, but rather at its success.[6]

A New Breed of Racism: Eliminating the Black Community.

Margaret Sanger was a racist, plainly stated. By her statements and programs, she clearly indicated her desire to segregate the black community and, if possible, to eliminate them altogether. Her first efforts were in the South, where white segregationists, racists, and supremacists would eagerly adopt a plan to stop the black community from "their reckless and irresponsible swarming and spawning."[7]

Linda Gordon, a pro-abortion feminist, writes of Sanger,

Sanger described her plan to stop the growth of the Blacks in the United States in a private letter to Clarence Gamble dated October 19, 1939. She spoke of a project that would "hire three or four colored ministers, preferably with social-service background, and with engaging personalities" to travel through the south and propagandize for birth control. "The most successful educational approach to the Negro is through a religious appeal. We do not want word to get out that we want to exterminate the Negro population, and the minister is the man who can straighten out that idea if it ever occurs to any of their more rebellious members." A steering committee from Margaret Sanger's group would supervise the project while very carefully appearing to give the control to the hand-picked local Blacks.[8]

No folks, what you've just read was not written by the Imperial Wizard of the Ku Klux Klan but by that true American pioneer Margaret Sanger.

To further expose her racism, let's examine her close associates. One, Dr. Lothrop Stoddard, served on the board of directors of the American Birth Control League for many years and authored the book *The Rising Tide of Color against White World Supremacy*. Stoddard, having traveled to Germany and met personally with Hitler, was a vocal supporter of the Nazis and especially their sterilization court.

Henry Laughlin was another of Sanger's collaborators and, in 1933, Sanger published an article of his in her *Birth Control Review*. Laughlin had authored Hitler's Model Eugenical Sterilization Law, for which he received an honorary M.D. from the University of Heidelburg in 1936. His article in the *Birth Control Review* advocated a similar policy of mandatory sterilization in the United States. There's no·doubt that this idea appealed greatly to Margaret and was an intrinsic element in her vision for African-Americans.

Finally, there was Dr. Ernst Rudin, the director of the Nazi Medical Experimentation program. Sanger actually commissioned him as well to write for the *Review*.

It is as tragic as it is odd that the current president of Planned Parenthood is Faye Wattleton, an attractive black woman with a social service background. Despite what Ms. Wattleton must know, she has allowed herself to be used by an organization that still targets blacks and has never renounced the racist statements and plans of its founder. In fact, in an interview with columnist John Lofton, Wattleton admits that Sanger advocated "Eugenics and the advancement of the perfect race."[9]

Plan for Peace

Sanger's machinations to purify the gene pool, however, did not stop with her programs against blacks. She, like Hitler, was determined to build a master race—with perhaps a little less violence.

In 1932 the *Birth Control Review* printed her Plan for Peace. One must wonder what war she was seeking to pacify. Regardless, she called upon the nation

- To keep the doors of immigration closed to the entrance of certain aliens whose condition is known to be detrimental to the stamina of the race, such as the feebleminded;

- To apply a stern and rigid policy of sterilization and segregation to that grade of population whose progeny are already tainted, or whose inheritance is such that objectionable traits may be transmitted to offspring;

- To insure the country against future burdens of maintenance for numerous offspring as may be born of feebleminded parents by pensioning all persons with transmissible diseases who voluntarily consent to sterilization;

- To give dysgenic groups in our population their choice of segregation or sterilization;

- To apportion farmlands and homesteads for these segregated persons where they would be taught to work under competent instructors for the period of their lives;

- To take an inventory of the secondary group such as illiterates, paupers, unemployables, criminals, prostitutes, dope-fiends; classify them in special departments under government medical protection, and segregate them on farms and open spaces as long as necessary for the strengthening and development of moral conduct.[10]

Notice the clever euphemisms and shrouded terminology. Make no mistake. She was referring to forced sterilization and concentration camps. What other phrase describes a "work camp" or a "farm" onto which individuals are herded against their will to work and to be "reeducated"?

Sanger's Plan for Peace obviously never materialized (thank God), so Margaret embraced a slightly less offensive means to reach her goal of the perfect race—*birth control*. Rest assured, Margaret Sanger's advocacy for birth control was motivated by the same bigotry and racism as her other more radical plans.

She stated plainly, "More children from the fit, less from the unfit—that is the chief aim of birth control,"[11] and "Birth Control: to create a race of thoroughbreds."[12]

She considered it folly to speak of eugenics without speaking of birth control. She wrote, "Eugenics without birth control seemed to me to be a house built upon sands. . . . The eugenists wanted to shift the birth control emphasis from less children for the poor to more children for the rich. We went back of that and sought to end the multiplication of the unfit."[13]

And again in this vein, "There is only one reply to a request for a higher birth rate among the intelligent and that is to ask the government to first take the burden of the insane and feebleminded from your back. Sterilization for these is the solution."[14]

Sanger's ideological alliance and personal friendship with those behind Hitler's eugenic agenda cannot be denied. Despite the growing evidence of Hitler's oppressive goals, indeed, two months *after* the Nazis had invaded Poland, the *Birth Control Review* commended the Nazi Birth Control Program as compared to that of the Italians, stating, "The German program has been much more carefully worked out. The need for quality as well as quantity is recognized."[15]

Amazingly, despite her bigoted, antichrist, master race message, Sanger's influence and that of her organization waxed rather than waned. She did have to abandon some of her rhetoric (though not her goals) when the world finally understood the evil nature of Hitler and his wonderful eugenic ideals.

In 1942, Margaret Sanger's Birth Control Federation of America hired a consultant, D. Kenneth Rose. Rose convinced Sanger (who had been opposed to a new name) that her organization did need a new name (and hopefully a new image).

The public was hostile to the eugenics movement's Nazi-like ideology, shared intrinsically with those promoting birth control. Hence, it became imperative to remove the birth control buzz word from the title. Yes, put on a new label! It's got the same poisonous, godless content but with a "new and improved!" euphemism to help package the poison. Planned Parenthood Federation of America was thus unveiled in 1942 and remained the only national organization promoting birth control until the modern child-killing movement of the late sixties.

Planned Parenthood: The New Branch of the Government

It soon became evident to Sanger and her cohorts that if she would ever realize her vision of controlling the birth of those human weeds (you know—you and me) that she would need to work within the system, not outside it.

Thus, in 1964, Planned Parenthood began a relationship with the government, particularly with taxpayer's money, which would eventually run into billions of dollars. Unbelievable as it is, despite the stated goals of Margaret Sanger and the incredibly outrageous tactics and educational literature used by Planned Parenthood to this day, they are not only respected but applauded by government officials at every level.

Let's examine some of these tactics and educational literature.

Sex Education

Sex education does not occur in a vacuum. Moral education is inevitably a part of any sex education program, if only by default. The nature of sex—how men and women have intercourse and procreate—is biological fact. But every current sex education curriculum contains far more than how our bodies work; it contains the blatant or subtle message of whom we can have sex with, how we can have sex, and when we can have sex. "Sex ed" will inevitably communicate a value system, a series of rights and wrongs.

Planned Parenthood teaches sex education in hundreds of schools across the country, and hundreds more school systems use curricula which they endorse or supply. Perhaps they adequately present the biological facts (I even doubt this); but what else are they teaching our children? Let's look at some of their other materials.

> Because some people, some religious and semi-religious groups dominated by elderly men, simply cannot deal rationally with sex. They can't talk about it rationally, can't think about it rationally, and above all can't give up the power which controlling other people gives them. They control other people through sex. What groups? The Roman Catholic Church . . . the Mormon Church . . .[16]

> Never use sex as a weapon. Never use "love" as a weapon. You wouldn't strangle a person—cut off their air—to force them to do something. So don't cut off love, either. People need it just as much as they need air. Relax about loving. Sex is fun, and joyful, and courting is fun, and joyful, and it comes in all types and styles, all of which are OK. Do what gives pleasure and enjoy what gives pleasure and ask for what gives pleasure. Don't rob yourself of joy by focusing on old-fashioned ideas about what's "normal" or "nice." Just communicate and enjoy.[17]

> Most people are heterosexual. Some people choose to be homosexual or bi-sexual. A few adults choose not to have sexual relations—which is okay, too. We have no right to condemn a person because of his or her sexual preferences. . . . Letting yourself be bothered by fear of homosexuality in yourself or others is irrational. [18]

> You can say to your male boyfriend, my parents won't be home til 2:00. Why don't you stop at Lucky's and get some condoms . . . . If you're out in Waller Park . . . and you've got about half your clothes off, and you say to your boyfriend, "Freddie, let's get our clothes back on and drive home and get my diaphragm and come back to the park." And the advantages of the pill are that a woman can take a pill for breakfast every morning and then later on that day nobody has to stop and do anything, nobody has to be embarrassed finding a diaphragm, putting on a condom or anything else.
> And let's face it when you males like to get into your females, it's fun, enjoyable. . . .[19]

These materials and their perverted philosophy have resulted in numerous real-life nightmares for young, impressionable students. Here are just two.

George Grant relates this testimony from a high-school teenager in his definitive exposé, *Grand Illusions*. A representative from Planned Parenthood had been asked to address this girl's health class on sex, contraception, pregnancy, and abortion. This woman, well-spoken and charming, clearly had other intentions. She was there to at least begin the process whereby these students' inhibitions and moral standards would be discarded.

Her presentation had three segments. She led off with a discussion on sexuality, beginning light-heartedly with jokes and innuendo but gradually becoming more and more explicit. The children were clearly embarrassed by her titillating and perverse dialogue; but her depravity only worsened. She then showed an explicit pornographic film which left nothing to the imagination. At one point the camera focused on the woman's trembling hands opening a condom package. Catherine stared at the screen in horror.

Finally, this nice woman from Planned Parenthood asked the children to perform a little hands-on training in perversion. Having passed out condom packages to each of the girls, she instructed the boys to hold up one finger so that the girls could practice contraception application. She described all of these activities and discussions as totally normal and totally good.

The girls apparently did not agree. Following the presentation, several of the girls began sobbing; others ran outside and threw up; one even fainted.[20]

Their nightmarish intentions are further demonstrated by a piece of Planned Parenthood literature promoting a "Safety Dance" held on May 11, 1989, in Burlington, Vermont. The dance concept was developed by Jay Friedman, sexuality educator of Planned Parenthood of Tompkins County (New York).

Here are some promotional highlights given to teachers, inviting them to come.

Safety Dance: A Safer Sex Dance Party

Description and Outline

A fun and exciting musical extravaganza guaranteed to keep you dancing while learning about sexuality and safer sex. This educational and entertaining event features games, crazy condoms and hot music with sexual messages. Includes a danceable history of sex and rock 'n' roll, and up to four hours of sexually-explicit dance music interspersed with sex educator's response to "Dirty Dancing. . . ."

"Puttin on the Condom" (adapted from "Condom Comfort" in Positive Images: A New Approach to Contraceptive Education by Brick and Cooperman).

During the course of the evening each person receives and wears a nametag depicting a different step in condom use. During this activity, participants arrange themselves in a line (or a circle) according to how they think a condom is used (if there are a large number of participants, have several groups perform the activity at the same time, and compare results!) After the line is formed, have the participants read off their tags in order. Acting out the steps can increase the fun of this activity. The nametags are labelled as follows:

Safer Sex Continuum activity:

- Physical attraction
- Think about having sex
- Talk about having sex
- Decide to use a condom
- Pool money . . . or more foreplay
- Go to a condom store
- Decide what kind to buy
- Take box off rack
- Pay cashier
- Decide where to store them
- Decide to have sex
- Need to use a condom
- Open package
- Penis hard?
- Place condom on penis
- Fall in love (throughout, or at all?)
- Leave space at tip
- Roll condom down penis
- Enough lubrication?
- If no, use KY jelly
- Intercourse
- Ejaculation
- Hold on to rim of condom
- Withdraw penis
- Remove condom
- Loss of erection (two of these)
- Decide where to throw condom away
- Trash it

- Wash penis
- Relax (throughout)

- Feel good? (throughout)
- Partner have an orgasm? . . .

Participants tape placards containing a "sexual activity" on a wall ranking them from least risky to most risky for HIV infection.

- Massage
- Slow Dancing
- Fantasy
- Dressing/undressing one another
- Dry Kissing
- Skinny-dipping/moonlight swimming
- French Kissing
- Erotic films and magazines
- Sex toys
- Walk along beach
- Body paints
- Cruising/parking
- Hugging
- Showering together
- Backrubs
- Masturbation
- Making out/petting
- Mutual masturbation
- Flirting
- Oral sex on a woman (cunnilingus)
- Wrestling

- Oral sex on a woman with a dental dam
- Saunas/Jacuzzis
- Stargazing
- Oral sex on a man wearing a condom
- Candlelight dinner
- Intercourse with a condom (and foam)
- Incense
- Oral/anal contact (rimming)
- Phone sex
- Anal intercourse without a condom
- Fast dancing
- Anal intercourse with a condom
- Intercourse without a condom
- Eating fresh strawberries dipped in chocolate/sensuous feeding
- Snuggling in a beanbag chair eating chocolate chip cookies. . . .

Condom Relay Race:

Description: A fun, "competitive" activity enabling participants to become comfortable handling condoms.

Preparation: This activity requires one condom (unlubricated, or lubricated with plenty of tissues handy!) per participant, and several bananas (firm, not ripe).

Directions: Divide into a comfortable number of teams (8–10 players works best) and have teams form parallel lines. Each player receives one unopened package containing a condom. The first player in each line also receives a banana. When commanded to start, the first player gives the second person in line the banana to hold, opens the package, and rolls the condom onto the banana. the first player then rolls the condom off. The second player then gives the third person in line the banana, and the process continues until the last in line runs to the front of the line and puts the condom on the banana held by the first person in line, who may then eat the banana. . . .

> Developed by:
> Jay Friedman, Sexuality Educator
> Planned Parenthood
> of Tompkins County
> 314 West State St.
> Ithaca, NY 14850

I still shake my head in disbelief every time I read this brochure. This is the *real* Planned Parenthood. This is not sex education; it is mind manipulation and coercion.

The content of these examples is sickening enough. What is worse, however, is the methodology of these sex education programs. Those techniques do not work through the intellect but rather through one's raw emotions as they force open discussions about perversion and sexual immorality in a group setting. The students are unable to defend their position intellectually; thus their will is broken, their convictions undermined, and their consciences seared. How would you feel as a fifteen-year-old girl putting a condom over the taut finger of a fifteen-year-old boy? What would that do to your self-image, your sense of dignity, or even your understanding of right and wrong?

Sex education expert Sondalyn McKasson has written, "[Such] role playing is an indirect, manipulative method of transforming attitudes and behavior. Hence, it is a method of coercion, not instruction."[21]

Economist and social analyst Jacqueline Kasan concurs.

The objectionable feature of these programs now being promoted by Planned Parenthood is not that they teach sex, but that they do it so badly, replacing good biological education with ten to twelve years of compulsory *consciousness raising* and *psycho-sexual therapy,* and using the public schools to advance their own *peculiar worldview*[22] [emphasis added].

Increased Child-Killing

As Planned Parenthood charges down its path of human carnage, it keeps strumming and strumming one ever-present, hypnotic tune, "We need sex ed and birth control. They lower the need for abortions." It's crazy how many uninformed Christians believe this, not to mention the average non-Christian who still believes that Planned Parenthood is a good, decent outfit.

The fact is this: The nationwide implementation of Planned Parenthood-style sex education programs over the past twenty years has been accompanied by a 230 percent increase in teen-age abortions.[23] The programs are completely fraudulent and ineffective in preventing teen-age pregnancy.[24]

Now, *finally,* Planned Parenthood, through the Alan Guttmacher Institute (a well-known Planned Parenthood front group), admits this to be true. They conclude a 1986 study,

> The final result to emerge from the analysis is that neither pregnancy education nor contraceptive education exerts any significant effect on the risk of premarital pregnancy among sexually active teenagers—*a finding that calls into question the argument that formal sex education is an effective tool for reducing adolescent pregnancy* [emphasis added].[25]

Everywhere Planned Parenthood and their partners in crime go, there is an increase in teenage sexuality, sexually transmitted diseases, pregnancy, and abortion. Margaret's dream of making the world in her own image has been frighteningly successful. Occasionally, the birth rate decreases. Why? Because the unborn children have been neatly disposed of—murdered in their mothers' wombs.

Planned Parenthood is a colossal failure. Their self-proclaimed need to exist, more birth control equals less abortions, is nothing more than a blatant lie—chaff in the wind. Their foundation is sinking sand.

Not to worry, though. As long as most Americans and politicians continue on with their Alfred E. Neuman smile and "Don't confuse me with the facts" attitude, Planned Parenthood will continue poisoning minds, promoting perversion, killing babies, and making big, big bucks at it.

Please understand, Planned Parenthood is utterly committed to child-killing. *It is not a side issue for these death-merchants.* Child-killing is a fundamental element in their "methods of fertility management," and they are the nation's single largest abortion provider.[26] They also view the providing of such child-killing services as "the best way to demonstrate . . . advocacy."[27] For Planned Parenthood, killing children is a political statement.

In January 1990, Planned Parenthood made quite a political statement when they appointed Dr. Kenneth Edelin as chairman of the Planned Parenthood Action Fund, their new political action committee. Ten years ago, Edelin was convicted by a Boston jury of manslaughter for strangling a baby who had survived Edelin's attempt at an abortion. Although the jury's verdict was later overturned, God's judgment remains the same: This man murders children, born and unborn. What does this say about Planned Parenthood and its future agenda?

Folks, these institutionalized killers must be stopped!

To Hell with Parents

Planned Parenthood is not only determined to devalue and destroy your children; they are also determined to do it with or without your permission. Their attitude is simple: If you parents don't like us giving birth control and abortions to your children, to hell with you.

Virtually, every time a state legislature enacts a parental notification law, in which parents must be informed of (and in some cases consent to) their minor daughter's abortion, Planned Parenthood rushes to obtain a court injunction barring the law from being enforced. In fact, Planned Parenthood's *1987 Annual Report,* boasts of successfully undermining parental rights in Georgia, Missouri, Minnesota, California, Utah, and Pennsylvania.[28] Moreover, a recent Planned Parenthood fundraising letter appeals for money to keep working against what they mockingly call "squeal laws"—laws guaranteeing parents the right to know what their children are doing.

This proven track record of parental betrayal makes a mockery of Faye Wattleton's acceptance speech for her Humanist of the Year award. She stated, "Parents have to be helped . . . to pass on their family's values. And because many parents just can't do that, sexuality education must be a fundamental part of school curricula from kindergarten through twelfth grade in every school district in the country."[29]

Is this Orwellian doublespeak or what?

Parents have to be helped. Yes, those poor, ignorant, religious, old-fashioned parents just have to be helped to pass on their family's values. That is, unless those values are too religious and conflict with the loose sex, homosexuality, abortion, anything goes message we preach. In that case, we will fight parents tooth and nail in the courts. (It's for their own good.) Meanwhile, we must be sure to brainwash— I mean, liberate—their children into true sexual freedom by teaching them Margaret Sanger's sexual philosophy (and techniques) from kindergarten to twelfth grade.

Our children would probably be safer playing in the street than left in the hands of Planned Parenthood.

Not Content to Teach

Brainwashing our children, however, is not enough. Planned Parenthood's goal is to provide not only abortions without parental consent but also birth control. Enter school-based clinics.

Faye Wattleton also said in that acceptance speech, "Easy access to contraception must be another priority. . . . We must establish many more school-based health clinics that provide contraceptives as part of general health care."[30]

Local schools virtually always have a staff nurse to provide for the general health care of the students. Planned Parenthood, however, wants more. They want to distribute condoms and the pill and provide counselling and abortion referral during school hours. This doesn't sound too appealing to local parents. So Planned Parenthood, in collusion with the pro-death school officials (faithful duespayers to the National Education Association), establishes a "school health clinic" which really duplicates already existing services, with one small difference. This new health clinic imports the message and wares of Planned Parenthood. When a girl or boy comes in for a sprained ankle or a runny nose, the health attendant takes the opportunity to talk about birth control and abortion.[31]

Planned Parenthood Vice President Louise Tryer says, "Every medical contact should be utilized as an opportunity to offer the option of contraception."[32] Planned Parenthood itself emphasizes that "when a student comes to the clinic ostensibly for other reasons, the clinic staff can take the opportunity to see if the student wants to discuss sexual behavior."[33]

Surprise! You Foot the Bill

If seeing your children or the children in your neighborhood polluted by Planned Parenthood outrages you, cheer up. It only gets worse. You get to pay for it! That's right. In fact, of the nearly $300 million Planned Parenthood Federation of America and its affiliates grossed in 1987, over $110 million was paid by you and me through federal, state, and local taxes.[34]

At the federal level alone, it is estimated that Planned Parenthood receives over $30 million a year through Title X program funding, over $8.5 million through Title XIX, over $12.5 million through Title XX funds, and over $3 million through Title V. These figures are staggering!

All of these funds were intended to be used in sex education and birth control programs for the poor. Under Title XX regulations, however, there are no stringent financial eligibility requirements; eligibility for the program is determined nearly entirely by the abortion counselor.[35]

This gaping loophole sets the stage for the following scenario replayed every day throughout America: women are simply convinced that they are needy, and then Planned Parenthood gouges the taxpayer. For instance, if a woman walks off the street into a Planned Parenthood clinic for a pregnancy test and pays cash, the average charge is a little over sixteen dollars. (This, by the way, is the same test that you can purchase for ten dollars at any drug store or have done at any pro-life pregnancy center for free.) Now, if she doesn't have the cash or, more importantly, if the counselor *persuades her* that she doesn't have the cash, Planned Parenthood bills Title XX almost fifty-eight dollars!

How Can These Things Be?

We're paying for our own demise. The government supports Planned Parenthood with our tax dollars so that they can distribute dangerous drugs, abortions, and sordid lies to our children without our knowledge or consent. When we work to pass legislation to protect our children's welfare, these death activists lobby against us and, failing that, seek court injunctions to overturn the laws our elected officials have duly enacted.

The bewildering question is how? How could an organization so sordid and corrupt have such a clean reputation? How could their founder, a close associate and ally of many Hitler and Marxist disciples, have buildings named after her, banquets held in her honor, and be heralded as "an American pioneer in the truest and noblest self-sacrificing sense?"[36] How could such an institution bilk millions of dollars a year from *us*—American taxpayers—to finance the undermining of *our* families, the destruction of *our* youth, and the murder of *our* children?

It's been an amazing use of smoke and mirrors, an Orwellian perversion of words and their definitions, and the faithful obeisance of co-conspirators—a conspiracy we pray will soon be exposed and crushed.

Planned Parenthood will ultimately be exposed, vilified, and crushed under the weight of its sin. God-fearing Americans and the Lord of Hosts will prevail against this hateful organization. Surely, "He who sits in the heavens laughs, the Lord scoffs at them" (Psalm 2:4).

4

THE NATIONAL ORGANIZATION OF WOMEN AND OTHER HARD-CORE FEMINISTS

W hat do child-killing, Marxism, lesbianism, witchcraft, and "vibrators" (for female masturbation) have in common?
You guessed it: the National Organization of Women (NOW).

One of the most important and powerful symbols of wimin's spiritual strength is our blood. menarch, menstruation, and menopause have long been regarded as the most mystical aspects of wimin's power; the power to renew life . . . so why do we, as wimin witches, continue to participate in this mockery of our truest selves? we've cried outrage at the gynocide of the burning times, we've struggled to peel away the patriarchal whitewashing of our goddesses, but still we go along with this denial of our primordial power . . . [we should] insist that pagan/witches/wimins gatherings have a 'blood hut' where bleeding wimin come to create and share power . . . as wimin, we can no longer afford to be uninformed and in the dark about our primal connection to life itself. as witches, we must no longer suppress our bodies' most mystical powers.[1]

NOW Revealed

Tom Minnery of Focus on the Family Ministries actually attended the NOW 1989 national convention to spy out the land. He was shocked. In the vendors' area, a large crowd had gathered around one particular booth. Curious to discover what the interest was about, he squeezed to the front where he found a woman displaying different vibrators for use in masturbation.

At this convention, NOW's current president, Molly Yard, unveiled their latest step in oppression and cruelty—a two-child-per-family limit to conserve our dwindling resources (the big lie). After all, the Rockefeller Tower has been sold to the Japanese; and Molly only makes over fifty thousand dollars a year. We've got to do something!

Where in the world did these people come from? What have they already accomplished? What more do they want?

We cannot understand the incredibly rapid deterioration of our nation, our families, our churches, and the entrenched state of child-killing without understanding the role of the NOW and other radical feminists. These women and their various organizations are deliberately unwinding the very fabric of our culture and weaving their own evil and vile pattern to replace it. In less than three short decades they have made incredible, frightful advances in their godless agendas.

What is tragic is how feminism has damaged the standing of women in virtually every area of our society. Mary Pride, a godly female author (whose book *The Way Home* is must reading for Christian couples), writes,

> Today's women are the victims of the second biggest con game in history. (The first was when the serpent persuaded Eve she needed to upgrade her lifestyle and "become like God.") Courts rip away our protection via "no-fault" divorce, non-existent alimony, and joint custody. "Women's" magazines follow in the footsteps of *Playboy* and *Hustler,* degrading us to the level of unpaid prostitutes by glamorizing uncommitted sex. Employers are losing their commitment to providing our husbands with a living wage, reasoning that we, their wives, can always get a job to make up the slack. Cigarette and alcohol manufacturers gleefully haul in big bucks from the exploding new women's market, while our cancer and alcoholism rates skyrocket. Community colleges everywhere are scrambling to cash in on the huge wave of "displaced homemakers," meaning women who

have been ditched by their husbands and are now forced to earn bread and rent money. All in the name of Liberation.[2]

Unfortunately, not everyone has seen through the empresses' new clothes; and very few have had the courage to point out the nakedness of feminism and its leading voices.

Who are these people? Exactly what do they want?

Betty Friedan and the Feminine Mystique

Most feminists point to Betty Friedan's book, *The Feminine Mystique* (published 1963), as the birth of the popular movement known as the Women's Liberation Movement. While feminist literature and goals had been around for centuries (the struggle for dominance began at the Fall), it was in the early sixties that they began to affect literally every area of American life.[3]

From the beginning, the overtly stated and oft-repeated goal of the feminist movement has been to destroy the traditional family unit. They wish to tear down the traditional home consisting of a man serving as husband, father, protector, and breadwinner; a wife serving as mother and homemaker; and obedient children.

To the feminist, the Biblical role of a wife—submitting to a loving husband, bearing children, staying at home (at least while the children are pre-school age), and volunteering in various church or civic activities—is literally oppression and virtually death to millions of downtrodden and unfulfilled women.

> It is urgent to understand how the very condition of being a house-wife can create a sense of emptiness, nothingness, in women. There are aspects of the housewife role that make it almost impossible for a woman of adult intelligence to retain a sense of human identity, the firm core of self or 'I' without which a human being, man or woman, is not truly alive. For women of ability, in America today, I am convinced there is something about the housewife state that is dangerous.[4]

Friedan and others continually used highly charged, provocative words and images in their message of liberation for oppressed women. Friedan compared the plight of motherhood/homemaker to being in a concentration camp: "[T]he women who 'adjust' as house-wives, who grow up wanting to be 'just a housewife,' are in as much

danger as the millions who walked to their own death in the concentration camps."[5]

The Fuel of Hate

Betty Steele, a self-avowed moderate feminist, wrote an alarming
book, *The Feminist Takeover,* chronicling the virtual takeover by feminism and feminists of critical areas of life in the United States and
Canada.

In her work, she insists that Canada has already passed from a
patriarchal society to a matriarchal one. The question now is how to
deal with some of the family and cultural chaos and restore some
balance. She does not profess to be a Christian, and her book contains some dangerous ideas. However, it *remains* an excellent exposé
of the dangers of radical feminism. As an insider's view of the movement, it is invaluable.

Steele dedicates an entire chapter to exposing the feminists' deliberate promotion of hate and vengeance toward all men. "Male chau-
vinist pigs" became the whipping boys of the feminists, who skillfully
stereotyped men as hateful oppressors to motivate wives to abandon
their husbands and single women to reject the idea of marriage and
the traditional role of a wife and mother. Steele further exposes the
destructive and threatening nature of feminist hatred, arguing that the
hatred of men and the militant vengeance have been the most evil
and unjustified aspects of the Women's Liberation Movement.[6]

But her voice and those of other "moderates" are largely ignored.
Anyone who has read feminist literature or been associated with a
group of radical feminists knows the venomous hatred and contempt
so many of them have for males.

Valerie Solanis wrote this in her SCUM (Society for Cutting Up
Men) manifesto:

> [Men] are a biological accident; the Y (male) gene is an incomplete
> X (female) gene, that is, has an incomplete set of chromosomes. In
> other words, the male is an incomplete female, a walking abortion,
> aborted at the gene state. . . . [She added,] the male, because of his
> obsession to compensate for not being female combined with his
> inability to relate and to feel compassion, has made of the world a
> shitpile. [Later she writes,] the sick, irrational men, those who at-
> tempt to defend themselves against their disgustingness, when they
> see SCUM barreling down on them, will cling in terror to BIG

Mama with her Big Bouncy Boobies, but Boobies won't protect them against SCUM; Big Mama will be clinging to Big Daddy, who will be in the corner shitting in his forceful, dynamic pants.[7]

Pamela Kearan further exhorted,

If hatred exists (and we know it does), let it be of a robust variety. If it is a choice between woman-hating and man-hating, let it be the latter. . . . It is a difficult stance because it requires a fidelity to what is real in us and neither innocuous nor attractive to oppressors, to that part of you which turned you on to feminism in the first place. That part which is really human and cannot submit.[8]

But their hatred does not stop with men. They also disdain and hate women who enjoy and desire the Biblical role of wife and mother, who refuse to follow blindly down the path of destruction. They scornfully refer to them as "house slugs." Solanis describes them in this manner:

[Housewives] have cast their lot with the swine . . . have reduced their minds, thoughts and sights to the male level and who, lacking sense, imagination and wit can have a value only in a male 'society', who can have a place in the sun, or, rather, in the slime only as soothers, ego boosters, relaxers, and breeders. . . .[9]

Roots of Bitterness

Most feminists readily admit, in their writings and personal conversations, that they possess a root of bitterness stemming from a relationship with a man who betrayed his responsibilities as either a father or a husband. Additionally, much anger arises from some inequity or injustice they experienced simply because they were women. This obviously places some of the blame on arrogant, foolish men who have committed evils—some of them very significant—against women. Many of these women need inner healing of this root of bitterness which causes them to hate all men. Many men need to repent.

Lesbianism. A growing percentage of hard-core feminists are hard-core lesbians. They obviously wield much power within the NOW, judging from the fact that the 1989 NOW National Conference had four workshops on lesbian-related topics:

- Lesbians of Color: Dealing with Discrimination's Triple Whammy

- Sexual "McCarthyism": Combatting the Military Witchhunts (Rooting lesbians out of the military)

- Lesbian Rights: Agenda for the 1990s

- Lesbian Rights Task Forces: Overcoming Obstacles to Action.

The teaser on the latter workshop read,

> Although lesbian rights is one of NOW's four major priorities, many chapters and states have a hard time finding activists to work on the issue, despite the fact that a significant number of NOW members are lesbian or bisexual. What gets in the way? How much is a rational reaction to a homophobic society and how much is internalized homophobia?[10]

Evidently, they haven't even yet overcome the natural repulsion toward homosexuality in their own ranks, despite their large numbers. In 1985, then-president Eleanor Smeal conceded that 25 percent of the delegates to that year's national convention were lesbians.[11]

These lesbian feminists are not in any way content to be closet homosexuals. They are determined to force their godless lifestyles on the rest of society. Mary O'Brien wrote that the "basic tasks of feminism are well defined: Destroy Capitalism, End Patriarchy, Smash Heterosexism."[12] With the cursed advent of *in vitro* fertilization, lesbians can now obtain children without any relationships with males. In Canada, lesbians are already bearing children in this manner, and their American counterparts are probably not far behind.

Marxism. Many feminist leaders are openly, unashamedly Marxist. As Steele points out,

> Only the feminists would seem to have a comprehensive picture of the coming years and our new society. They apparently see the sexes equal and androgynous with babies still being produced (sometimes by artificial insemination as in a stud culture, promoted by lesbians), but always the responsibility of the government, with universal child care according to Marxist edict.[13]

One leading book written by feminists north of the border, *Feminism in Canada*, has these words in the introduction: "All the contributors agree . . . that feminism is revolutionary and that the feminist revolution will be a total one, leaving no aspect of social life un-changed."[14]

And lest anyone tell you that Canadian feminists are an abnormal breed of feminists, think again. The strong presence and acceptance of communists at the 1989 NOW convention shows otherwise.

Day care and public education are critical in the ·feminist pro-gram for brainwashing our children and bringing about a Marxist/so-cialist state. The NOW Convention offered a workshop entitled "To-ward a Child-Care Policy." The leading line in the teaser stated, "Establishing a comprehensive, US child-care policy is essential to all of America's children."[15] Why? Isn't mommy's care good enough? Well, no, if mommy isn't training little Johnny and Susie to be sexu-ally-neutered socialists.

We cannot underestimate the havoc and destruction already wreaked through statist public education indoctrination. Kids can nei-ther read nor write; but they can fornicate, rebel against authority, and flounder in the sea of humanist amorality. With the clamor for state-run day care and more hours in state-run schools, we can only expect more calamity.

Make no mistake—the feminists want to own, mold, and control your children, or at least bridle you so that you train them how "Big Sister" wants. One feminist advocate of Zero Population Growth writes,

> The right to breed implies ownership of children. This concept is no longer tenable. Society pays an ever larger share of the cost of raising and educating children. The idea of ownership is surely affected by the thrust of the statement that "He who pays the piper calls the tune."[16]

Mary Pride exposes the vile heart and intentions of the godless, statist public education system.

> The public schools, you see, are the coercive utopians' catechism classes. Since coercive utopians refuse to reproduce themselves the normal way, public education becomes their avenue for passing on their beliefs to the next generation—through other people's chil-dren. Public school is their private school. Whether the cause be de-veloping "world citizens" as opposed to patriotic Americans, "sexually active" as opposed to moral teenagers, Socialists instead of believers in free enterprise, or feminists instead of Mommies, there are text-books designed to teach it and a curriculum designed to enforce it.[17]

Marriage. Betty Friedan likened being a married housewife to being in a concentration camp. Gloria Steinem, another famous American feminist, described marriage as "the only gamble most women take" and as "a way of reducing two people to one and a half."[18] American feminist Shulamith Firestone wrote, "[Marriage] is organized around and reinforces a fundamentally oppressive biological condition." She advocated that we forego "our concepts of exclusive physical partnerships," that children be born to a unit, and that the blood tie of a mother to her child eventually be severed.[19] Sheila Cronan concluded, "Since marriage constitutes slavery for women, it is clear that the Women's Movement must concentrate on attacking this institution. Freedom for women cannot be won without the abolition of marriage."[20]

It's no wonder that so many feminist leaders are single, divorced or never married. Granted, these radical feminists do not represent every woman who holds to certain elements of feminist ideology (for example, ending the exploitation of women in pornography, equal pay for equal work—both legitimate goals); but they represent the tip of the spear. They are the leaders who steer the ship and feed their footsoldiers their philosophical chaff. So many women in the camp with the feminists may find their labors and contributions supporting goals with which they disagree. These footsoldiers should pick their comrades more carefully.

"Liberated" Sexuality. To me, the abandonment of sexual restraints is one of the most contradictory, harmful elements of the feminist revolution.

In their determination to rid America of "Victorian" morality, the feminists have encouraged sexual sins of all kinds: multiple partners, homosexuality, adultery, fornication, and so on. And what sin-bent male would not revel in women's newfound "freedom"? Now men can have illicit sexual relationships without commitment, love, and longevity. These feminists have handed the exploiting male his one-night stands on a silver platter. No longer must a man seek to be strong, protective, chivalrous, and worshipful of the child-nurturing sex; he can be a predator in search of his next sexual experience with a liberated woman.

This is having very negative ramifications for women as they reach and pass thirty. One major study showed a single woman in her thirties had very, very little chance of marrying—and that at a time when most of them were tired of the revolving door of relationships and wanted to get married. But the available men in that age group don't want marriage. Thus, the liberated woman is now condemned to liberation from the oppression of marriage. They made their bed; now they must sleep in it—with whoever they can find.

The feminist liberation, in its clamor to be free from exploitation because of their sex, actually furthered their own sexual exploitation. In the forties and fifties, "nice girls" did not sleep around. Now, supposedly "nice girls" do sleep around. In days gone by, if a man got a woman pregnant, the noble thing—what was expected—was to marry her. Now, threatening to leave, he tells her to kill the baby. If she keeps the child, she often raises it alone. The man is off prowling for another liberated woman and is often avoiding any financial responsibility for the child. This is a tragedy for women.

Grand Illusions

For all the exposure and impact feminists have had, their movement is not as large as one might imagine. For example, the NOW has a membership of approximately 160,000. This fails to even rank in the top three women's groups in America. Indeed, Concerned Women for America has six hundred thousand members, nearly four times that of NOW; and these six hundred thousand are adamantly opposed to NOW's godless agenda and their radical feminism.

Then why do we hear only of the NOW and their radical feminist ideology? Well, where do you hear about them? Television, radio, and newspapers. And where do you think all those liberated women reporters and editors and their sympathetic male comrades stand on the agenda of radical feminism? The NOW and the secular media have been in a love affair since NOW's birth. The coverage and credence they receive is grossly disproportionate to their size; but through the secular media they wield an incredible amount of influence.

For instance, compare the media coverage of the 1989 NOW Convention with that of the Concerned Women for America. In July, fifteen hundred pro-death NOW delegates gathered in Cincinnati and received evening network coverage from ABC, CBS, NBC, and CNN. On November 4, 1989, over fifty thousand participated via satellite in CWA's tenth anniversary celebration and were addressed by President Bush's drug czar, William Bennett. Media coverage was noticeably absent; their bias is not. Nor is their intended message: "NOW represents the women of America. Get it?"

NOW's influence and poison has also infiltrated our culture through our colleges and universities. Yes, whole battalions of radical feminists are presently lecturing and discipling the next generation of our nation's leaders. In so-called "Women's Studies" curricula, day in and day out, eager, young, impressionable minds are readily indoctrinated with their hedonistic, Marxist ideology. Christian author Dr. George Gilder contends that every year over twenty-five thousand co-eds become dedicated feminists through these radical seminary programs.

While the feminist elite is fairly small, they have quickly exerted incredible influence over our culture and lives through these two means. They quietly have seized "the robes" of elementary through university education; and they noisily have clamored in front of the camera or microphone as their friendly feminist reporter delightfully repeats their lying rhetoric, day after day, night after night.

Children. The Waterloo for the radical feminist is children. Feminist author Mary O'Brien writes in *The Politics of Reproduction* that a woman's reproductive role is "nature's traditional and bitter trap for the suppression of women."[21]

We already read Shulamith Firestone's statement that children should be born to a unit and that the blood tie of the mother should be severed. She also demanded "the freeing of women from the tyranny of their biology by any means available" and continued, "Childbearing could be taken over by technology."[22]

To the feminists, children are more than an inconvenience; they are a cruel trick of nature. Or worse, they are rude and uninvited intrusions into a woman's life, keeping her from full consciousness of her self and denying her the lifestyle, career goals, financial status, and freedom of movement that she wants.

So what does one do with one of these little angels who disrupts one's devilish lifestyle? Kill it.

Understand this: Feminism will always demand child-killing. As you well know, abortion is the core of NOW's agenda; but let me reveal to you just how committed these women are to the right to execute their offspring.

On national television, I have pressed Faye Wattleton and Molly Yard to denounce third-trimester abortions. These abortions kill children during the seventh through ninth months of development, children who are capable of living outside the womb. These women refuse to do so.

I pressed Molly Yard on the "Oprah Winfrey Show" to denounce sex-selection child-killings, in which about 90 percent of the unwanted babies killed are girls (perhaps future feminists). She refused. In fact, Molly ended up turning off her receiver and yelling like a cheerleader, "It is her choice! It is her choice!"[23]

Other feminists have adopted a practice perhaps even more perverse: planned pregnancy/planned abortion. Reportedly, these women become pregnant with no intention of carrying their child to term. The reasons are varied: to prove their fertility, to test the commitment of their lover, or to experience a rite of passage similar to menses and childbirth. Feminist writer Leslie Savan also adds that the practice can be a means of retaining both one's femininity (by getting pregnant) and one's feminism (by killing your child).[24]

Obviously, though, feminists do not want to kill every child they conceive (as we've seen with the lesbians who are impregnated through in vitro fertilization). They just want the freedom to kill the children they don't want, have the one or two children they do want, and then be able to dump them into tax-funded, Marxist-oriented day care. They need all this freedom so that they can go on fulfilling themselves, raising their consciousness, and serving the goddess. And they insist we do the same.

While I was on "The Oprah Winfrey Show," I asked Molly Yard what she thought about China's birth control program, which she knows is a government-mandated one-child-per-family limit and relies upon coerced abortion for those who fail to comply. She launched into a lengthy defense of China's barbarism, stating, "I consider the Chinese government's policy [on birth control] among the most intelligent in the world." I turned to the audience and said, "A woman who will sit here and say that that government is right when it imposes a one-child-per-family will one day turn around and tell you that you can have one child per family! Talk about government intrusion. . . . That is terrifying."[25]

Well, she has. At the 1989 NOW convention, she unveiled her new agenda: two children per family. She knows this will lead to forced child-killing, but apparently she doesn't care.

She is doing it under the guise that we are running out of resources. Hence, we aren't killing children; we're saving the planet.

This is a smokescreen, a bold-faced lie. Again, in *The Way Home*, Mary Pride thoroughly and factually debunks this myth.[26]

The NOW has always claimed that a majority of Americans believed in killing children. Yet they are frantic at the Webster decision (which did little to undermine Roe). Why? Because they know that they don't have a majority. Columnist Joseph Sobran pointed this out in his caustic piece, "Molly Yard's Phantom Majority."

> If the feminists really believed that the majority was with them, they would not have been unduly disturbed that the Court had widened the discretion of state legislatures. They would have, in fact, regarded the legislatures as a friendlier forum than the conservative Court.[27]

Now Molly Yard and her sisters have lost their sustaining elite and the will to produce that phantom majority they have been claiming. The trouble is that they don't really believe in it themselves.

The truth is that feminists have always used (and abused) the courts to ram their godless agenda down the throats of the rest of us. They are continuing their abuse in court this very hour against Operation Rescue. They have us in a major RICO lawsuit along with Joe Scheidler and others in Chicago. And they have successfully sued us in New York and are seeking three hundred thousand dollars in attorneys' fees. Their stated goal is to bankrupt us, to drive us out of business.

They can't beat us in the street; they can't beat us in debates; they can't beat us in public opinion about child-killing; so they turn to tyrant judges to quietly crush us beneath the weight of federal judiciary. It's a tactic that has worked well for them in other areas. Why not here?

Witchcraft. One only has to read the headlines or watch Geraldo to know that there is a revival of witchcraft going on in America. The poem I quoted at the beginning of this chapter is anything but abnormal. I'm not saying that every feminist is in favor of blood sacrifice to Satan (although some are). I am saying that a very strong contingent within feminism is involved to one degree or another in some form of ancient, occult practices, part of which we commonly refer to as witchcraft.

For those who think these the words of a madman, look at one of the workshops at NOW's last convention:

Feminist Spirituality

This workshop will examine the status of both the feminist and patriarchal religious communities, and will discuss ways to continue laying the spiritual foundations for a new society. Topics will include
words and symbols, creating centers for equality, and ideas from the
Book of Feminist Spiritual Wisdom.[28]

What kind of spiritual foundations and new society do you think
they're speaking of? Do you want to live in it? On April 23, 1976, the
first national all-women conference on women's spirituality was held
in Boston, Massachusetts. Naomi Goldenberg, a feminist, reported:

After listening attentively to two addresses . . . the audience became
very active . . . they chanted, 'The Goddess is Alive—Magic is Afoot.'
The women evoked the Goddess with dancing, stamping, clapping,
and yelling. They stood on pews and danced bare-breasted on the
pulpit and amid the hymnbooks.

In fact, the women were angry at all religions of the fathers and
took this opportunity to mock and defy those religions in a church
they had rented for the occasion. . . . Proclaiming that the 'Goddess
is Alive' in a traditional church setting is proclaiming that . . . being
female is divine. . . . [29]

As feminism indoctrination has been on the rise, in one college
campus after another, courses on women's spirituality have become
common. The following course description is not uncommon.

417 Women's Spirituality

Exploration of women's spirituality beyond traditional, patriarchal
religions. The significance of the ancient Goddess traditions for
women today, individual spirituality as a manifestation of personal
power, and the transformation of spiritual power into political
power.[30]

Anyone who still doubts the feminist/witchcraft connection
should just come to one of our rescue missions in some large cities.
In the San Francisco area, women dressed as witches and calling out
incantations against Christians have been at several rescues.

In Burlington, Vermont, many of the supporters of Vermont
Women's Health Center are avowed witches. These female sorcerers
have arrived at rescues in cultic dress, beating drums, blaspheming
Jesus and crying out strange words and incantations, apparently trying

to conjure up demons. One has to wonder what happens with the blood of the innocent children murdered in this killing center.

If anyone doubts that feminism is at its very core anti-Christ, listen again to Naomi Goldenberg's commentary on the goal of feminism: "The feminist movement in Western culture is engaged in the slow execution of Christ and Yahweh. Yet very few of the men and women working for sexual equality within Christianity and Judaism realize the extent of their heresy."[31]

I have had many, many conversations with hard-core feminists and have shared the gospel of Jesus Christ with them. Virtually every feminist I have ever spoken with makes a point to refer to God as "she." They truly believe in "the goddess"—whatever false god or demonic delusion that might be.

Poison in Our Water

If the influence of feminism was limited to the unbelieving, that would be bad enough and would require our efforts to combat their lies. But tragically, feminism has crept into the church and raised its ugly head, demanding that we abandon or compromise Biblical truth and bow down to the feminist ideology.

The greatest and most tragic impact of feminism within the church is its impact on the family, particularly our attitude toward children. Scripture consistently regards children as a blessing, proclaiming that we are blessed to have many children and that we should "be fruitful and multiply." But millions of Christians have unconsciously bought the lie that children are a nuisance, an imposition, a financial liability, and a burden that inhibits our lifestyles or (God forgive us) our "ministries." Furthermore, to have too many children is foolish, unwise, and irresponsible. None of these anti-child attitudes can be supported by Scripture. In fact, they fly in the face of Scripture. But being a compromised Christian in the "me generation" has its identifiable consequences.

So we dutifully follow Margaret Sanger and Molly Yard's advice and take drugs or use devices to prohibit us from receiving God's least wanted blessing—children—while we get ahead financially, get used to married life, and so on. After that second, or if we're really radical, third child, we submit willingly to sterilization. (Gosh, I hate that word.) We are the very people Margaret Sanger wanted to sterilize, and we've willingly submitted ourselves to her godless attack on the church. If someone could laugh from hell, she undoubtedly would.

Many of our married women with working husbands (who earn enough to support the family) then put the child with a sitter or day care and return to work. These Christian women disregard the clear dictates of Titus: ". . . that they [older women] may encourage the young women to love their husbands, to love their children, to be sensible, pure, workers at home . . . that the word of God may not be dishonored" (Titus 2:4–5). We put money ahead of nurturing our children.

Then (please forgive my bluntness), we send our children to god-less, state schools where they are exposed to God (and the human-ists)-knows-what. Do we need to wonder why so many of our young people fall away from the faith when they are in their teens? When will we wake up!

Divorce is rampant in the church. We get married and divorced for self-centered reasons rather than under Biblical guidelines. We entertain the teaching of heretics—who call themselves Biblical femi-nists—in our midst.

Frankly, one reason the church has tolerated child-killing for over twenty years is because the antichild attitude in the church has been a poison that has left us lethargic and uncaring. We must now repent of our own attitude toward children and return to a Biblical view of chil-dren: "Blessed is the man whose quiver is full of them" (Psalm 127:5).

Back to the Feminists

I, for one, am sick and tired of hearing the feminists' godless agenda. I'm sick of their ideology's fruits: The murder of unborn babies and the destruction of born children in the various ways discussed. I loathe hearing them whine for millions of dollars in day care money or millions to take care of the hundreds of thousands of emotionally disturbed children, many (if not most) of whom are disturbed be-cause daddy is gone or mommy is on her second (or third) marriage. Feminist ideology has helped destroy the family and the culture and they want the taxpayers to pump more money into their havoc-ridden programs and ideologies. Forget it!

I have some advice for the feminists. Do yourself a favor. Turn to the Lord Jesus Christ for the forgiveness of your sins and learn what God has intended you to be as a woman—the beautiful crowning point of creation. Stop reducing the exalted position of women. Stop betraying your children. Repent, turn to God, and times of refreshing will come to you from the Lord.

If you will not repent and are determined to die in your sin, then do us a favor. Don't have any children. Go ahead and fulfill the curse of God by sterilizing your womb. And then along with your shut womb, shut your mouths. Don't try to tell us anything about raising children. Anyone who promotes the wholesale slaughter of children has forfeited any right to talk about the children who escaped your knife. Be silent. You've already helped destroy an entire generation. How many more must suffer under the tyranny of your folly?

WHAT IS THE ACLU?

Attending the amusement park as a child was always an enjoyable experience for me. One of the funniest events of the day was the tour through the house of mirrors. As a youngster, I was amazed that the image in the mirror was actually me. Seeing our normal, healthy bodies turn into hilarious distortions of humanity drew sustained laughter and an inevitable second (and third) look.

As an adult, I still get a kick out of the house of mirrors, but it no longer amazes me. I know that the image in the mirror is a bent reflection of the truth—hence a deception.

What would amaze me, however, would be to take a distorted, abnormal, unhealthy image, and through a clever bending of the reflection, transform it into a thing of beauty; or at least, something admirable and healthy. That is exactly what has happened with the American Civil Liberties Union (ACLU). The ACLU, through an incredible use of mirrors, has been able to hide its vulgar, grotesque, even hideous image from an unwary public and to this day manages to present itself as healthy and normal—as American as baseball.

But, thank God, the mirror is cracking. Far from being American or civil or standing for liberties, the ACLU is a cauldron of evil. As we shall see, the ACLU is an enemy of Christ, of righteousness, and of freedom; it is a self-conscious adversary of the family, the church, and ultimately a free government.

The ACLU is the world's oldest, largest, and most influential association of lawyers, political activists, and social reformers.[1] For more than seventy years[2] it has claimed a single-minded devotion to "protecting" the Constitutional rights of every citizen in the United States through lobbying, legislation and, most especially, litigation.[3] As we shall see, their claim to protecting the Constitution would be laughable were it not for their achievements.

I have relied heavily on the excellent book by George Grant entitled *Trial and Error* (Wolgemuth & Hyatt, 1989), for much of the material in this chapter. For permission to use his thorough research I am very grateful.

Remarkable Successes

Along the way, the organization has achieved a number of frighteningly remarkable successes—more often than not, dramatically transforming the nature of America's legal and judicial system for the worse. With only 250,000 contributing members,[4] seventy staff lawyers,[5] and a budget of approximately fourteen million dollars,[6] it has established more standing court precedents than any other entity outside the Justice Department[7] and has appeared before the Supreme Court more often than anybody else except the government itself.[8] A few of its landmark cases include:

1925, The Scopes Monkey Trial: The ACLU launched its manipulated test case strategy against the State of Tennessee's education standards, locating a small-town biology teacher to act as plaintiff and a showcase lawyer to focus national attention on the issue. Despite the fact that the ACLU and its high-profile defender, Clarence Darrow, lost to the state's attorney William Jennings Bryan, the publicity proved invaluable.

1973, Doe v. Bolton: In this manipulated test case, the ACLU led the legal fight that, in conjunction with the infamous Roe v. Wade ruling, eventually overturned the laws against child-killing in all fifty states.

1982, Arkansas Creationism Case: Fifty-six years after it had argued against educational exclusionism in the Scopes Trial, the ACLU reversed itself, fighting *against* the right to teach various views of origins in public school classrooms.

1983, The Akron Case: The ACLU successfully fought to overturn the right of localities to regulate medical safety. Moreover, they fought *against* informed consent for women considering abortion of their child. So much for an informed "choice."

1986, Jager v. Douglas County: The ACLU was able to forbid religious invocations before high school football games. For one of the first times, the lawyers successfully used endorsement language instead of the traditional establishment language—the implication being that the government is not only forbidden to establish or institutionalize religion; it is forbidden to endorse or condone it as well. In other words, praying for players' safety before a game is unconstitutional and hence illegal.

1987, The Bork Confirmation: Abandoning all pretense of political neutrality, the ACLU led the smear campaign designed to deny Judge Robert Bork confirmation to the Supreme Court.

1988, Civil Rights Restoration Act: The Washington office of the ACLU led the year-long legislative battle to overturn the Supreme Court's Grove City decision, thus requiring institutions receiving federal grants to extend privileged service access to homosexuals, abortionists, and drug abusers.

1989, Equal Access Act: The ACLU was successful in making voluntary school prayer or Bible study meetings *before or after* school the one exception to the federal Equal Access Act of 1984. So while students may gather in public schools to discuss Marxism, view Planned Parenthood films, play Dungeons and Dragons, listen to heavy metal rock, or hold gay activist club gatherings, *they are not allowed to pray or read the Bible together.* We expect this in Russia. Is this what America is about?

By any standards these achievements are remarkable. And, considering the fact that the ACLU no longer has to take many of its cases before the bench—its influence is so great that even a threat of a lawsuit is often enough to change policies, reshape legislation, and redirect priorities in case after case[9]—those achievements are even more remarkable and dangerous.

The ACLU is not simply a corporate entity. It is not simply a political action committee. And it is not simply a legal advocacy group. It is a cause that men rally to, sacrifice for, and find identity in. It is a movement. It is a cabal. It is a faith, albeit a heretical one.

A Deceptive Image

It is crucial to comprehend this basic, fundamental fact if we are to make any sense of the ACLU's glaring paradoxes and outright contradictions: The very thing that makes the ACLU so unpopular—its heretical faith—is also what makes it so successful and respectable.

The American Civil Liberties Union does not advertise itself as a cause. Nor does it advertise itself as a movement or a faith. Instead, it advertises itself as an advocate of truth, justice, and the American way. It advertises itself as the lone defender against prejudice, tyranny, and brutality.

What it advertises itself as, and what it actually is, are two entirely different things. The fact is, what the ACLU wants and ultimately does utterly betrays what it says. The image you see in the mirror is a carefully drafted deception. That discrepancy is the key to properly adjudging and understanding the organization.

The ACLU says it "has only one client: the Bill of Rights." [10]   It advertises itself as doggedly impartial, caring only about the integrity of the Constitution itself.[11] But the facts say otherwise. The radical labor and social dissent movements (such as communism) have always been the ACLU's primary clients, the Constitution notwithstanding. In its very first annual report, the ACLU described itself as "a militant, central bureau in the labor movement for legal aid, defense strategy information and propaganda."[12] It went on to assert that along with the International Workers of the World and the Communist Party, it was the "center of resistance" for radical groups in America.[13] In its advertising fliers, it argued that "the union of organized labor, the farmers and the radical and liberal movements, is the most effective means . . . whereby rights can be secured and maintained. It is that union of forces which the American Civil Liberties Union serves."[14] Thirteen years later, the organization reaffirmed its commitments to the radical cause stating that "the struggle between capital and labor is the most vital application of the principle of civil liberty."[15]

In 1976, Aryeh Neie, then the executive director of the ACLU, broadened the client base of the organization, saying that it was the "legal branch of the women's movement."[16] In fact, as the years went by, the ACLU would identify with virtually every subversive dissent movement that appeared on the national scene: communists, anarchists, socialists, terrorists, homosexuals, lesbians, pornographers, Nazis, abortionists, and atheists.[17]

Even a cursory glance at the caseload of the ACLU demonstrates that it is far more interested in pursuing its godless ideological agenda than it is in defending the Constitution.[18]

The ACLU says that it is wholly nonpartisan.[19] It advertises itself as an objective organization that is "neither liberal nor conservative, Republican nor Democrat."[20] Instead, it is "a public interest organization devoted exclusively to protecting the basic civil liberties of all Americans."[21] But the facts say otherwise.

Roger Baldwin, the founder and leading force in the ACLU until his death in 1981, asserted the partisan nature of his agenda saying, "I am for Socialism, disarmament, and ultimately for abolishing the state itself as an instrument and compulsion. I seek social ownership of property, the abolition of the propertied class, and sole control by those who produce wealth. Communism is the goal. It all sums up into one single purpose—the abolition of dog-eat-dog under which we live."[22]

In case anyone didn't tell Roger, communism and the freedom embodied in the United States Constitution cannot peacefully coexist—in fact they are enemies.

In recent years, the ACLU has revealed its blatant partisanship time after time. It vehemently opposed the Vietnam War.[23] It demanded unilateral nuclear disarmament.[24] It called for disinvestment in South Africa.[25] It violated its own policy in order to stymie the nomination of William Rehnquist to the Supreme Court.[26] It steadfastly opposed the Nixon administration and was the first organization to call for his impeachment following Watergate.[27] During the eight years of the Reagan administration, it blasted the president with one invective after another.[28] It led the fight to defeat the confirmation of Robert Bork to the Supreme Court.[29] It frequently writes speeches for candidates that it likes.[30] And it even issues scorecards on legislators, evaluating their performance according to the ACLU's own ideological yardstick.[31]

As Phil Donohue has said, "Quite simply, the ACLU has a politics, and that politics is liberalism."[32] Liberalism in this sense is a very kind word.

The ACLU says that at the time it was set up, during the furor of the First World War, "freedom of speech didn't exist."[33] It then goes on to messianicly advertise itself as the only "nationwide, non-partisan organization dedicated to preserving and defending the Bill of Rights."[34] But the facts say otherwise.

John Haynes Holmes, one of the ACLU's original Board members, confessed that the organization was only "using the civil liberties issue," and that its real interest was "the cause of radicalism."[35] He went so far as to say that the ACLU was "manipulating cases as a means toward certain ends, namely, the advancement of labor and the revolution."[36] Roger Baldwin himself said that "civil liberties, like democracy, are useful tools for social change."[37] So when the tool of liberty is through being used, throw it away. Put tyranny in its place.

Perhaps that explains the curious inconsistency of the organization in its defense of the Bill of Rights. For instance, the Second Amendment of the Bill of Rights says that "the rights of the people to keep and bear arms shall not be infringed." But according to the ACLU Policy Guide, "the possession of weapons by individuals is not constitutionally protected."[38] The Tenth Amendment of the Bill of Rights says that "The powers not delegated to the United States by the Constitution, nor prohibited by it to the states, are reserved to the states respectively, or to the people." But in 1985, the ACLU castigated the president and the attorney general for suggesting that Tenth Amendment provisions be enforceable by law.[39] Over the years, the ACLU has variously opposed the enforcement of clauses in the First Amendment[40] and the Fifth Amendment.[41] It has defended the free speech, transit, and assembly rights of nuclear protesters[42] but has denied those same rights to abortion protesters.[43] It has fought for the right to strike for unions[44] but it has fought against the right to work for individuals.[45]

The ACLU says that "the Constitution as originally conceived was deeply flawed."[46] In fact, it was not until the organization came along that the American ideals of freedom and justice could be realized. "The ACLU," it brazenly asserts, "was the missing ingredient that made our constitutional system finally work."[47] And so, it shows no hesitation in advertising itself as "the ignition for the constitutional engine, the key that makes it run."[48] It is terrifying to think where the engine will propel us with the likes of the ACLU guiding the way.

Part of this sense of self-importance stems from the ACLU's discovery—and enforcement in the courts—of the right to privacy.[49] Everything from wiretapping to fingerprinting, drug testing to lie detectors, and breathalizers to airport security measures have been ardently opposed by the organization on the basis of this right.[50] Similarly, everything from child-killing to euthanasia, homosexuality to pornography, and drug use to prostitution have been adamantly defended.[51]

Apparently, however, this liberal notion of privacy does not extend to everyone. Take the case of Illinois Congressman Henry Hyde. A prominent foe of child-killing in the House and the author of federal legislation to limit the use of tax dollars for the killing of unborn children, Hyde rankled the ire of ACLU officials. So, they plotted a course of retaliation: They hired a private investigator to report on the congressman's leisure activities, to monitor his mail, and to compile a three-hundred-page dossier on his private life.[52] A main part of their accusation and hence his crime was that he is a devout Roman Catholic.

The ACLU has found exceptions to the right to privacy for any number of its adversaries as well: nonunion workers,[53] conservative judges,[54] police,[55] pro-lifers,[56] Christian evangelists,[57] parents of teens,[58] and concerned teachers.[59]

The ACLU says, "Unless we defend the rights of the sons of bitches, we'll lose our own."[60]   Thus, it advertises itself as America's watchdog for the underdog—as the beachhead defense for citizens who face civil rights deprivation, regardless of who they are or what they believe.[61] But the facts say otherwise.

The ACLU only rushes to the aid of those that contribute to its cause, its movement, and its faith. The perception that it has a diverse portfolio of cases scattered all over the ideological map is, very simply, a myth. Although the organization has occasionally ventured out of the Left's territorial waters to defend such groups as the Ku Klux Klan,[62] the John Birch Society,[63] and even the Jews for Jesus,[64] without exception those cases have been carefully contrived either as public relations show pieces or as back-door precedents for their own agenda.[65] In other words, they have been little more than a means to an end.

Roger Baldwin admitted as much when he wrote,

All my associates in the struggle for civil liberties take a class position, though many of them don't know it. I too take a class position.

It is anti-capitalist and pro-revolutionary. I champion civil liberty as the best of the nonviolent means of building the power on which the workers' rule must be based. If I aid the reactionaries to get free speech now and then, if I go outside the class struggle to fight against censorship, it is only because those liberties help to create a more hospitable atmosphere for working class liberties. The class struggle is the central conflict of the world; all others are incidental.[66]

So the incidental case that the ACLU might deign to undertake for a nonradical, a conservative, a Christian, or an ordinary citizen— in Baldwin's parlance a reactionary—is little more than an incidental means to create a more hospitable atmosphere for its pet Leftist causes.

Abortion Stance

The ACLU is an unapologetic advocate of child-killing on demand.[67] Very simply, the organization is at the forefront of the legal battle over the sanctity of human life. It has handled more than 70 percent of all medical ethics cases in United States courts.[68] It has participated in one way or another in every abortion case that has appeared before the Supreme Court.[69] And it has been unyielding in its insistence that the government provide the medical atrocities of abortion, infanticide, and euthanasia as a service to all citizens out of the tax largess.[70]

The ACLU's commitment to child-killing is so ardent that they have eagerly abandoned their own guidelines in an attempt to crush, or at least bankrupt, Operation Rescue.

Despite the fact that the ACLU guidelines state that "orderly, non-violent protests such as sit-ins are not a trespass on private property but rather a constitutional right to express opinion," pro-life rescuers have been consistently denied that right, and the ACLU has advised abortion chambers to dogmatically enforce trespassing violations.[71] When Operation Rescue came to Los Angeles in March 1989, the ACLU opposed us with unrelenting fervor. Carol Sobbells, pro-abortion feminist and attorney for the ACLU, met with Police Chief Darryl Gates, insisting that they vigorously enforce trespass laws and that we be arrested at any rescues. She also met with two city councilmen and Mayor Bradley for the same reason, boasting of their support.

The ACLU then completely betrayed its own policy—and remained faithful to child-killing—secured an injunction against rescues, and sued us. They won some preliminary battles and were awarded $110 thousand in attorneys' fees (thus trying to bankrupt us). Judge Tashima ultimately ruled in our favor and vacated the injunction, but the ACLU appealed to the Circuit Court of Appeals, which immediately re-instated the injunction. The case may go on for years. The ACLU is committed to child-killing at all costs—even in the face of blatant contradictions with its own civil liberties principles and moral rhetoric. And those contradictions abound:

- It has said that it condemns any lack of respect for human life.[72]

- It says that it abhors anything that might give society the unmistakable message that life ceases to be sacred when it is thought useful to take it and that violence is legitimate when it is thought justified by pragmatic concerns that appeal to those having the legal power to kill.[73]

- It argues that "A civilized and humane society does not deliberately kill human beings."[74]

- It asserts that teaching "the permissibility of killing people to solve social problems is the worst possible example to set for any society."[75]

Its own ardent pro-life rhetoric notwithstanding, the ACLU has maintained its unequivocal pro-death position since Roger Baldwin—the ACLU's founder and leading light—and Margaret Sanger—Planned Parenthood's founder and leading light—first became comrades-in-arms back in 1915. This irony is never reconciled in its literature. Instead, the official ACLU Policy Guide ambiguously states that the organization can offer "no comment on the wisdom or the moral implications" of pro-death activities, arguing that such matters fall into the nether realm of "free speech and privacy rights." Accordingly, over the years the ACLU has sought to:[76]

- Abrogate all state and local laws regulating abortion trafficking—even before Roe v. Wade and Doe v. Bolton were heard before the Supreme Court.

- Require states to effect living will statutes legalizing consensual mercy killing for the terminally ill or permanently disabled.

- Ban informed consent requirements that would inform women of the many medical risks inherent to abortion procedures and allow them to have access to information about fetal development.

- Decriminalize assisted suicide.

- Deregulate abortion procedures through the entire nine months of gestation, making abortion the only completely unregulated surgical procedure in all of medicine.

- Disallow spousal consent laws concerning child-killing.

- Disallow parental consent laws concerning child-killing.

- Refuse even parental notification requirements concerning child-killing.

- Oppose regulations that require reasonable and humane treatment of the children that survive abortion procedures.

- Require federal, state, and local funding for abortion and birth limitation services for all citizens.

- Coordinate its judicial, legislative, and educational efforts with Planned Parenthood, the Hemlock Society, the National Abortion Rights Action League, the National Abortion Federation, the Alan Guttmacher Institute, and other radical pro-death advocacy groups.

These judicial demands are claimed as basic civil rights and fundamental civil liberties for women, terminally ill patients, or the permanently disabled. Of course, the ACLU somehow fails to mention the civil liberty concerns of the children that are ripped limb from limb inside their mothers' wombs, or are starved to death on the neonatal wards of our hospitals, or are burned by poisonous solutions, or are experimented on in research laboratories, or have their organs harvested from their bodies one by one. It also fails to mention the civil liberty concerns of parents, spouses, communities and tax-paying citizens who are forced into a position of either helpless complicity or total incognizance by its pro-death policies.

And as if all that were not bad enough, the ACLU takes its pro-death commitment one step further still: actually enjoining the civil liberties sanctions on pro-life groups that oppose abortion, infanticide, and euthanasia. It seems that some civil liberties are guaranteed by the First Amendment only to those citizens that happen to agree with the ACLU's liberal worldview and social agenda. For instance: though the policy guide says that "the ACLU supports the right to picket in any circumstances, by any method, and in any numbers," it has often fought to limit the circumstances, methods, and numbers for peaceful pro-life protests.[77]

The ACLU officially deplores espionage tactics in all other circumstances and situations, but when it comes to pro-life protesters, it condones implementing special surveillance measures, compiling dossiers on individuals and photographing potential opponents for later litigation.[78]

It has often defended antiwar, nuclear, and ecology protesters when they have crossed state lines to incite riots, but in the case of peaceful pro-life protesters, it has advised the enforcement of federal racketeering statutes—or RICO laws.[79]

Thus, as a result of its foursquare commitment to the pro-death ideology, the ACLU has been forced to contradict not only its carefully phrased moral rhetoric but its most cherished and fundamental principles as well. But it is ultimately being consistent with its own roots—for those who hate God, love death (see Proverbs 8:36). And the ACLU certainly does both.

6

HIRED ASSASSINS AND THEIR BLOOD-BOUGHT PROPHETS

Viewing again and again the grainy black-and-white films of the Nazi concentration camps has made the endless piles of corpses familiar to many of us. The familiarity, however, does not diminish the gruesome reality. These documentaries undoubtedly also include footage of the death camp's research laboratories in which innocent human beings were used like lab rats for perverse and cruel tortures in the name of scientific advancement. Children and adults were injected with various poisonous chemicals; some had portions of their brain removed; others were dropped into pools of freezing water and carefully monitored as they succumbed (*the Dachau Freezing Experiments*, 1942); many were asphyxiated in high-altitude (zero-oxygen) experiments; following hysterotomies, the surviving children were jabbed and poked with needles to test reflex actions; others had their limbs and sexual organs removed without anesthesia.[1]

And who was wielding the knife of cruelty? Doctors.

Primum Non Nocere

Doctors had become executioners and murderous barbarians. Even prior to the death camps, the Nazis had quietly accomplished the

71

execution of the aged, the retarded, and the insane with the complicity of the medical community. These medical madmen had taken the
godless ideologies of Darwin's survival of the fittest and Hitler's master race to their logical conclusions—the murder of the weak and
defenseless.

Now the scenario of brutality is being repeated with new players
and a new country. Once again, the medical community—doctors—
have become the executioners. Once again, helpless victims—this
time, the unborn—are subject to the cruelty of inhumane experimentation: excruciatingly painful dismemberment, dissection, and inevitably death.

Those who are called to heal are again wielding the instruments
of death. This is a disgrace to the practice of medicine. Make no
mistake. These abortionists are hired assassins. As Deuteronomy 27:25
says, they receive a bribe to kill innocent people. Specifically, they
rake in their blood money and kill defenseless babies. Yes, they are
murderers.

Referring to abortionists as murderers causes some Christians to
cringe. They think it is too harsh. Some pro-lifers question if it is
true. They are killers, but are they murderers?

First of all, the question must be argued from the victim's vantage
point and not the murderer's. For example, could it be said that the
Nazis were not guilty of murder because they believed that the Jews
whom they killed were less than human? That is ridiculous. Likewise,
the question of child-killing must be argued from the children's perspective. Are the babies made in the image of God? Yes. Are they
judicially innocent of any capital offense? Absolutely. Therefore, to
deliberately, with forethought, kill an innocent child in the womb is
murder under God's law. The person who kills the child is a murderer; and yes, the mother is an accomplice to the child's murder. It
can be argued that she acted in ignorance; so clever are the lies of
the abortionist, i.e., "It's not a baby; it's a small mass of tissue."

These abortionists have betrayed their profession and their calling
to be healers. What a glorious profession the doctor has! What a privilege to be able to understand so much of human anatomy and to
bring healing to diseased bodies. These men and women are trained
to set bones, to diagnose and treat infections, and to repair any number of internal disorders or external breaches. Thank God for doctors.

The primary ethic of medicine is—or was—*Primum Non Nocere,* first, do no harm. The original Hippocratic Oath—which doctors took for centuries—stated within it, "Similarly, I will not give to a woman an abortive remedy."[2]

Evidently, though, at some point certain doctors with a hand in framing medical ethics decided it was time to edit the oath of centuries in order to accommodate the murderers within the profession. The latest emendation of the oath by the American Medical Association was adopted in 1980 as the *American Medical Association, Principles of Medical Ethics.*

Preamble

The medical profession has long subscribed to a body of ethical statements developed primarily for the benefit of the patient. As a member of this profession, a physician must recognize responsibility not only to patients, but also to society, to other health professionals, and to self. The following Principles adopted by the American Medical Association are not laws, but standards of conduct which define the essentials of honorable behavior for the physician.

Principles

I. A physician shall be dedicated to providing competent medical service with compassion and respect for human dignity.

II. A physician shall deal honestly with patients and colleagues, and strive to expose those physicians deficient in character or competence, or who engage in fraud or deception.

III. A physician shall respect the law and also recognize a responsibility to seek changes in those requirements which are contrary to the best interests of the patient.

IV. A physician shall respect the rights of patients, of colleagues, and of other health professionals, and shall safeguard patient confidences within the constraints of the law.

V. A physician shall continue to study, apply and advance scientific knowledge, make relevant information available to patients, colleagues, and the public, obtain consultation, and use the talents of other health professionals when indicated.

VI. A physician shall, in the provision of appropriate patient care, except in emergencies, be free to choose whom to serve, with whom to associate, and the environment in which to provide medical services.

VII. A physician shall recognize a responsibility to participate in activities contributing to an improved community.[3]

Blood-Stained Hands

Scripture says, "There are six things the Lord hates, Yes, seven which are an abomination to Him . . . hands that shed innocent blood" (Proverbs 6:16–19). Abortionists are an abomination to God. They are vile in His sight. Can they be forgiven? Yes, of course, because the shed blood of Jesus is able to wash away all sin. But in the meantime, they are abominable in God's sight.

Then it should go without saying that these miserable wretches should have absolutely no part in the care of our family, especially the delivery of our children. Why would we allow the hands that murdered a defenseless baby—perhaps that very morning—to then deliver our children? It is insane. It is wrong. Abortionists have betrayed the practice of medicine, and they must have no part in delivering our children.

Do you know if your doctor is an abortionist? There's only one way to find out—ask. Call the receptionist and try to schedule an abortion, or ask the doctor himself the next time you visit him. If he or she is an abortionist, find another physician immediately. Tell him why you are doing it—either by phone, letter or preferably in person—and tell him the truth. He is killing innocent children and needs to repent. As long as he kills babies, he will have no part in your medical care.

What about an ex-abortionist who has quit killing children? That is a matter for each Christian to decide. Did he quit because it hurt his image and his finances? Does he still refer women to have their children killed? Has he had a conversion experience? The answers to these questions should weigh heavily into such a decision.

Blood-Stained Halls

Doctors are not alone in their treachery. Hospitals have betrayed their callings as well. Those that allow children to be killed on their premises have become veritable death camps. (It always gives me an eery feeling to visit the sick in a hospital where children are killed—I wonder if one is in the process of being killed at that moment.) It is a tragedy—a cultural defeat for us—that places originally dedicated to healing and convalescing are now also locations of deliberate death.

These hospitals that second as death camps should be stringently boycotted, except perhaps in extreme emergency. We should steadfastly refuse to have our children in hospitals where other children are killed—perhaps on the same floor! Catholic hospitals are consistent in honoring the sanctity of human life, and we ought to use their services as often as possible.

These hospitals, however, are not fortresses. They are susceptible to public pressure. Boycotts and picketing of hospitals allowing children to be killed have resulted in many hospitals changing their policy. Most hospitals who allow child-killing do not get much money from the venture. They do, however, receive a far larger portion of their income from delivering children. If they are properly boycotted, the hard cold dollars and cents unprofitability of allowing child-killing will sway some hospitals to stop allowing butchery under their roofs.

Likewise, many physicians who kill children do it very infrequently. Their main practice is normal, legitimate ob-gyn services. For example, in Binghamton, New York (my home town), in the early 1980s, half the ob-gyns killed children occasionally in their offices. We, however, mounted a major campaign to pressure them to quit. We picketed their offices; we exposed their killing practice in fliers. Their patients started leaving them, so most of them quit killing children. They just didn't want the pressure and the image of being an abortionist.

Our enemies will argue (and some naive Christians may agree) that these bullying tactics are not nice. But remember, we are not talking about whether someone is a Republican or Democrat, whether or not they drink martinis, or whether or not they pay their taxes. We are talking about murder: the cold-blooded execution of innocent, defenseless children for money. Abortionists are hired assassins. A few short years ago they went to prison for their deeds, a punishment which they fully deserve. If we refuse to take a stand against and expose murderers of children, then what do we believe? What God do we serve? No, we are not bullies. If anything, we're wimps.

The American Medical Association

The American Medical Association is an ardent supporter of child-killing, and it has sound financial reasons. The child-killing industry nets over $500 million per year. With the growing, ghoulish trade of harvesting and selling fetal body parts, the death industry will net in the billions.[4]

Not Historically Pro-Abortion

But it wasn't always so. In fact, in the last century it was the AMA who led the battle to criminalize abortion. And contrary to the current lie that they sought only to protect maternal health, they acted because they knew abortion killed innocent children.

In 1857, the AMA appointed a committee on criminal abortion. The committee presented its report at the twelfth annual AMA convention in 1859. The report stated, ". . . with strange inconsistency the law fully acknowledges the fetus in utero and its inherent rights for civil purposes; while personally and as criminally affected it fails to recognize it and its life as yet denies all protection." [5] Following the release of the report, the AMA passed a resolution protesting the "unwarrantable destruction of human life" through abortion and called on legislators to make child-killing illegal from conception.[6]

The AMA's commitment to end abortion continued. In 1871, a pamphlet released by the AMA denounced in vitriolic fashion physicians who performed abortions. Marvin Olasky quotes from the tract, "We shall discover an enemy in the camp. . . . It is false brethren we have to fear; men who are false to their professions, false to principle, false to honor, false to humanity, false to God." These doctors went on to describe abortionists as "these modern Herods," "educated assassins," and "monsters of iniquity."[7]

What a tragic loss that the current members of the AMA have completely betrayed their fathers. In 1970, they caved in to pro-death pressure and legitimized child-killing. Their stated policy on child-killing now reads, "The Principles of Medical Ethics of the AMA do not prohibit a physician from performing an abortion in accordance with good medical practice and under circumstances which do not violate the law. . . ."[8] Doctors can now kill children in accordance with the law through the day of birth in most states.

Advanced Technology

The double tragedy of this pro-death stance and that of the American College of Obstetricians and Gynecologists is that, unlike 1859, today we see the living child in the womb through sonograms and fetoscopy. We can watch the child swim, suck his thumb, sleep, wake with a start at a loud noise and cock his ear to hear pleasing music. Not only can they see the child, but doctors can also treat the child. The preface of the sixteenth edition of *William's Obstetrics* (a standard medical text published in 1980) reads, "Happily we have entered an era in which the fetus can be rightfully considered and treated as our second patient. . . . Who would have dreamed—even a few years ago—that we could serve the fetus as physician?"[9]

The technology and advances made since that preface are astounding. In fact, Dr. Nathanson points out that the field of fetology is advancing more rapidly than any other discipline in the realm of medicine.[10] The unborn child is a patient! What kind of physician tears his patient limb from limb?

Questions abound regarding these unholy developments in the medical profession. Why have physicians abandoned righteous medical ethics? Why do so many kill their second patient? Why would they participate in the gruesome and violent death of another human being? How can they continue, having seen the baby's tiny hands and feet or even a whole dead child after it had been expulsed from the womb? The answer may be obvious to many, but it bears telling.

The love of money. An abortionist can make hundreds of thousands of dollars, even millions, doing assembly-line child-killing. A ten-minute procedure costs a patient from $250 to $400. Figure it out—there's a lot of money to be made. A parade example is a doctor in California, who owns twenty-five abortuaries in that state alone. He is a multi-millionaire, owns several lavish homes, thoroughbred racing horses, and a private jet. All were bought with blood money. A young physician just out of medical school has to struggle in a private practice. As an abortionist, he can leap into a six-digit income overnight. The temptation is clear.

Truth and Integrity Die

The death ethic has taken its toll on the integrity of the medical profession. In 1978, the Akron City Council passed an ordinance de-

signed to protect women seeking abortions. Among the provisions of
the measure were informed consent regulations. A physician was legally responsible to make all relevant information available to patients, colleagues, and the public. They had to tell a woman that her
twenty-two-week-old child was viable, that abortion is a major surgical
procedure and can result in sterility, and *that the unborn child is a
human life from conception.*[11]

All of these requirements are medical and scientific facts. Yet the
medical community, in a sick *betrayal* of choice, fought to keep the
women in the dark. (How can people make intelligent choices if they
are ignorant of the facts?)[12]

The law was contested and brought before the Supreme Court.
The American Medical Association, the American College of Obstetrics and Gynecologists, the American Academy of Pediatrics, and the
Nurses' Association of the American College of Obstetrics and Gynecologists all joined to file an *amicus curiae* (friend of the court) brief
asking that the law be struck down. What a deplorable act of treachery! The medical community was asking the Supreme Court to deny
women the right to know the truth. The Court, acting as the great
lapdog of the killing industry, did as requested: *they ruled that a woman
does not have the right to know the facts about and dangers involved in
abortion.* God will reward them.

Dr. Nathanson gave this scathing rebuke to his colleagues who
are promoting and participating in the holocaust—despite their medical training and knowledge that the children are human.

> I accuse the policy-making bodies of the American Medical Associa-
> tion; the American College of Obstetricians and Gynecologists; the
> American Medical Women's Association; the American Psychiatric
> Association; the New York Academy of Medicine; the American
> Academy of Pediatrics; the Nurses' Association of the American Col-
> lege of Obstetricians and Gynecologists; and the 170 medical school
> deans, departmental chairmen and professors of obstetrics and gyne-
> cology throughout the nation of a willful and conscious disregard of
> the massive and still-growing data identifying the pre-natal person as
> a living, valuable, and fully protectible human being. I accuse them
> of abandoning the canons and principles which lent legitimacy to
> their organizations, and caving in to trendy political fashion of the
> moment. I accuse them of a heinous abuse of their professional trust
> in failing to protect this unborn patient in their charge. I accuse
> them of voluntary collaboration in an unprecedented surgical holo-

caust against these mute and defenseless victims, and I accuse all physician members of these organizations who fail to speak up against this unspeakable crime of complicity in that crime.

History will not forgive them.[13]

Well said, Dr. Nathanson.

Many in the pro-abortion medical community have cried out (and the pro-abortion press has gladly spoken the lie) that they are most qualified to speak on the subject of child-killing. They argue that it should be legal because they are the doctors and they know best. Dr. Nathanson offers this caustic response to such logic:

> . . . as if the Institute of Electrical and Electronics Engineers were to hold itself out as an expert in the question of capital punishment merely because an electric chair is utilized as the instrument of destruction. I am perfectly willing to concede that obstetricians and gynecologists are in general the personnel who wield the instruments in the process of abortion and undeniably have the technical expertise to comment upon the uses of the machinery. But in the complex arena of public policy (in this case the legal and ethical acceptability of permissive abortion) they possess no special insights.[14]

We must pray that godly ethics will be restored to the medical community. Upright, pro-life physicians must work to do the same and labor to wrest the reins of power from the hands of those promoting death and acting as the social executioners of this brave new world. It is a tragedy that the major medical associations and organizations have been made to tow the pro-death party line—despite the contrary medical evidence.

A hopeful sign is the once again growing stigma attached to abortion and the title "abortionist." As reported in the *New York Times*, abortionists are in many cases now viewed as second-class physicians; and many physicians simply refuse to perform abortions.[15] Let us pray that this contempt for abortionists rises to such a degree that the medical community no longer endorses the murder of children but condemns it.

NARAL

NARAL, the National Abortion Rights Action League, was founded in 1966 by Lawrence Lader. (At that time it was called the National Association for the Repeal of Abortion Laws, still NARAL.) Throughout its existence, NARAL has been on the cutting edge of changing laws regulating abortion and developing the public relations ploys necessary to make abortion rights an American staple.

Lader had been a free-lance journalist and publicist in the mid-sixties and proved a brilliant public relations genius for the death advocates. He understood that for child-killing to be made legal, the pro-death forces needed broad, strong support in the media. Therefore, they needed to frame the issues in such a way that the press would become advocates and promoters of the death ethic. Lader effectively framed the issue and did gain the favor of the media. His entire program, however, was based on distortion.

A former co-conspirator of Lader, the aforementioned Dr. Nathanson was a founding board member of NARAL, served on its executive committee, and at one point was the chairman of its medical committee. Nathanson was an insider. When he joined the pro-life ranks, he brought with him a wealth of first-hand knowledge about NARAL—their tactics, their deceptions.

False Statistics

One common deception and perhaps the most effective is that five to ten thousand women per year died from illegal abortions. Dr. Nathanson readily confesses that the founders of NARAL pulled this out of thin air as a nice, round, shocking figure.[16] The incredible effectiveness of this deception is evident in that it is still quoted by the media and believed without question whenever a reporter discusses the dark days of back-alley abortions.

The actual number is far less. In 1981, Dr. Thomas Hilgers testified at the Hatch Amendment hearings (an amendment which would give states the right to decide laws on child-killing) concerning child-killing prior to 1973. Dr. Hilgers at the time was associate professor of obstetrics and gynecology at the Creighton University school of medicine in Omaha and was director of the Creighton University Natural Family Planning and Educational Research Center. He and his colleagues had done years of demographic research concerning pre-Roe child-killing. Their studies revealed that from 1948 until 1973, an average of 250 women per year, not five to ten thousand, died from illegal abortions.[17]

Others had earlier presented the truth, also to the deaf ear of the press. In 1968, Dr. Herbert Ratner employed census data to demonstrate that there were only 114 deaths in 1963 that "were due to abortions that were criminal, self-induced, or without legal indications."[18] Even proabort Dr. Mary Calderone, former medical director of Planned Parenthood, acknowledged that in 1957, "There were only 260 deaths in the whole country attributed to abortions of any kind."[19]

Nathanson points out that with the advances in surgery and medication, the number would probably be reduced to seventy-five or so.[20] (That many die per year from safe and legal abortions.)

Another deceptive figure thrown around before Roe was that one to two million illegal abortions were performed annually. This, too, was a fictitious figure created by NARAL for public consumption.[21] Hilger testified that between 1940 and 1967, the actual average was ninety-eight thousand per year. This is still a tragedy and a moral outrage but is demonstrably less than the 1.6 million children who now are murdered. This crystallizes a simple truth: Most women will not resort to back alleys if child-killing is illegal; they will bear the children to term.[22]

So the next time you see a NARAL commercial or hear a NARAL spokesperson talking about the one to two million illegal abortions per year and the subsequent deaths of ten thousand women, know this: *they are willfully distorting the facts.*

Those of you who have access to the media need to challenge them when they parrot the lying figures fed them by NARAL and friends.

NARAL's deliberate deception did not end with those lying figures. A NARAL position paper entitled *An Outline for Action* shows how NARAL used deception concerning the false connection between the absence of legalized abortion and child abuse. The paper concedes,

> Among our shock pictures might be those of battered children with attested case histories, or of infanticide cases. *Although the link between battered children and the unwanted child may not be too firm statistically* [italics added] and infanticides are not common, we may have to stretch the point if need warrants it.[23]

NARAL also deceived and manipulated the public through polls, stating in the minutes of a high-level meeting on January 9, 1971,

"careful wording of questions is essential to achieve favorable results. . . . " [24] Beyond the normal chicanery of polls (which most of us
have become accustomed to), however, Nathanson admits that
NARAL actually created polls that did not exist in order to sway Catholics to a pro-abortion position,

> To sweeten the appeal and support of those wavering Catholics who
> wanted to look around and see others of their ilk joining us NARAL
> supplied them with fictitious polls and surveys designed to make it
> appear as if American Catholics were deserting the teachings of the
> church and the dictates of their consciences in droves.[25]

The Catholic Strategy

The preceding efforts to deceive Catholics were a small part of the
NARAL's master plan concerning Catholics. While NARAL did try to
persuade nominal Catholics to be pro-death, their Catholic strategy
was quite contrary and essentially one of utter bigotry. The plan was
to promote the Catholic hierarchy as the enemies of freedom and as
religious zealots bent on ramming their dogma down the throats of
an unwilling America.

The January 9, 1971, strategy meeting yielded these notes concerning Catholics:

> The major opposition to abortion law repeal comes from the Roman
> Catholic Church and groups like the Right to Life Committee, or-
> ganized and funded by the Catholic church. All present had seen
> evidence of opposition tactics in the form of election campaigns
> against proponents of abortion law change, pastoral letters, etc. Sug-
> gested ways to contend with this opposition were to support actively
> those Catholics who support abortion law repeal, to emphasize the
> minority opinion within the church (Daniel Callahan, *Abortion Law,
> Choice and Morality*) and separation of religious conviction from legis-
> lative judgment as proposed by such notables as Robert Drinan, S. J.
> and Cardinal Richard Cushing. The opposition argument of abor-
> tion law repeal promoting promiscuity can be exploited to expose
> the immorality of the pregnancy as punishment philosophy.[26]

On May 12, 1972, NARAL issued a public statement which was
the outworking of their use-the-Catholics-as-a-whipping-boy strategy.

> Only one conclusion can be made: that the Catholic hierarchy is
> determined to bend the country to its will over abortion. What hap-

pens to all human rights in the next few years depends on what happens to abortion. If the Bill of Rights is to survive, we must never allow Cardinal Cooke to rule our bedrooms. We must never allow Catholic dogma to take over a legislature as it has just done in New York, and try to force every women to bear a child against her choice.

We have learned a terrible lesson: the Catholic drive is unrelenting, and this is only the beginning. We must start next week to match the most powerful lobby in the nation with equal force and similar tactics. We must match money with money in Michigan, our two points of concentration. We must match them with professional political staff and skilled organizers. The Catholic lobby succeeded in New York by concentrating a massive attack on a carefully chosen list of spineless legislators and terrorizing them with the votes of controlled Catholic blocs. . . . [27]

Had there been the equivalent of an Anti-Defamation League for Catholics, NARAL never could have gotten away with its bigotry.[28] Or for that matter, if the media had an ounce of integrity, it would have derided NARAL's hateful bigotry. Nathanson ruefully pointed out that if the word *Catholic* had been replaced with *Jew* or *black* the outrage from the media would have destroyed NARAL.

Overall, the tactic was a great success for NARAL and the death forces. They still employ it today; but since the revival of activism among fundamentalists and evangelicals, NARAL now refers disparagingly to both Christians and Catholics as those wild-eyed religious fanatics who seek to breach the wall of separation of church and state.

National Abortion Federation

The National Abortion Federation (NAF) is not as high profile as NARAL but is more intrinsically tied to the killers. It is supported primarily by child-killing providers.

Following in those well-worn steps of deceit, the NAF recently participated in some sleight-of-hand tricks of its own. The Rescue Movement was having much success around the nation. We had been generally able to keep an abortion mill from killing children for an entire day of the rescue. Because of this, the NAF released a secret memorandum on confronting Operation Rescue. Included within it were instructions to lie to the media, if necessary, insisting that no abortion appointments were missed or, at least, that the mill was able to see all women who wanted to be seen. They kill children for a living. Why wouldn't they lie?

Conclusion

The medical community has cancer. It is not incurable, but it will take some serious treatment before healing comes. Along with the prayers and pressure from without, pro-lifers within the medical community must become far more vocal. We must stop worrying about offending those whose hands drip with the blood of innocent children or their ideological comrades in surgical garb. It's time for that spirit of courageous determination that sought out the false brethren and the educated assassins to once again embolden pro-life physicians and medical professionals.

NARAL and NAF are going to continue shoring up the killers with their lies and bigotry. We must remember that they are professional liars, child-killers, and anti-Christs who hate God and love death. At every opportunity we must expose them and their lies to the willfully gullible media and the manipulated public. God help us. It's a big job.

PART THREE

THE ALLIES

ABC, NBC, AND CBS: MINISTRIES OF PROPAGANDA

How does one drain the ocean? He doesn't! How could I possibly chronicle in detail the gross abuse and distortion of television media concerning the "coverage" of child-killing in one chapter? I can't. It could not be done in a whole book. I would venture that it could not be done in an entire volume of books, so vast is the guilt and complicity of secular television media with the killers. Hence, I will point out a few glaring abuses and hope that you become a little better equipped to realize when you are being manipulated and deceived.

Deliberate Propaganda

First, we must know our enemy. You don't have to be a prophet to recognize that much of television—both entertainment and "news shows"—has become a veritable pipeline of anti-Christian sleaze. This does not happen by magic nor random chance. It is deliberate.

To Whom Are We Listening?

In 1980, the now famous (or infamous!) Rothman/Lichter report was released. They interviewed 240 journalists and editors who were considered the media elite—high echelon men and women at the three

major networks, the three leading news magazines, and the three
leading newspapers.

The study found, among other things, that 86 percent of them
seldom or never attend church. (That's the foundation—or lack
thereof—that they build on.) Only 25 percent favored prayer in public schools; 75 percent approved of homosexuality; over 50 percent
believed adultery was acceptable and, concerning child-killing, 90 percent believed abortion was a woman's right.[1] A more current study
would most probably be even worse—a 1982 Rothman/Lichter study
of those graduating from the prestigious Columbia School of Journalism revealed that over 96 percent believe that a woman has a right to
an abortion.[2]

We need to remember that most of those who pull the levers—or
hire the writers—at television networks are radically out of step with
most of America and are often self-proclaimed enemies of righteousness, Christian truth, and morality. They may be likened to the false
prophets of Jeremiah's day who despised the right ways of the Lord
and strengthened the hands of those who did evil.

These members of the media elite determine,

- How child-killing is reported

- How often it is covered

- What about it will be emphasized

- Who in the struggle will be highlighted (and who will be deni-
  grated or ignored).

It should not surprise us that both the children and the pro-life
movement rarely receive a fair shake in the media. These are the bad
guys. The simple truth is this: *Child-killing could never have been legalized
or remained so for so long without intensive propaganda* from the media. It
was, in fact, through the television media that our conscience as a
nation was deadened to the reality of child-killing. Throughout the
1960s, 70s, 80s, and now 90s, television entertainment and news has
fed American viewers a steady diet of pro-death rhetoric and drama.

The Crusade Begins

CBS began its crusade in 1962 with "The Benefactor," an episode of
their series, "The Defender". The show portrays an abortionist, the
benefactor, as a sympathetic public servant crusading for legal abor-

tion and, in the meanwhile, braving persecution to help young women in trouble. This was the first such drama which failed to characterize an abortionist as "the heavy." Despite protests from both paid advertisers and the public, Frank Stanton, CBS president, described the play as "a very fine, realistic and honest dramatization." The prodeath propaganda machine was gearing up for the long haul.[3]

There were two television news broadcasts of note in the 1960s. In 1965, CBS, again leading the way, presented "Abortion and the Law," one of a series of "CBS Reports" narrated by Walter Cronkite. The upshot of the show was two-fold.

First, it appears that its content was composed from a NARAL press release. The *New York Times* reviewer Jack Gould commented, "The program was a comprehensive summary of the medical, moral, and legal aspects of the problems stemming from the epidemic rise in prematurely terminated pregnancies." He continued, "The presentation . . . estimated that about a million abortions in defiance of state laws were performed annually in the United States . . . About 350,000 a year suffer post-operative complications, and 5,000 a year die."[4] Lies, lies, lies.

Second, Gould commented on CBS's editorial position, "The program . . . did not quite come out in favor of changing the laws, but in effect did take the next closest step. CBS favored a public dialogue on what once was regarded as a taboo subject."[5] CBS may not have; but its ally in the unholy media alliance, the *New York Times,* picked up the slack. Their editorial entitled "The Cruel Abortion Law" followed the CBS broadcast.

> The bitterly cruel choices forced upon individual women and on the medical profession by overly restrictive law were movingly presented in the Columbia Broadcasting System's documentary television program on abortion . . . Surely civilized civilization demands a liberalization of abortion law.[6]

In other words, "Thanks for the propaganda; we needed some more ammo."

ABC joined the fray in 1969 with its documentary "Summer Focus," also reviewed by Jack Gould in the *New York Times.* I quote his two lead paragraphs to demonstrate again the utterly incestuous relationship between the print and broadcast media concerning child-killing.

The American Broadcasting Company's documentary series, "Summer Focus," gave a sensitive and persuasive report last night on reform of abortion laws.

The power of television is to intensify personal emotions and experience. This impact tilted the scales overwhelmingly in favor of abortions conducted under medical supervision in sanitary hospitals, rather than illegal operations performed with crude instruments by the untrained.[7]

The show was a study in contrast: legal child-killing is associated with "medical supervision in sanitary hospitals"; illegal child-killing, with "illegal operations . . . crude instruments . . . the untrained." ABC further contrasted two pregnant women suffering from German measles; one has her child killed and goes on to have other healthy babies; the other can't get an abortion and bears a deformed child. (The *Times* described this child as "a helpless ward of society.")

Not missing a point on the NARAL fact sheet, "Summer Focus" purposefully included the viewpoint of the Roman Catholic Church. ABC had pitted the repressive Papists against a respected Baltimore surgeon. Unbiased journalism? I think not.

Gould was correct. Yes, this documentary was persuasive. It also was pro-death propaganda whose credits should have included a dedication to Margaret Sanger.

CBS followed their 1965 documentary in 1978 with Bill Moyers' report "The Politics of Abortion." The emphasis of this broadcast was upon the efforts of pro-lifers to impose their peculiar religious beliefs on secular society. The message preached by Moyers sounded familiar: "You can't legislate morality." Well, Bill, you get an A+ for following the pro-death party line. (Does Bill feel the same way about laws against rape or murder?)

Enter the Comedians

In the 1970s and 80s, the networks' entertainment divisions stepped up their propaganda campaign. Beginning with CBS's two-part "Maude" episode broadcast in 1972, a string of sitcoms and dramas dulled us to the horror of child-killing (i.e., NBC's "Buffalo Bill," CBS's "Cagney and Lacey").

This was accomplished in two ways. First, the issue of child-killing was the subject of silly and coarse humor. It was not presented as a life-or-death issue but something to laugh about. Viewers lost any understanding of the seriousness of abortion—of child-killing. Secondly, the focus of these shows was always on the women in their plight. Television does intensify our emotions; and these stories created much sympathy for the woman with an "unwanted pregnancy" while ignoring the unborn child whose life is in jeopardy.

Yes, they've promoted child-killing. They've spewed out, month after month, year after year, pro-abortion rhetoric and lies; and they've steadfastly refused to show the victims of the holocaust—the innocent murdered children.

Staggering Influence

Much has been said about the role of television media in turning the hearts and minds of the American people against the Vietnam conflict. The nightly presentations of dead and wounded American men, combined with what became a persistent anti-war editorial theme, had its desired effect. Popular support for the effort eventually waned and was replaced by strong sentiment against United States involvement in Vietnam. To be sure, this did not affect the ideological stance of all Americans; but tens of millions were affected, nevertheless.

Just ponder the impact on our nation if night after night the television media covered the war against children. Imagine seeing the bodies recovered from the dumpsters; viewers confronted with close-ups of the over sixteen thousand babies discovered in a garbage container in southern California. Envision the in-depth exposés of the various hideous types of abortion procedures and the children's futile struggle for their lives. Listen to the testimonies of the multitude of physically scarred and emotionally devastated mothers who believed the abortionists' lies. Imagine the exposés of the lavish lifestyles abortionists have built for themselves from blood money. Do you see the point? Child-killing could never survive the bright light of truth; the vast majority of our nation's people would reject it out of hand and demand its immediate end.

But tragically, the television media has become the willing slave of the death industry. They do not expose the truth; they hide it. They report half-truths and fabrications and omit the truth. They are cowards; they fear showing the American people the truth. They are ministries of propaganda, reducing a life-and-death issue to quick pan shots of marches and pro-abortion sound-bites. They forever speak of "safe and legal" child-killing, ever calling the babies by some word that dehumanizes them and deadens our consciences to the horrid, murderous reality.

The Myth of Neutrality

I have spoken with many reporters who confidently professed to me that they were unbiased and objective in their coverage of an abortion story. They weren't deceiving me; I wonder if they were trying to fool themselves. Fortunately, some in the television industry have had the integrity and boldness to admit that neutrality is a myth.

Robert Bazell of NBC stated in 1986, "Objectivity is a fallacy. . . . There are different opinions, but you don't have to give them equal weight."[8] Irving R. Levine, also of NBC, stated, "The reporter has got to determine, ultimately, what is valid and what is not."[9] Linda Ellerbee, now of TBN, was far more blunt: "There is no such thing as objectivity. Any reporter who tells you he's objective is lying to you."[10]

So if a reporter doesn't think tens of thousands of injured women constitute a valid argument about how "safe" legal abortions are, too bad for the truth.

This *myth of neutrality* begins with the network corporations—the buck stoppers. This is plainly revealed in their corporate giving. In fact, each of the major television networks financially supported the NOW Legal Defense and Education Fund in 1988.[11] Furthermore, ABC's parent company, Capital Cities, also donated one thousand dollars in 1986 to arch-feminist Gloria Steinem's Women's Action Alliance.[12] Even more outrageous, CBS Executive Vice-President Barbara Corday actually organized a major fund-raising event to pay for a nationwide media blitz prior to the Webster arguments before the Supreme Court in April 1989.[13]

Now think for a minute. How ridiculous is the very thought of having an "objective" or "balanced" report concerning child-killing! You start with the truth, remembering that God's Word defines truth—abortion is murder. From there you proceed. Imagine seeing a reporter on your television screen: "This is the body of a twenty-two-week-old baby girl who was murdered by saline solution. Now we're going to talk with the murderer. We want to hear why he thinks it's a positive thing that her life has been snuffed out." Or to put it in another time framework, can you conceive of a German television station doing a balanced documentary in 1942 on the murder of millions of innocent people in gas chambers? Either one will spout propaganda or speak the truth.

Roe v. Wade

A perfect illustration of television propaganda and brainwashing of the masses was NBC's feature movie "Roe v. Wade," which aired May 15, 1989. If you missed it, you didn't miss much—only more of the typical pro-abortion dribble.

First of all, consider the timing. It aired while the Supreme Court was considering the Webster case and considering overturning Roe. The debate about child-killing in our nation had reached a pitch surpassing that of the late sixties and early seventies. Pro-lifers were making undeniable gains. It was then that NBC decided to film, promote, and air the drama. Thomas Sowell wrote, "Anyone who believes the airing of this film at a time the Supreme Court is considering a case which could limit or overturn abortion on demand is pure coincidence is a potential customer for a bridge in Brooklyn."[14]

Consider some of the other glaring tactics:

- Not once was an unborn baby pictured on the screen. In 1973, such pictures were readily available. Once again, NBC lied by omitting the central figure (target) in the abortion debate; they simply ignored the child about to be murdered. There's nothing like unbiased media coverage.

- The two women in the film, Jane Roe (Norma McCorvey) and Sarah Weddington, the feminist attorney, are portrayed as heroines. Their words and expressions were designed to evoke sympathy and support from the viewing audience.

- The film denigrates adoption. Norma says, "I can't give up another baby. What could it possibly be like to have a kid out there gettin' his butt kicked and you don't even know?" In other words, the kid is better off dead. At least then she knows where it is. At one point Weddington soapboxes, "You shouldn't have to bear a child and give it up to strangers." It's too bad for the "strangers" (it sounds like a dirty word)—those two million couples longing, hoping, and praying that young women will give life and not death to their "unplanned" children. Why not positively portray adoption as life for the child in a loving home with parents anxious to have children but unable to for medical reasons?

- Pro-lifers—embodied in the attorney's resisting the death of McCorvey's child—are portrayed solely as callous men. Note the absence of any sincere and articulate pro-life women, women who constitute more than half our ranks. At one point a pro-life attorney actually says to his beer-drinking buddy, "The Court is gonna hafta choose between a woman and her baby." After all, pro-lifers care nothing about women.

This is the core of our enemy's "media strategy." Ellen Goodman, arch-feminist columnist for the *Boston Globe*, wrote in 1985, "Questions about the life of the fetus dominate the talk shows. Bernard Nathanson's sonogram of a fetus being aborted was replayed on the news with hardly a word questioning his premises." She understood then that she and her co-conspirators had to captivate their audiences again with the "life stories of the thousands of women" facing crisis pregnancies.[15] "Roe v. Wade" is an answer to her plea. All in all, the film was a brilliant piece of pro-death propaganda.

The program's pro-death message was completely reinforced by the NBC News panel discussion that followed. The discussion, hosted by pro-abort Tom Brokaw, proved to be a sham. He consistently interrupted the pro-life participants, Olivia Gans, director of American Victims of Abortion, and Congressman Christopher Smith (R-NJ); he refused, save once, to refer to us as "pro-lifers," preferring the "anti-abortionist" label; finally, the NBC reporter covering viewer reaction actually referred to a group of pro-lifers as "so-called pro-lifers," an even more outrageous slam, suggesting that we are not who we say we are.

One particular exchange is telling. Olivia Gans had the courage (or did Tom think gall?) to open the program by asserting, "It's also very important tonight to understand that we've just watched two hours of pro-abortion propaganda. . . ." Brokaw quickly interrupted her, "Miss Gans, Miss Gans . . . I'm going to tell you something . . . That is a statement without foundation." Wow! There's a pillar of conviction! He then turned to the rabid proabort Anna Quindlen to prop up his teetering defense, asking, "Did you see it as propaganda?" She responded, "No, I didn't see it as propaganda. But I must say, Tom, that I saw it as a very powerful case for legalization of abortion."

What's the difference! I like Jerry Rubin's analogy, "Gee, Herr Goebbels, did you see the 1936 Nazi documentary "Triumph of the Will" as propaganda?" "No, Tom, but I must say that I saw it as a very powerful case for Hitler and the Master Race."[16]

The movie "Roe v. Wade" was just another—albeit expensive—railroad car in a long train of efforts by the television media to railroad the public into its pro-death camp.

Another glaring indictment of the media's pro-death agenda was the April 9, 1989, "Mobilization for Women's Lives" in Washington, DC. The build-up for this march for continued legalized child-killing was so incredible that it was as if the press were preparing for a Super Bowl. In fact, CNN actually covered much of the day's activities live. Year after year, tens of thousands of pro-lifers have braved the winter cold of Washington on January 22 with often only a thirty-second mention. But when a group of screaming proaborts get together on the eve of the Webster decision, it receives free publicity for days and live coverage during the event. What a disgusting sham.

CNN tipped its pro-abortion hand even further on April 28, 1990. Somewhere between 300,000 to 500,000 men and women came to Washington, D.C., to the Rally for Life. CNN gave the rally none of the extensive coverage it gave to the death-marches.

Post-Webster

The television media was on a roll. Indeed, their post-Webster coverage has been more of the same propaganda. Story after story has portrayed the freshly invigorated and motivated pro-death forces. One night, I watched an NBC story on child-killing and felt like I was watching a NARAL commercial. In fact it was, because NBC had graciously shown long sections of new NARAL commercials as part of its "unbiased" coverage. This trend continued with network coverage of post-Webster legislative and political activity.

Indeed, as pro-life activists rushed to introduce legislation to restrict child-killing in many states, the networks selectively judged the importance of the results. For instance, when subcommittees controlled by pro-death legislators in the Florida House consistently blocked all of Governor Robert Martinez's initiatives in early October 1989, the national media paid close attention.[17]

ABC, NBC, and CNN led their October 10 broadcasts with the story; and CBS gave it sixth billing. On October 11, ABC, NBC, and CBS all included references to the story in their opening segments. The network morning shows also gave a great deal of air time to predicting, reporting, and analyzing the pro-death victory. ABC's "Good Morning, America" and CBS "This Morning" each had thirteen stories or interviews on the legislation over a four-day period. NBC's "Today" aired twelve such segments. Each of the networks spouted the pro-death party line that the votes indicated a major shift in national opinion on child-killing, despite the fact that the only members who actually voted on the abortion restrictions during the entire session were on these sub-committees controlled by pro-death forces.[18]

But what about the pro-life victories in Pennsylvania and Michigan? According to the Associated Press, the expected media blitz in Pennsylvania never materialized. Where were the over five hundred journalists who spent two weeks in Tallahassee? Apparently, the pro-life victory didn't fit their agenda.[19]

Well, what did the networks have to say concerning the passage of abortion restrictions by the Pennsylvania House on October 22, 1989? Or the Michigan senate's passage of parental consent legislation? Very little. The evening newscasts buried the Pennsylvania story; ABC placed it in seventh while CBS relegated it to twelfth. NBC incredibly failed even to mention the vote until the following day when Andrea Mitchell begrudged one sentence in her report on President Bush's veto of Medicaid funding for abortions. The morning shows included nine mentions of the vote, compared to the thirty-eight segments on Florida.

Similarly, the Michigan vote was silently spiked. Although CNN made it their third story, ABC and NBC actually ignored it altogether. Mitchell did manage to give the story one line in her report on Medicaid on October 25. Disregarding the pro-life victories, she recapped her report, "The pro-choice movement believes it has won public support and a powerful weapon to use against the President."[20] The networks have similarly ignored or belittled pro-life legislative advances in South Carolina, Wisconsin, and Alabama.

Now who could forget the defeats of would-be Governors Courter and Coleman in New Jersey and Virginia, respectively? The press attributed it solely to the pro-life position of the candidates. The truth is that both candidates ran inept campaigns (so say Republican insiders), waffling on their pro-life commitments, causing many pro-lifers to stay home on election day or, at least, to refuse to work for their candidacy.[21]

Furthermore, Marshall Coleman was hampered by a media blackout. Eight television stations in northern Virginia actually refused to air last-minute ads sponsored by the National Right to Life Political Action Committee which revealed Wilder's deep-seated pro-death stance. These same stations ran ads by NARAL endorsing Wilder and attacking Coleman. Some have argued that, given the close margin of the race, the media in northern Virginia actually determined the outcome of the election. Mediacracy, anyone?[22]

If your only source of news were the television, you would think that pro-life candidates had lost every race since *Webster* was decided. This is simply not true. In fact, since the July 3 decision, pro-life candidates have won twenty of the twenty-seven state races in which their opponents were clearly pro-death.[23]

- On August 29, 1989, Ileana Ros-Lehtinen, a strong pro-life candidate, won Florida's eighteenth district seat in a special election to fill the seat of the late Claude Pepper. Her opponent had made abortion the issue of the campaign by labeling Mrs. Ros-Lehtinen, "one of the most ardent anti-choice members of the (state) legislature."[24] Here's further proof that this was a pro-life victory: NARAL had supported her opponent with the maximum legal financial contribution.[25]

- On August 12, 1989, pro-life Democrat Pete Geren won Texas' twelfth district seat in the special election to replace ex-Congressman Jim Wright, defeating the pro-abortion candidate Jim Lane.

- On August 8, 1989, pro-life candidate David Oetting was elected in Missouri's 121st state legislative district with over 60 percent of the vote.

- On August 22, 1989, pro-life Republican Mike Gunn won a vacant seat in the Mississippi legislature.

- In Alabama's thirty-second district, pro-lifer Albert Lipscomb gained a vacant Senate seat.[26]

- On October 17, 1989, Gene Taylor, a proponent of the Human Life Amendment, won election to the House of Representatives from Mississippi.[27]

I ask, where were the networks? Do only token pro-death victories in southern California rate coverage?

The Rescue Movement

Operation Rescue has received some measure of network media coverage, including evening broadcasts and weekly news shows such as "48 Hours" and "20/20." The exposure, however, has been a long time coming and pales in comparison to that which would be accorded to an animal rights or antinuclear movement of similar national breadth and impact.

For instance, our first series of rescues in New York City in May 1988, in which over nine hundred rescuers participated, received no national secular media coverage at all. Outrageously, far smaller and less tumultuous demonstrations against South Africa have received greater publicity by the networks. Pro-lifers apparently had not yet caught the fancy of the pro-death media.

A similar cover-up occurred during our Holy Week rescues held in Los Angeles March 22–25, 1989. Although we were covered by three of the four major networks, CBS "This Morning" and " Evening News" viewers didn't hear one word about our activities. Still true to their liberal agenda, however, "This Morning" did find the air time on March 28 to show three lonely demonstrators protesting nuclear power at Three Mile Island.[28]

Unfortunately, our relationship with network media tends to be a no-win situation. The media either ignores us or skewers us. Two prime examples of the latter were the "20/20" and "48 Hours" news broadcasts. Yes, they did show some of the brutality in Atlanta; for this we are grateful. The image, however, that they presented of the Rescue Movement was clearly slanted. We were described as "The New Crusaders" and as "foot soldiers of the Lord." In other words, we're religious fanatics only seeking publicity for our efforts to oppress women with our peculiar religious beliefs. That's us, according to the likes of Dan Rather and Barbara Walters.

With our experience we expect no more and no less from our friends in the media.

Brutality Coverage. The television media has also played its part as a black cloak. When the brutality of Atlanta first occurred, CNN and ABC News showed the abuse; CBS and NBC did not. Since then, police brutality has grown; but the coverage remains sparse.

Fortunately, the NBC "Today" show did do a segment on police brutality with Senator William Armstrong, West Hartford Police Chief

McCue and video footage of some of the worst of the brutality. This remains only a miniscule portion of the coverage and, more importantly, the outrage that the network media should have shown.

More often, the media simply ignores the plight of beaten rescuers. For example, while we were watching Russian KGB beat Soviet citizens for conducting a candlelight vigil outside KGB headquarters, Maryland police were bludgeoning pro-lifers with night sticks for peacefully singing and sitting outside an abortion mill. The national media failed to even mention the event.

Radio. Our nation's airwaves are far from free from the biases of the pro-death ministries of propaganda. In fact, the same corporations which own the three major television networks also own radio networks and individual radio stations which serve as additional "delivery systems" for their disinformation. Two particular stories highlight the networks' commitment to toe the pro-death party line in their "radio ministries."

In 1978, the NBC radio network actually refused to carry a broadcast of "The Lutheran Hour" that contained a sermon entitled "The Sanctity of Life," whose message opposed child-killing. NBC claimed that the sermon violated a long-standing company policy prohibiting the sale of air time to any group that would use it to express their views on a controversial issue.[29]

Apparently, NBC, as well as CBS and ABC, claimed that such issues can receive the fairest examination in their news and public affairs programming. NBC said in a statement, "The public interest goal addressed by this policy seeks to provide the public with information on controversial issues under the auspices of disinterested journalists rather than advocates that have the means to buy time to express their views."[30]

Are they serious, "disinterested journalists"? What an outrage! Over 90 percent of them believe a woman has a right to have her child killed. Dishonest, yes! Disinterested, no!

Pro-Life in a Pro-Death Business

A second revelatory testimony concerns Vincent Benedict. Benedict had been with CBS for thirteen years in various capacities, slowly moving up the corporate ladder. Eventually, he was appointed vice-president and general manager of CBS-owned station WOGL-FM in Philadelphia, where he worked until he was fired—fired because of his pro-life editorials.[31]

Benedict had been bold enough to occasionally take a stand for the unborn in the editorials he produced for WOGL. The CBS brass would have none of it. After Benedict ignored several warnings to tone down his editorials, he was called to New York and told that he was fired. As he explains it, "The excuse given me was I was 'burned out' and I was 'tired.' But the truth is, I was a pain in the neck to CBS because I dared to be pro-life in a pro-death business."

This is a man who worked in the business for thirteen years. Listen to him; don't be deceived. Major network media is a pro-death business. Nearly every decision—from their choice of labels for the opposing sides to their choice of stories to cover and not cover—is made in the context of advancing their pro-death agenda.[32] These networks are surely the ministries of propaganda (and in many cases, the treasury) for the pro-death cause.

THE PRINT MEDIA: THE LAPDOGS OF THE DEATH PEDDLERS

T here was a time when the print media was pro-life.

> The enormous amount of medical malpractice [the common euphemism for abortion] that exists and flourishes, almost unchecked, in the city of New York, is a theme for most serious consideration. Thousands of human beings are thus murdered before they have seen the light of this world, and thousands upon thousands more of adults are irremediably robbed in constitution, health and happiness. ("The Evil of the Age," *The New York Times*)[1]

> The "perpetration of infant murder . . . is rank and smells to heaven." ("The Least of These Little Ones," *The New York Times*)[2]

No, you are not dreaming. These biting pro-life messages were trumpeted by the *New York Times*. In fact, at one time the *New York Times* was probably the leading pro-life voice in the nation.

Historical Stance

Nineteenth Century: Pro-Life

During the 1860s, 1870s, 1880s and the first-half of the 1890s, the *Times* read like many pro-life periodicals of today. For example, in

1871, a *Times* reporter, Augustus St. Clair, was assigned to do under-cover reporting of the abortion industry. St. Clair did a marvelous job exposing the greed and vice of abortionists as well as the death of children and, at times, their mothers. Additionally, when Madame Restell, the nation's leading abortionist, was scheduled for trial, the *Times* quoted the prosecutor's comments on Restell's prestigious home: "Every brick in that splendid mansion might represent a little skull, and the blood that infamous woman has shed might have served to mix the mortar."[3]

And the *Times* did not stand alone. For example, the *National Police Gazette* quoted a doctor describing abortion as child murder and as a brutal and revolting act. He added, "[T]he law provides punishment for it when it can be proved."[4] A *Gazette* story entitled "Hellish Earll" skewered an abortionist and began with this hard-hitting message:

> The civilization of today is opposed to babies, and its basest product is the abortionist. He is the human hyena, and the living, quivering flesh of foolish or unfortunate womanhood is the grave from which he tears his prey. He lives upon the crushed and mangled bodies of tender, breathless infants.[5]

As time passed, the *Times*, the *Gazette*, and papers all over the country became more and more vigorous in their attacks on the child-killing movement of their day.

The founders of the *New York Times* (1851), Henry Raymond and George Jones, were professing Christians, as was Louis Jennings, the editor at the *Times* who led the attack on child-killing.[6] Unfortunately for the babies and mothers of today, the *Times* has abandoned the faith of its fathers. Today, it is among the most vicious defenders of infant murder—as *Times* editor Jennings accurately called abortion.

There were inconsistencies in newspapers, to be sure. Not all were as strong in their attack on abortionists as others, although some did become stronger after they cut the purse strings to the death business. For even though advertising for abortion was against both federal and state laws, abortionists cleverly worded advertise-ments; and some jurisdictions were slow or negligent to uphold the law. A typical abortion ad might read, "All Female Monthly irregulari-ties are restored, from whatever cause, by my genuine remedies; real process, without medicine, never fails to regulate in one day."[7]

As strong antiabortion sentiment grew throughout the 1870s and 1880s and abortion laws grew tougher, the *Times* and newspapers across the country were reporting on the arrests and trials of doctors who were killing children. Headlines such as "Twenty-One Murdered Babies" were followed by lead sentences stating that "the bodies of 21 infants who had been killed before birth" were found in the basement of Dr. Isaac Hathaway with only a few spadefuls of dirt covering them.[8] The *Gazette* also covered the story, headlining their article, "Demon Doctor: Blood Curdling Discoveries in a Philadelphia Physician's Cellar."[9]

What can be viewed as tragedy in the pro-life cause occurred when the *Times* was sold in 1896 to Adolph Ochs. It was then that the paper's motto became, "All the News That's Fit to Print." Ochs developed the advertising slogan, "It does not soil the breakfast cloth." Since news about child-killing definitely soils the breakfast cloth, the *Times'* coverage of abortion virtually ended for two decades. Other papers, however, continued their efforts to expose the truth, but abortion was being driven underground.

Twentieth Century: Shift to Pro-Death

A major shift in the coverage of abortion began at the beginning of the twentieth century. The babies slowly dropped out of the picture. Stories on abortion still were covered, primarily when women "died of an illegal operation" performed by Dr. So-and-So. But concern for, advocacy of, and reporting on the dead child, previously associated with abortion, waned and waned.[10]

Into the 1950s, abortion coverage focused on injured and dead mothers, greedy doctors, and the corrupt, bribed officials who protected them. It was then that a second major shift began. Due to some brilliant public relations tactics by abortion proponents, the press began to positively entertain the idea of relaxing laws against killing unborn children. In 1955, Planned Parenthood sponsored a meeting concerning abortion, which was chaired by Alan Guttmacher. Many influential pro-abortion doctors attended. In that meeting, although virtually all agreed they wanted no restrictions on child-killing, all also agreed that the public simply wouldn't tolerate such a proposal. (And they viewed public sentiment as critical.) They thus recommended relaxing abortion laws in cases of rape, incest, child-deformity, major maternal health problems, and for the emotional health of the mother. They knew this would deaden the conscience of America—getting them accustomed to child-killing—and would consequently lead to unrestricted child-killing.

They left the meeting with a carefully thought-out public relations plan of attack: talk to the press about the rigidity of current abortion laws, the lack of compassion for mothers facing hard-case pregnancies, the plague of maternal deaths at the hands of back-alley butchers, safe versus unsafe abortions, etc. The meetings were edited and published in book form, which *Time* magazine and *Coronet* (another popular magazine) reviewed favorably. The shift of the press to pro-death advocacy had begun.

Toward this end, as the debate over child-killing entered into the 1950s and 1960s, these promoters of abortion made the claim that the antiabortion movement of the last century—the press, the politicians, the physicians (led by the AMA), the public—and the subsequent laws outlawing child-killing from the moment of conception were solely for the benefit of the mother's health. This was and remains *a bold-faced lie*, with absolutely no factual foundation. The clear consensus of that day was that abortion was murder—it killed an innocent, defenseless baby.

It is true and tragic that not only thousands of children died but also hundreds of mothers as well. Most women, however, died from infection, since antibiotics were not discovered until the 1940s. Another lie proclaimed from the fifties through today is that when child-killing was illegal—and should it be made illegal again—that quacks—back alley butchers—would be killing the unwanted products of conception of desperate women. This again is primarily a lie. The records of abortionists' arrests from 1870 through the 1950s and 60s shows that the vast, vast majority of abortionists were practicing physicians gone astray for the love of money.

Through the end of the nineteenth century, newspapers covered the arrests and trials of doctor after doctor, not quack after quack, who had illegally aborted a woman's child and oftentimes killed the mother in the process. Mary S. Calderone, past medical director of Planned Parenthood, concurs, stating in 1960 that 90 percent of child-killings were done by licensed physicians.[11] The portrayal of most abortionists as greasy mechanics working after hours is simply a public relations ploy—a lie—to elicit sympathy for the pro-abortion movement. It has been incredibly effective.

A Growing Crescendo. The pro-abortion movement slowly gained converts and steam in the press through the late fifties and especially in the sixties. More and more editorials portrayed our laws against abortion as cruel, too rigid, and in need of reform.

Throughout the sixties and early seventies the secular press fell into line with Planned Parenthood and NARAL's agenda, with a growing crescendo clamoring for freedom of choice and the liberalizing of abortion laws. The *New York Times*, once the leading defender of the children, became the leading advocate for child-killing. It consistently printed its own pro-death editorials and ran huge stories on the pro-death movement. Lengthy paragraphs were given to quotations from pro-death leaders with nary an opposing or, at least, intelligent argument from the pro-child position.

Newspaper after newspaper across the country did the same, publishing stories that were little more than pro-abortion propaganda. Abortionists were portrayed as heroes and as humanitarian servants risking their practices and their freedoms to help oppressed, desperate women—quite a turn from the headings of "Demon Doctor." They hammered Catholics, continued to deride back alley abortions, emphasized the hard cases, and ignored the child being killed.

Roe v. Wade. When the Supreme Court legalized child-killing through the day of birth on January 22, 1973, the chorus of praise that ascended from newspapers was virtually unanimous. Editors cheered and claimed that the issue was settled, that politicians and the nation could move on to other pressing matters. The *New York Times* recently described the ruling as "one of liberty's landmarks."[12] One lone voice in the wilderness was the *Orlando Sentinel*, whose editorial response to Roe was quite prophetic.

> The devaluation of morality induced by abortion could, and in all likelihood will, have far-reaching effects. Among them are the promotion of promiscuity, depersonalization of the concept of life and activating the destruct button on the family unit as we know it . . . And what of the woman herself? Abortion by whim could have grave future consequences to her. There is enough unavoidable pain in living without inflicting on oneself, in a period of extremity, the haunting memory of a child that might have been.[13]

(One outrage of the Roe coverage and the post-Roe coverage was the number of papers that said that the Supreme Court legalized child-killing only in the first trimester. From time to time, this erroneous fact still comes through the keyboard of some lazy journalists.) And so, Roe was history. It was officially open season on children in the womb. The papers applauded.

But child-killing was far from a settled issue, as the press would soon learn—much to their chagrin. The press often complained bitterly that abortion had to be an issue at all in political races, especially in the 1980, '84, and '88 presidential campaigns. They have often chided the Christian right for single-issue politics and the so-called abortion litmus-test. Well, apparently since Kate Michelman laid down the gauntlet to legislators, "Take our rights, lose your jobs," such politics is fine with the pro-death press.

The truth is that child-killing is the most heated, divisive blight on our nation since slavery; and it will never be settled as long as it is legal. No doubt, long after child-killing is once again illegal (or God ends it by ending the United States), there will still be those who believe in child-killing just as there are those today who still believe in slavery.

Related Issues

The debate over child-killing clearly centers on whether or not it is acceptable for us to murder our offspring. There are, however, numerous related issues which certainly merit honest investigation and reporting by the press but which have been greatly neglected. Most secular print media outlets have simply become the lapdogs of the abortion industry.

Abortion Dangers

The pro-death public relations experts played one theme so loudly and for so long that very few have questioned it. At every opportunity they recited their mantra, "Legal abortion equals safe abortion," (for the women, obviously, not the children). Consequently, reporters have generally failed to investigate the truth and ask the hard questions. What does abortion really do to women? How do the abortionists and the abortion industry view and treat women? What conditions really exist in these safe abortion mills?

One very odd series of true investigative reporting appeared in the *Chicago Sun-Times* in 1978. I say odd because the *Sun-Times* spent so much of their resources to expose the vile abortion trade in Chicago, despite the paper's own explicitly pro-abortion editorial stance. The series, in fact, was researched for five months and ran for two weeks. As Marvin Olasky points out, "No major metropolitan newspaper had spent such resources on an abortion exposé since the *New York Times* put out its memorable "Evil of the Age" article in 1871. For the *Sun-Times*, as for the *New York Times* a century earlier, the effort paid off."[14]

The first article ran on November 12, 1978, and set the tone for the entire series. It detailed the gamut of abortion mill corruption, portraying the mill owners as "abortion profiteers" and their mills as, just that, mills—not clinics. The article described "counselors who are paid not to counsel but to sell abortion with sophisticated pitches and deceptive practices." An administrator is quoted instructing receptionists, "We have to corral the patients." Another mill owner stated it plainly, "No matter how you put it, we're in the business of selling abortions. Use a positive approach. It's not, 'Do you want a termination, but *when*?'"[15]

The insatiable greed of the profiteers was also documented. The article described abortions being performed on women who were not pregnant and, in lurid detail, the helter-skelter nature of one mill's treatment rooms. The killer was shown dashing from procedure to procedure, not "washing his hands or donning sterile gloves." In one case a killer's dog actually "accompanied the nurse into the operating room and lapped blood from the floor." The article (and the entire series) plainly showed, "For the abortion profiteers, there is money to be made and no time to waste."[16]

The articles were very damaging to the abortion industry in Chicago, and the proaborts were furious with the paper. As the series wore on, the *Sun-Times* continued to reaffirm its pro-death stand and did puff pieces on Planned Parenthood and HERS killing center, evidently to appease their wrath.[17]

There is no reason to believe that the conditions at so many Chicago abortuaries are unusual; in fact, they are undoubtedly typical. Thousands of women have come forward in agony, traumatized over the murder of their child, and lamenting the horrid conditions and pressure from counselors they experienced in their safe and legal abortion.

Tens of thousands have had moderate (infection, scarring) to severe (future miscarriages, sterility, hysterectomy, near death from blood loss) complications from their simple procedure. Most abortionists require that women sign a waiver warning them of these and other complications.

Of course, the hundreds and perhaps thousands of women who lie in the grave because of a post-Roe abortion give silent witness to the safety of abortion.

The Dreaded Complication

Again, virtually no press coverage has been given to the abortionists' dreaded complication: a live birth. This press silence occurs in spite of several hundred live births that occur annually from botched assassination attempts.[18] A small percentage of these children actually survive and grow to maturity, often with the scars received from the attempt on their lives.[19]

Some abortionists follow through with their murderous intentions after the child is born alive. One such case involved Dr. Kenneth Edelin (who was recently appointed as chairman of the board of the Planned Parenthood Action Fund). In 1973, he tried unsuccessfully three times to abort the child of a seventeen-year-old black girl. (Edelin himself is a fair-skinned black, the fact of which would later play an important part in the press.) He finally gave up using saline solution and resorted to a hysterotomy—a Caesarean-section with the intent to kill the child. The little boy was born alive, and Edelin strangled him to death. In 1974, he was indicted for manslaughter; and in January 1975, he was brought to trial.

The pro-abortion *Boston Globe* dutifully played its role as lapdog, painting Edelin as a humanitarian, harassed by racists; the prosecution's witnesses were representing the antiabortion position; the defense witnesses were supposedly experts. One Edelin supporter said, "There is no question in my mind; the media went all out for Ken."[20]

But the jury was sequestered and didn't have the benefit of the daily pro-abortion, pro-Edelin press input. They convicted him of manslaughter on February 18th.

The press went wild. The editorial slant first taken by the *Globe* erupted in other newspapers across the country: the case was not about "abortion or manslaughter but . . . [about] racism, and a judgement from the perspective of the Catholic church."[21]

Of course, this is poppycock, but it reveals something both frightening and sad about the state of the press.

Blind Commitment

Blindly following the *Globe*'s lead, editorials across the country denounced the verdict. *Most of these papers never even had a reporter in the courtroom.* This willingness to express outrage, despite lack of firsthand knowledge of the facts, shows that they were more committed to ideology than truth. In the big picture, the cold-hearted, stone-faced refusal of the press to report or expose anything negative, abusive, indecent, or dangerous about child-killing shows that they truly are lapdogs, or worse, the *willing ideological slaves* of the pro-abortionists. That is a tragedy. It is also frightening.

The Purse Strings

The blind commitment of the press to the death industry is further exposed by the financial giving of their corporate bosses. Here's a brief run-down on major media's support of the abortion mills and their apologists:

- Times-Mirror Foundation (owns *Los Angeles Times, Newsday, Baltimore Sun*) (1982–86) $1,000 ACLU Foundation $50,000 Planned Parenthood

- New York Times Company Foundation (1982–86) $15,000 Feminist Press, Inc. $19,000 NOW Legal Defense and Education Fund $24,500 Planned Parenthood

- Philip L. Graham Fund (*Washington Post—Newsweek* empire) (1983–87) $30,000 Women's Legal Defense Fund

- Capital Cities Foundation (a chain of newspapers) (1986) $5,000 NOW Legal Defense and Education Fund $1,000 Women's Action Alliance (funded by Gloria Steinem).

Furthermore, Gannett Company (*USA Today*), *USA Weekend*, Capital Cities, the New York Times Company, and the Washington Post Company each supported the NOW Legal Defense Fund in 1988.[22] (This is the same year in which the NOW launched a huge lawsuit against pro-lifers in Chicago, a story which received pathetic, pro-NOW coverage. What else can you expect?)

What You Never See

On May 7, 1987, Joseph Scheidler and the Pro-life Action League held a press conference in front of an abortuary where they displayed dead babies, the gruesome reality of an abortion. These babies had been retrieved from the dumpster of that very abortion mill. The reporter covering the event for the *Chicago Sun-Times,* Lynda Gorov, wrote, "Look closely, [an antiabortionist] urged. Go ahead, look real close. I couldn't." Not only could she not bring herself to see the victims of abortion—dead babies—but she and her editors are determined that *you* will *never* see those dead babies.[23]

Have you ever seen a clear picture of an aborted child in your paper? The editors often say it's too distasteful, yet they don't hesitate to show tragedy and human suffering of every other ilk. Or what about a healthy, living *in utero* child of ten, twelve, or sixteen weeks? You probably never have, unless it was an advertisement paid for by pro-lifers. Why? Because a photo of a twelve-week *in utero* child makes chaff of all pro-death arguments that a baby isn't really a baby. They don't want the public to see who is being aborted (murdered). As long as they can reduce the child to dehumanized words and hence images (fetus, uterine contents), they can hide the reality that they are promoting and protecting the greatest holocaust ever experienced on the planet and that they are crucial collaborators.

When someone takes the stand at a trial, they take an oath to tell the truth, the *whole* truth, and nothing but the truth. To not tell the whole truth, to omit facts or information pertinent to the case, is to lie. Every newspaper that refuses to print pictures of abortion's victims—either dead or alive—is a bold-faced, calloused liar.

And the God of heaven shall avenge the blood of the innocent on all who sought to ignore their cry and who participated in the coverup of their murder. Since the media is purposely hiding this holocaust, they are more than accomplices; they are themselves *criminals.*

For those who believe this a little harsh or overstated, what would you say of Goebbels, the Nazi minister of propaganda, and all the editors and their newspapers who hid the holocaust in Germany from the German citizens? Were they not accomplices? Were they not criminal in hiding the truth—abandoning the innocent to violent death?

Likewise, American editors and journalists of American papers will one day bear the scorn of history's light. More importantly, each one will give an account to God who made those children and commanded, "You shall not murder" and "You shall not bear false witness." And perhaps, just perhaps, a few of them will receive some degree of justice here in this life or at least the scorn and villification they deserve.

The March for Women's Lives

The *New York Times'* coverage of the NOW's death march on April 9, 1989, was particularly up close and personal. The reason? Linda Greenhouse, who covers the abortion issue as part of her beat, actually participated in the march despite the *Times* strict *written* policy against "any undertakings . . . that create or appear to create a conflict of interest." This is the same Linda Greenhouse who in 1970 wrote concerning the passage of liberal abortion laws in New York state, "At last it seemed, abortion had been placed where it belonged—in the legal category of a tonsillectomy, with no more red tape, committees, humiliation, or exploitation."[24] What is even more outrageous is that the *Times* may continue to allow her to cover the abortion issue despite her long-standing pro-death commitment and more recent indiscretions.

As Dan Doheny of National Right to Life commented, "Would you send a reporter just back from his Ku Klux Klan meeting to cover civil rights violations in Alabama? Would you send someone back from a vacation in South Africa to cover an anti-apartheid rally? Would you send a reporter with a fur coat to cover an animal rights demonstration?"[25] Perhaps this explains why the *Times* was cited in 1978 by the National News Council, a private media watchdog, for bias in the reporting of two stories concerning abortion. The stories were essentially slams against Catholic legislators. *Can anyone say NARAL?*[26]

Other reporters participated in the march as well, including *Washington Post* reporter Sharon Walsh and *Post* magazine Senior Editor Amanda Spake. Thankfully, Walsh has been forbidden from ever covering abortion for the paper. In response to the furor, *Post* Executive Editor Benjamin Bradlee issued a directive: "We once again remind members of the newsroom's professional staff that it is unprofessional for you to take part in political or issue demonstrations." After perus-ing the memo, another Death marcher, *Post* Science Editor Boyce Rasberger wondered, "How can the *Post* permit reporters and editors to express their opinions in the news through op-ed pieces, news analysis and regular columns but prohibit the same people from ex-pressing their opinions through the right of peaceable assembly?"[27]

Bingo. Rasberger spills the beans. There is no objectivity. Every facet of a paper's presentation of the news is skewed. Regarding child-killing, this bias is generally deeply pro-death. Ironically, the *Post* sul-lied its own professionalism by providing a map and schedule for the march in its Sunday edition, which it has never done for the March for Life in sixteen years.[28]

The bias of the entire industry was revealed in the actions last year of the Newspaper Guild. The Guild, a union representing over twenty-five thousand reporters across the country, actually passed a resolution at their 1989 convention supporting abortion rights and joined with the ACLU in an amicus brief attacking the Missouri stat-ute under scrutiny in the Webster case. Talk about political involve-ment. Talk about unprofessionalism. This is outrageous.

Bias by the Book

It has also been recently revealed that the pro-death bias in some of the major print media's use of the prochoice and antiabortion labels is not mere happenstance. Rather, it is strict policy:

- The *Los Angeles Times'* style book requires reporters to describe pro-lifers as antiabortion and pro-deathers as prochoice. This pol-icy was reinforced in March 1989 during the Holy Week rescues in Los Angeles. A memo was actually circulated reminding the staff that these phrases were the only acceptable labels used by the paper.[29]

- The city editor of the *Chicago Tribune* quite bluntly states, "[It] de-pends on the event. If it's prochoice, that's what we say. And if it's pro-life, we use 'antiabortion.' "[30]

- The *Washington Post* no longer identifies [pro-life] groups as they wish [only pro-death groups]; they have chosen the labels "abor-tion rights" and "antiabortion."[31]

Deathspeak

Another blatant example of pro-death reporting can be found in the July 17, 1989, edition of *Newsweek*, the first issue released following the Webster decision.

For *Newsweek* reporter Ann McDaniel, the focus in this debate ought to be on a woman's right to make one of the larger decisions of her life and the women who each year choose abortion as the best way to resolve their personal dilemmas. Chief Justice Rehnquist's opinion is viewed as chilling and as adversely affecting the poor, the young and uneducated, perhaps making it all but impossible for poor women or teenagers to get abortions. Where is the footnote to a speech by Molly Yard or an article by Kate Michelman?

A boxed note does reveal some sympathy for the unborn child. The note, describing home-remedy abortions, comments that such do-it-yourself methods are dangerous. "Sadly, many home remedies could damage a fetus instead of killing it." How terrible! The victim in this war on the unborn would be wounded instead of killed! God help us!

The Latest Coverup

The most recent omission of the secular press is the incredible rise of the Rescue Movement and the police brutality and judicial tyranny that has accompanied it.

In order to give you a framework in which to see how truly unprecedented the Rescue Movement is, let's look at these facts. The *Wall Street Journal* has reported that less than ten thousand arrests occurred in the entire black Civil Rights Movement.[32] In contrast, in just two years (May 1988 through May 1990), over 40,000 arrests have occurred in the Rescue Movement; and individuals have risked arrest another sixteen thousand times without being taken into custody by the police. Moreover, it is likely that more clergy have been arrested in this movement than in any other movement in American history.[33]

Yes, Operation Rescue has received a good bit of media; but it is pitifully small in light of how much activity has happened. For example, if 40,000 had been arrested for protesting apartheid in South Africa, can you imagine the amount of coverage that would have occurred?

The press has at times begrudgingly covered rescues, often placing us on some back page. Beyond this limited coverage received by rescue activities, there has been a near blackout of the police brutality that has been endured by rescuers. In the same month in which the press reported and denounced the billy beatings at a peaceful candle-light vigil inside Czechoslovakia, rescuers were brutalized by police in Maryland. Did the media expose the Maryland police?

In the same month in which our press denounced the massacre at Tiananmen Square—and well it should—rescuers were having limbs broken by police in West Hartford, Connecticut. I am not comparing broken limbs to death. Rather, I wish to contrast the coerced silence which the Chinese press must endure—they are forced to cover up the abuse—and the self-imposed silence of the American press which has chosen to look the other way or even to cover up what police have done in Atlanta, West Hartford, Pittsburgh, Los Angeles, San Diego, and elsewhere. Does anyone believe that if Molly Yard, Betty Friedan, and friends had been sexually molested in a Pittsburgh jail (as women rescuers were) that there would *not* have been a hue and cry from the press? But the press is so committed to death that they are willing to ignore a level of brutality that hasn't been seen in over twenty years. They have become in so many ways the willing slaves of death.

If the press is willing to cover up these crimes because of ideological commitments, what else will they cover up? The press is suppos-edly the watchdog of the people. What happens when the watchdog sees someone being victimized and doesn't bark? What if the watch-dog secretly rejoices because he despised the victim's ideology?

Do you have any idea how many churches and Christian schools have been harassed by the government and how little the press has covered it? Or, worse yet, how these events have been reported with the same anti-Christ bias shown against the babies? Do you know how many Christian families have been harassed by the social service orga-nizations for raising their children according to Biblical standards? Has the press rushed to their defense? We have already seen that they are more committed to ideology than truth or justice. How shall we fare when we are committed to some other Christian principle that they hate?[34]

THE COURTS:
A NEW BREED OF TYRANTS

J ustice Harry Blackmun pensively sipped his second cup of coffee. Today, he would make history. It was January 22, 1973. He had authored the Supreme Court's majority opinion for the Roe v. Wade decision that legalized child-killing up to the day of birth in all fifty states.

He knew that this ruling had nothing to do with the Constitution for which our forefathers fought and died. He knew that this ruling was in fact judicial fiat, legislating law. As Potter Stewart wrote to Blackmun in an internal memo, "I appreciate the inevitability and the wisdom of the dicta [establishing the trimester demarcations] in the Court's opinion, but I wonder about the desirability of the dicta being quite so inflexibly 'legislative.'"[1] Blackmun knew, as Justice White said in his dissenting opinion, that this was a flagrant display of "raw judicial power."[2]

But none of that mattered. He was a visionary making history. Besides, as Justice Charles E. Hughes said, "We are under a Constitution, but the Constitution is what the judges say it is."[3] As Justice Oliver Wendell Holmes also said, "[Law] is the majority vote of that nation that could lick all others."[4] (You know, kinda like a street fight.)

Blackmun had won the right to kill children, fair and square, by a vote of 7–2 (Blackmun, Warren Burger, Lewis Powell, Jr., William O. Douglas, William J. Brennan, Jr, Potter Stewart, and Thurgood Mar-

shall concurring; Byron White and William Rehnquist dissenting).
Roe was law. Roe was truth. And Roe opened the bloody door to the
slaughter of tens of millions of innocent children.

Yes, as Mr. Blackmun and the other six justices who voted with
him emerged from behind the tall black curtain in their flowing
black robes, they made history. But when history casts its final editorial light, how will it view Mr. Blackmun?

A Rude Awakening

It's been a rude awakening for me and for thousands of my pro-life
compatriots. I envisioned the American judicial system as the citadel
where justice would prevail, a fortress where fairness would reign. I
naively imagined judges who were impartial, who wanted all defendants to have a fair trial, who truly wanted justice. The thought of a
police officer taking an oath, getting into the witness box, and then
lying never even occurred to me. I knew that district attorneys wanted
to convict criminals. I did, however, expect them to play by the rules
and to truly want the innocent to go free. Let me tell you the simple
truth—it just ain't so.

One of the stated grievances in the Declaration of Independence
and justifications for the revolution of the thirteen colonies against
Britain was tyranny, which included tyranny in the courts.

> He has obstructed the administration of justice, by refusing his as-
> sent to laws establishing judiciary powers. He has made judges de-
> pendent on his will alone, for the tenure of their offices, and the
> amount and payment of their salaries. For protecting them (armed
> troops), by mock trial, from punishment for any murders which they
> should commit on the inhabitants of these states. For depriving us,
> in many cases, of the benefits of trial by jury. For transporting us
> beyond seas to be tried for pretended offenses.

Over the past two hundred years we have drifted slowly back to
the rule of tyranny—a place where many judges have become little
gods unto themselves. Not only pro-lifers have seen the gross injustices in our judiciary—parents dealing with family court and social
services and child-custody cases, child-molesters (prisoners call them
baby-rapers) being released, blacks being handed harsher sentences
than whites, the poor being treated more harshly than the rich, mur-

derers plea bargaining to manslaughter and being paroled onto the streets in seven years or less.

Tragically, the courts have often become the bedrock of injustice and institutionalized anarchy in America. This is not always true, thank God. But the courts are quickly becoming the citadels of injustice. The American public is surely losing respect for this institution, and rightfully so.

The Supreme Court

We live in a day when the Supreme Court has virtually become a ruling oligarchy; their power extends far beyond what the framers intended. They have created constitutional rights out of thin air, or have built on the ever-shifting sand of *stare decisis* (court precedent).

The Supreme Court has repeatedly betrayed justice, overturned laws instituted by the duly-elected officials, and substituted their own laws (even though the Supreme Court is not supposed to make law). They have repeatedly ignored the intentions of the framers of the Constitution and run roughshod over laws and practices of public morality that have been with us for decades and even hundreds of years.

Behind the Veil

Just take a quick look at some of their practices. Some obviously are more egregious outrages than others. The Supreme Court made reading the Bible and prayer in public schools, a practice which had been going on for over two hundred years in America, illegal. The Supreme Court legalized pornography and helped unleash the sexual violence against women and children associated with it. It is inconceivable that the framers intended this when they spoke of freedom of the press. The Court struck down the Baby Doe regulations (designed to protect handicapped newborn children), effectively saying that parents and doctors can withhold food and medical treatment from handicapped babies and leave them to die. They struck down laws against dial-a-porn in spite of the will of parents and the evidence of the harm it was bringing to children. They struck down an ordinance in Akron, Ohio, that made it mandatory for the abortionist to warn a pregnant woman of the dangers to her accompanied with aborting a child. The Court instituted forced busing. The Court legalized flag-burning, even though our soldiers die in battle holding that flag. The Court also recently proclaimed that creches on public property during Christmas are illegal.

If the Supreme Court had been here on July 4, 1776, I'm sure they would have outlawed the Declaration of Independence. Its several references to God surely violate the separation of church and state.

Thomas Jefferson saw the danger of the Supreme Court becoming a ruling oligarchy and quickly called for an amendment to the Constitution barring the Supreme Court from ruling on United States' foreign policy. He also said,

> The opinion which gives to the judges the right to decide what laws are constitutional and what not, not only for themselves in their own sphere of action, but for the legislative branch and executive also in their spheres, would make the judiciary a despotic branch. . . .[5]

In 1788, Thomas Treadwell and Judge Robert Yates prophetically wrote these words in response to Federalist Paper 78:

> The Supreme Court under this Constitution would be exalted above all other power in the government, and subject to no control. . . . I question whether the world ever saw, in any period of it, a court of justice invested with such immense powers, and yet placed in a situation with so little responsible [sic].
>
> There is no power above [the judges], to control any of their decisions. There is no authority that can remove them, and they cannot be controlled by the laws of the legislature. In short, they are independent of the people, of the legislature, and of every power under heaven. Men placed in this situation will generally feel themselves independent of heaven itself.[6]

Unfortunately, their warning went unheeded, and now we are watching the Supreme Court's rulings tear asunder the moral fibre of our nation. The Supreme Court, more than any other legal body, has contributed to the moral cancer and anarchy ravaging our nation.

Rejecting the Word of the Lord

The greatest crimes against humanity committed by these tyrants were Roe v. Wade and other subsequent pro-death rulings which legalized child-killing up until the day of the birth! Over twenty-six million children have been brutally murdered since 1973. That is more people than all Central American countries combined and more than the cumulative 1989 populations of Montana, Idaho, Wyoming, Utah, Colorado, North Dakota, South Dakota, Nebraska, Kansas, Minnesota, Iowa, and Arkansas. Moreover, it is more than four times the number of Jews massacred by the antichrist Hitler.

The Supreme Court struck down the laws of all fifty states, including those in the few states that had passed liberal child-killing laws as early as 1967 and 1969. Think of the insanity: child-killing is transformed overnight from a century-long felony to a fundamental constitutional right. This is unalloyed tyranny.

Please understand something. The issue is not liberal judges versus conservative judges. I have been beneath the heel of both liberal and conservative judges, and let me tell you—they feel pretty much the same. Perhaps the only difference is that the liberal judge is more tolerant when he puts his heel on your neck! I don't want conservative judges! I want judges that fear God and believe that what God gave Moses at Mount Sinai is the bedrock of our society!

No doubt many books could be written about the death of justice in our judiciary, at every level and for every imaginable offense: criminal, civil, or family-related. My many hours in court and many months in jails have exposed me first-hand to the desperate shape of our justice system.

The problem is actually quite simple. Most judges have abandoned the Bible as the foundation of law and justice and have little fear of God in their rulings. Many have become pompous little gods unto themselves with egos as big as the world. Like the judge of the importunate widow (see Luke 18), they fear neither God nor men: "Behold, they have rejected the word of the Lord. So what wisdom do they have?" (Jeremiah 8:9, NKJV). Judges who do not fear God and honor His Law are ultimately unfit to be judges.

Nowhere is this more evident than in the legal actions against those who are attempting to end the slaughter. Indeed, since it was the courts that primarily brought us child-killing, it has been the courts that have feverishly sought to prop up the death industry, punishing with vigor all those who dare to try to topple this fortress of bloodshed. Generally, federal, state, county, and city judges have blindly followed in the blood-stained path of the Supreme Court; but, thank God, not always.

With a blind commitment to perpetuating this holocaust, they steadfastly ignore anything or anyone that might point out the obvious: *abortion is murder,* our nation is in the midst of a bloody holocaust. Moreover, many judges seek to crush all opposition to child-killing. For those who think this an overstatement, let the facts be plainly shown.

Betrayal of Justice

What has now become the infamous McMonagle RICO case[7] involves pro-life rescuers. RICO stands for the Racketeering Influenced and Corrupt Organizations Act. These laws were designed to combat organized crime organizations such as the mafia. Michael McMonagle and twenty-six others were tried and found guilty under civil RICO statutes in federal court. They lost their appeal at the Third Circuit and appealed to the Supreme Court. The Court has openly criticized the sloppy use of RICO, and Chief Justice Rehnquist himself referred to the folly of the McMonagle case in a commentary in the *Wall Street Journal.*[8]

However, in a stunning defeat and a betrayal of justice for pro-life forces, the Supreme Court, on October 10, 1989, announced its decision not to review the case and to allow the lower court's ruling to stand. Only Byron White dissented, advocating that the Court should have ruled on the case in order to resolve the conflict over RICO's use in suits where there is an "absence of any economic motivation on the part of the defendants."[9]

What makes this case such a flagrant abuse is three-fold:

1. The rescuers had no criminal intent.

2. The rescuers had no financial motives for their activity.

3. They received no financial benefit from their activities.

These motives and benefits are supposed to be the basis for a RICO prosecution. Furthermore, in a pretrial ruling, the original trial judge, Judge McGirr-Kelly, precluded the pro-lifers from even testifying regarding their intent. Did this judge even read the statute?

And so, attorneys for the abortion mill are seeking to obtain $2,600 in damages, $42,000 for added security, and $65,000 in attorney's fees. Additionally, because they are refusing to pay, these pro-lifers are being assessed $18 per day in interest. McMonagle and crew are now convicted racketeers for trying to save babies. Welcome to pro-life justice.[10]

At the time of this writing, I am currently being sued under RICO statutes in at least five cities, besides civil lawsuits in another fifteen cities, *some of which I've never even been to.* In others I have never participated in any pro-life activities. And yet often the judges allow these ridiculous lawsuits to proceed, despite the lack of evidence against me and others and the (or perhaps because of) finances and inconveniences they cost.

For example, not only have I never been to West Hartford, but also their chief piece of evidence in the RICO lawsuit against me is my first book, *Operation Rescue.* So much for free speech. What is even more outrageous is that the city originally sued under RICO *The Orange County (New York) Post—for editorializing against the police brutality.* Apparently, the city fathers were offended when the paper referred to their police officers as "northern rednecks." So much for freedom of the press. Welcome to pro-life justice.[11]

Civil Courts

On Sunday afternoon, June 11, 1989, police officers stormed into the worship service of New Christian Community in Virginia Beach, Virginia, in order to serve summonses for a $1.3 million lawsuit brought by Hillcrest Clinic, a local killing center at which several rescues had occurred. This lawsuit named the seventy-three individuals, including five pastors, who had participated in the April 29, 1989, rescue at Hillcrest.

Virginia Beach, Virginia. It followed an earlier (June 1988) temporary restraining order issued by Judge John Winston which had barred pro-lifers from even approaching the clinic's grounds. For his violation of that court order, Don Varela, pastor of New Community Church, was sent to jail indefinitely by Winston on June 22, 1989. He had refused to agree not to participate, incite, discuss, encourage, or plan any future protests on the clinic's property. After serving thirty days in jail, Varela finally did relent for family reasons and was released, although he did so only with full assurances that fellow rescue leader Jay Comisky would himself break the same order and assume Varela's place behind bars.

Comisky shortly did violate the restraining order and was arrested. The authorities, however, chose not to pursue the civil contempt against him; they prosecuted him on the criminal trespass charge only. Apparently, Varela's commitment swayed them not to attempt such high-pressure tactics again.

One must remember that these court proceedings were entirely civil proceedings, contrary to criminal charges. Judge Winston could have, without a trial or a conviction, imprisoned Varela (or Comisky) forever; there is no limitation placed upon a sentence for civil contempt.

Portland, Oregon. On January 25, 1990, in a scene reminiscent of Stalinist Russia and present-day Virginia Beach, eight pro-lifers—having been neither tried nor convicted—were sentenced to a Portland jail indefinitely. Each of the eight, Andrew Burnett, Catherine Ramey, Dawn Stover, Linda Wolfe, Sean Hahn, Norman Norquist, Marion "Doc" Hite, and Cathy Gorsline, was found in contempt by Multnomah County District Judge Nely Johnson for violating a preliminary injunction issued in the fall of 1989. The eight had violated the order by rescuing children on September 30, 1989, at Lovejoy Surgicenter.

On January 18, Judge Johnson had presented the rescuers with two options: either agree never to return to the Lovejoy abortuary to rescue or turn themselves in to the authorities for indefinite incarceration in the Inverness Detention Facility and Justice Center. At this writing, the eight have spent nearly three months in custody—and are now under house arrest. Appeal efforts are underway. It is outrageous that such preventive detention and prohibitive incarceration is being used against United States citizens. God help us.

Criminal Courts

I can only begin to describe the pervasive injustice faced by rescuers in criminal courts across the country. The outrage of these trials and sentences is deeply accentuated when one looks at the manner in which fair trials are regularly denied, the sentences given to members of other protest groups, and the sentences given to criminals.

Each time rescuers go to court, they hope for a fair trial. This means one thing: that the jury or judge will allow them to present evidence that they trespassed at an abortuary in order to save children from murder. We insist that we are not breaking any laws. It is not a crime to save a person's life or even to attempt to do so.[12]

For example, you spy a young girl thrashing about in a pool, no doubt drowning. Her yard, however, is fenced in, and there are numerous No Trespassing signs posted. How should you respond? Well, you would be breaking no law to jump the fence or even to knock it down in order to rescue her. In fact, even if you were mistaken and the supposed child was actually a life-like doll, your actions would still be justified. The legal terminology is just that: the justification or necessity defense. It means that the actor technically broke some law to prevent a greater harm or injury to another person (or thing).

We simply want to communicate to a jury of our peers the facts. We ought to be permitted to present as evidence the pictures of *in utero* babies and films of babies being murdered through suction abortions and other killing methods. It is our firm belief that such evidence would convince jurors that we in fact did trespass to prevent the grizzly death of innocent children and that they would consequently acquit us. When juries have been afforded such an opportunity or even when a few judges have looked at the facts (in non-jury trials), rescuers have generally been acquitted. Unfortunately, we are rarely given the opportunity.

Prosecutors almost always vigorously—and at times venomously—fight the rescuers' use of the necessity defense. Why? Because they know they will lose the case or, at least, get a hung jury. And unfortunately, when it comes to pro-life law, most prosecutors don't want justice, they want a *conviction*. And where prosecutors leave off, most judges pick up, typically ruling, "Abortion has nothing to do with this case. It is irrelevant to a trespassing case." These words are an affront to common sense as well as justice. It's saying, "The fact that you thought a little girl was drowning is irrelevant. This is a case about trespass!"

San Diego, California. A horrifying example occurred in January 1990 in San Diego, California. Cyrus Zal, a phenomenal pro-life attorney, was representing seven rescuers on charges stemming from a rescue on October 21, 1989, at Family Planning [Killing] Associates in La Mesa. Judge Larry Brainard freely granted the prosecution's *ad limine* motions. These motions set the boundaries of the trial, meaning they can exclude the issue of child-killing from being introduced.

Well, the prosecutor in this case went for it all. He was able to get excluded any reference to the necessity defense, freedom of speech, the defendant's religious beliefs, and even God. Such words as unborn, fetus, abortion, holocaust, and murder were also barred. The D.A. also tried to exclude "religious beliefs, God, and diety." Moreover, Judge Brainard forbade any corporate or silent prayer in or outside of the courtroom. He expressed his judicial philosophy in this manner: "There's no room in my courtroom for First Amendment rights."

Zal, however, fulfilling his obligation to bring the unborn child into the courtroom, disregarded the motions and continued to present the truth. He was rewarded by Judge Brainard with twenty contempt of court citations. If his appeal of the charges fails, Zal faces ninety days in jail and ten thousand dollars in fines.

Other officials in the San Diego criminal justice system hold similar opinions to Judge Brainard's. One prosecutor, Gordon Davis, commented during the course of a January 1990 rescue trial, "There's no place for these antiabortion people within a pluralistic society." Judge Victor Bianchini (who also presided over rescuers' trials) from the transcript of the trial concurs, "The absolutism of the pro-life movement is so inimical to, and destructive of, the democracy, the unwillingness to even engage in debate, I see the defendants' actions as having no moral basis in this democracy." Since Zal refuses to pay the fine that protects child-killing, Judge Brainard imposed an additional two hundred days in lue of the fines for a total of two hundred and ninety days. God save us from such judicial tyranny.

The bottom line is simple: pro-lifers regularly are denied fair trials by a jury of their peers. A jury is supposed to represent the conscience of the community. When we are denied the right for a jury of our peers to understand why we acted, then the judge and prosecutor are looking for a jury to merely rubberstamp their foregone decision: guilty!

Pensacola, Florida. By far and away, the most outrageous sentence came against a woman who could very well be the movement's most courageous defender of the children: Joan Andrews.

On July 22, 1986, Joan was found guilty in a bench trial before Judge William Anderson in Pensacola, Florida. She was convicted of burglary arising from a March 26, 1986, rescue at The Ladies' Center, in which she unsuccessfully tried to pull the plug from a killing machine.

She was sentenced to five years in prison! This happened on the same day that Judge Anderson sentenced two men who were *accomplices to murder* to four years in prison!

After serving nearly three years, Joan was finally released by the timid Governor Martinez, after he had received thousands and thousands of phone calls and letters over many, many months. Thank God for pro-life solidarity. Truthfully, though, Joan should never have served a day, and Governor Martinez exemplified much cowardice and compromise for months before he finally worked for her release.

Atlanta, Georgia. Michael McMonagle is the same racketeer, gangster, and pro-lifer you've been hearing about. Michael stood on trial before Judge Thelma Cummings in Atlanta, Georgia, from November 13–15, 1989.

On October 5, 1988, a rescue was in progress at Feminist Women's Health Center in Atlanta. Michael was not risking arrest at this rescue. He was standing on the sidewalk, using a bullhorn, asking police to be gentle with the rescuers. Without warning, he was arrested for obstructing a sidewalk and jailed with a $300 bond. He spent nine days in jail.

At the trial, the police lied on the stand, saying that Michael was encouraging people to break the law. Michael had video footage from *48 Hours* showing what he was actually doing. The film would have controverted the testimony of the officers.

Judge Cummings refused to let Michael show the video. It then became the word of an out-of-towner against that of several local policemen in uniform from Atlanta, complete with southern accents. The jury believed the police and found Michael guilty of aiding and abetting the obstruction of a sidewalk.

His sentence? The prosecutor requested twelve months in jail and one thousand dollars fine. The judge (maybe feeling merciful) instead sentenced him to forty-five days in jail and one thousand dollars fine. Michael said that he could not in good conscience pay the fine since he was not guilty of a crime. She then sentenced him to six months in jail! For obstructing a sidewalk!

Contrast this with the trial of another man before Thelma Cummings. As the jury deliberated his fate, Michael witnessed Cummings preside over a bench trial. The accused individual had placed a loaded gun to another man's head. The prosecutor, having reduced the charge from felony assault with a deadly weapon, managed to obtain a conviction on the misdemeanor illegal use of a gun. The sentence: ten days in jail and a one hundred fifty dollar fine. Again, welcome to pro-life justice.

A man threatens another man's life and gets ten days in jail; Michael is legally standing on a sidewalk and gets forty-five days in jail and a thousand dollar fine, which becomes six months in jail when he wouldn't pay the fine.

More on Atlanta. On October 24, 1989, Elizabeth Hall, having pleaded not guilty, was convicted in an Atlanta courtroom on a trespassing charge for rescuing children. Judge Jerry W. Baxter, disregarding her request for community service, immediately sentenced her to a year in jail, of which she would have to serve thirty days, and a five hundred dollar fine. Stunned, she said, "Your honor. I have a four-month-old nursing baby. My baby needs me. She has never had a bottle." The judge, granting her a thirty-day stay to wean her child, replied, "You should have thought of that before you did this." The tender mercies of the wicked are cruel. She appealed her case and was temporarily spared the ordeal of being separated from her baby.

Forgive me for mentioning my own kangaroo trial, but it bears telling.

I was tried before Judge John Bruner between September 25 and September 29 in Atlanta. As with most rescue cases, the judge refused the necessity defense, thereby ensuring I would not get a fair trial. I was railroaded through to a conviction and sentenced on October 5. Three things make this trial notable.

- First, the prosecutor Lee O'Brien professes to be a Christian. In his closing arguments he mocked me and rescue efforts, stating, "Mr. Terry thinks he's the savior of the children!" He quoted from the Bible, even referring to Jesus; and then he promptly asserted (implicitly) that a woman has a right to kill her child! Before my sentencing I rebuked Mr. O'Brien in court, "[He] has betrayed the faith, and the blood of the children is on his hands."

- Second, both the judge and the prosecutor saw portions of *The Silent Scream, Eclipse of Reason,* and a grotesque training film for abortionists. (The jury never saw them. I was making my offer of proof.) Apparently, as they watched the children being systematically murdered, they had hardened their hearts and concluded that abortion had nothing to do with my trial, despite the fact that I was arrested for trying to stop such barbarism. That's like saying to a worker in the Underground Railroad, "Whether a slave is a human being or not has nothing to do with this case. You are on trial for stealing another man's property!" How the purveyors of injustice are so willingly blind!

- Third, the prosecutor requested the maximum sentence of two years in jail and a two thousand dollar fine. He also offered the judge the option of imposing upon me a two-year banishment from the Atlanta area. (Is this America or Russia?)

The judge opted to sentence me to a one thousand dollar fine with a two-year suspended sentence and banishment. When I told him that I would not pay the fine, he sentenced me to the full two years. The two charges merged, and my sentence reduced to one year. After four months, an anonymous donor paid the fine, and I was released.

Compared to the sentences of other protest groups in Atlanta, our sentences have been outrageous. An anti-Ku Klux Klan group gathered in Atlanta during the Democratic National Convention to protest the Ku Klux Klan. They threw bricks, some of which hit the police. They were all fined one hundred dollars. A group of antinuclear protesters were also arrested during the convention. They served three days in jail, had a twenty-five dollar fine suspended, and went home. When disabled veterans sat-in at the federal building in Atlanta (coincidentally, during the week of my trial), President Bush himself called and asked that they not be arrested! Homosexuals lay down in the streets and were fined seventy dollars and released. Meanwhile, by comparison, we receive horrendously long jail sentences for trying to stop the murder of innocent children! We are truly political prisoners.

Tacoma, Washington. On April 10, 1989, fifty-two rescuers were convicted before Judge Rindal in Bellevue, Washington, on trespassing charges. Prior to sentencing, the judge declared that he would impose the maximum penalty unless the rescuers would promise not to rescue again anywhere in the United States for the next two years. The first to come before him was Penny Ackeret. Penny stood courageously and responded to his ungodly request, "No. No. I couldn't do that." The judge then said, "I sentence you to 365 days in jail, impose a five thousand dollar fine, and will suspend none of it." The entire courtroom was shocked, including the prosecutor, who had asked for only a one thousand dollar fine and a suspended sentence. The judge was so unnerved by the refusal of this brave woman to be coerced that he set aside Mrs. Ackeret's sentence and postponed any further sentencing until June 23.

The pro-life community responded. They began to call and write Judge Rindal, politely demanding he reduce the harsh sentences. In the next two months he received over one thousand letters and innumerable phone calls. When the sentencing hearing was reconvened, his attitude had been greatly altered. He sentenced the majority of the rescuers to a $1,000 fine and a two-year probationary period. This is a far cry from one year in jail and a $5,000 fine.

Burlington, Vermont. On Wednesday, October 5, 1989, fifty-four rescuers stood before Judge George Costes in a Burlington, Vermont, courtroom. They had already spent two days in jail, refusing to identify themselves in order to stand in solidarity with several rescuers who had been unjustly charged with bogus felonies. As the rescuers were arraigned before Judge Costes, they were asked to identify themselves. They, however, chose to remain silent, identifying with the children who have no voices. The judge was outraged and immediately sentenced all fifty-four to serve up to ninety days in jail for contempt of court! They eventually served thirty-nine days and were released, only giving their names after being assured by their attorneys that the bogus felony charges would be dropped.

The Role of the Bench

Allow me to introduce you to two judges whose rulings have not only hurt the pro-life movement but have also violated our constitutional rights.

Federal Judge Robert Ward. One federal judge is U.S. District Court Judge Robert Ward of the southern district of New York in New York City. It was in his court that the NOW brought suit against me and Operation Rescue in connection with our rescues in New York City in May 1988.

The judge not only forbade us from rescuing children (which is typical), but also ordered Operation Rescue and me to pay $25,000 a day per rescue to the NOW, Planned Parenthood, and individual New York City abortion mills! His final judgment, rendered October 27, 1988, read:

> Plaintiff's motion for civil contempt is granted. Defendants Randall Terry and Operation Rescue are adjudged in civil contempt of this Court's May 4 Order and assessed coercive civil penalties in the amount of $50,000. . . . These funds are to be paid to plaintiff National Organization for Women and disbursed among the remaining plaintiffs according to its discretion. [The remaining plaintiffs included Planned Parenthood of New York City, Inc., Eastern Women's Center, Inc., Planned Parenthood Clinic (Bronx), Planned Parenthood Clinic (Brooklyn), and the Planned Parenthood Margaret Sanger Clinic (Manhattan).][13]

Never in the history of the United States (that my attorneys or I are aware of) had a defendant's civil rights concerning fines or damages been so flagrantly violated, concerning the payment of fines or damages. For me to pay fifty thousand dollars to NOW and various killing centers would be akin to asking the NAACP to pay fifty thousand dollars to the Ku Klux Klan or the Jewish Defense League to pay fifty thousand dollars to the Young Nazis. He ordered me to pay for the murder of innocent children.

The entire court proceeding, including the trial, was a sham, a true kangaroo court. The judge suspended or ignored court rules that would have assisted our case and basically gave the NOW attorneys anything they wanted. This was what the signers of the Declaration called a mock trial.

During my deposition, my attorney advised me at many points to use my Fifth Amendment privileges, which are the Constitutional guarantees against self-incrimination. We withheld certain documents on the same premise. The judge then granted NOW a motion to compel, basically demanding that I answer all questions and turn over all documents, whether they might incriminate me or not. To add to this outrage, the judge told me and my attorney to pay sixteen thousand dollars for the cost of their motion to compel. I did not have the money, so my attorney (who was working for free!) was forced to pay it out of his own pocket!

We appealed the case, and on September 20 the Second Circuit upheld the entire decision, with the exception that the fifty thousand was to be paid to the federal treasury. This was barely an improvement. The federal government began the collection proceedings under the leadership of a pro-abortion lawyer in the U.S. attorney's office in New York City. On December 20, 1989, they seized our payroll and general operating accounts in Binghamton. Our national office in Binghamton has been forced by the federal government to severely curtail its activity and reduce staff from twenty-three to three.

Think about this: never, to our knowledge, has the United States government attempted to obtain $50,000 from any protest group, i.e., the SCLC, SNCC, NAACP, ACT UP, SANE, Greenpeace, animal rights' protesters, or the Days of Outrage.

Furthermore, violent groups such as the Underground Weathermen, Refuse and Resist, and the Marxist-Leninist Party of New York—who call for the violent overthrow of the government—have never been sued. The United States government has never sought $50,000 from them! What does this tell you? Is the government more committed to protecting child-killing than it is to preserving its own existence?

On February 27, 1990, Judge Ward issued another judgment on a second lawsuit against Operation Rescue brought by the NOW, Planned Parenthood, and the ACLU. These court proceedings had stemmed from rescues in January of 1989 in New York City.

Judge Ward ordered Operation Rescue, eleven other defendants, including Mrs. Adelle Nathanson, and me to pay $425,000 in fines for violating his court order not to rescue babies. Meanwhile, the homosexuals who sat in at St. Patricks's Cathedral in New York City were fined one hundred dollars each.

Just before going to print, the Supreme Court refused to hear our original NOW case out of New York City. That means Judge Ward's $50,000 fine stands. Also, the Supreme Court refused to give an emergency stay regarding an injunction obtained by the City of Atlanta which forbids picketing, sidewalk counseling, prayer, leafletting, etc. on a public sidewalk within fifty feet of an abortion mill in Atlanta. And we thought this was a pro-life Supreme Court!

District Court Judge Tashima. On August 8, 1989, rescuers in southern California went to District Court Judge Tashima requesting an injunction against the police use of nunchakus against rescuers. Pro-life attorneys cited as evidence United States District Judge Stanley Weigel's ruling on June 22, 1989, forbidding police from using pain-compliance against those protesting at the Concord Naval Weapons Station in Contra Costa, California. In fact, in that case, the judge actually awarded $50,000 to three anti-war demonstrators for injuries sustained in November 1987.

Judge Tashima, however, refused to protect the rescuers. Why? Rescuers had ignored his statewide injunction from the prior March barring them from rescuing children. His attitude appeared to be, "You people are going to break my order, and you want me to issue an order so that the police don't brutalize you? Forget it!"

District Attorneys. As we look at these cases of judicial tyranny, we must remember that prosecutors often play as evil a role as judges. For example in Binghamton, New York, rescuers were picked up, placed in wheelchairs, and wheeled to a bus. At this point most rose from the wheelchairs and walked onto the bus. For this crime they were charged with resisting arrest.

The head district attorney, Gerald F. Mollen, told the rescuers that if they would plea bargain, they could pay a $250 fine. If they went to trial, were convicted, and refused to pay the fine, he would request that the judge sentence individuals to six months in jail—*six months for being picked up and placed in a wheelchair.*

I called Mr. Mollen and politely confronted him with this injustice, pointing out how many child molesters get weekends in the Binghamton jail. He was angered by this comparison (while it should be *we* and the general public who are outraged) and stood fast to his guns. Thus, Judge Vitanza gave those convicted of resisting arrest—who refused to pay the fine—three months in jail, of which they served sixty days. Sixty days in jail for being placed in a wheelchair! Certain drug criminals, thieves, and child molesters get less time than that in Binghamton!

Lights in the Gross Darkness

In all fairness, there are judges who fear God more than men and who have done what is right, disregarding godless Supreme Court rulings. I must mention a few of them.

Judge Randall Hekman.[14] In late October, 1982, Kent County (Michigan) Probate Judge Hekman was confronted with a challenge to his convictions. Could he permit a pregnant fourteen-year-old girl, assigned to be a ward of his court, to undergo an abortion, *to have her child killed.* He could not. He stood for righteousness.

Although an appeals court later vacated Judge Hekman's ruling, its truth is not diminished.

I am asked by the law to totally disregard the poor, defenseless unborn child that grows and moves within his or her mother's womb.

Perhaps, for abortion cases, we need to call on judges who are indifferent to life and have no scruples about arbitrarily ordering the execution of innocent victims when they conclude the pregnant girl's existence would, in some tangible way, be thereby enhanced.

I wish to state emphatically that I consider the putting to death of an unborn child far more significant than asking a young woman who is 5 months pregnant to be inconvenienced for a few months more.

I consider my oath of office as a solemn trust. In eight years on the bench, I have not violated that solemn trust and I have no intentions of doing so in the future apart from cases like this that literally involve life and death. Where I am ordered to put to death innocent subjects for the expediency of others, I do refuse and will refuse to so act.

There are many other decisions of the Supreme Court which I find illogical, but I still follow them religiously due to my oath of office. However, when a decision threatens the life of an innocent being, I must apply a different standard.

Forty years ago in Hitler's Germany it was totally legal to torture, maim, cruelly experiment with and otherwise kill people of Jewish descent.

After the war, these same governmental officials were tried and many were executed according to the principles of a higher law.

To quote from one attorney at the Nuremberg trials: "A soldier is always faced with the alternative of obeying or disobeying an order. If he knows the order is criminal, it is surely a hollow excuse to say it must be obeyed for the sake of obedience alone."

There is no question in my mind that if I am ordered to initiate procedures to kill innocent life for the expediency of others, that is a criminal order which I cannot obey.

For the reasons contained in this opinion, the petition for the abortion is respectfully denied.[15]

Missouri Judges George R. Gerhard and Arthur Miorelli. On August 16, 1989, Associate Circuit Judge George Gerhard dismissed over eighty charges of trespassing and resisting arrest pending against twenty-one rescuers in St. Louis County Circuit Court—*based on the necessity defense.* This judgment followed the Supreme Court's Webster ruling which left intact the Missouri statute's preamble declaring that life begins at conception. His decision is a beacon amidst the darkness of judicial tyranny.

> My job as I see it is to render judgment in these cases based on the law and the evidence and the reasonable inferences to be drawn from the evidence. . . .
>
> The overwhelming credible evidence in this case is that life begins at conception.
>
> The sense of the people of the state of Missouri as expressed in Section 1.205 is that life begins at conception.
>
> The overwhelming evidence in this case, and indeed the judicial admission of the prosecutor, proves that abortion kills an unborn child. . . .
>
> Additionally, the evidence shows no exigent circumstances existing for the killing of these unborn children such as the health or life of the mother. . . .
>
> The Court finds that the credible evidence in these cases established justification for the defendants' actions. Their violations of the ordinances involved here were necessary as emergency measures to avoid the imminent private injuries of death and maiming of unborn children, which imminent deaths and maimings were occasioned through no fault of the defendants but occasioned by the operation of a lucrative commercial endeavor. The desirability of avoiding death and maiming of unborn children—persons—obviously outweighs the desirability of avoiding the injury sought to be prevented by the ordinances.
>
> The Court therefore finds the defendants . . . not guilty of the charges against them.[16]

Little more than a week later, on August 24, Judge Arthur Miorelli acquitted five more rescuers, ruling, "No question that abortion is a significant imminent harm. There's no adequate remedy but to go onto property and block doors."[17]

Judge Bill Constangy. Similarly, on May 22, 1989, Mecklenburg (North Carolina) County Judge Bill Constangy acquitted six rescuers on trespassing charges after he permitted the necessity defense to be argued. Although Constangy neither released a written decision nor commented himself on his reasons for acquitting the rescuers, pro-life and pro-death forces understood. As pro-life attorney Tom Bush said, "It's an extremely important decision. A sitting trial judge has recognized as a matter of law that life begins at conception."[18]

The local ACLU and other pro-death public defenders were so outraged by his courageous stand for truth that they instigated an attack on him on a separate but closely-linked issue. In fact, they filed suit against him, demanding that he stop praying at the opening of his court sessions! His prayer clearly reflects his humility before God and dependence on God's wisdom which, I'm sure, influenced his decision.

> O Lord, our God, dear Father in Heaven, we pray this morning that you will place your Divine Guiding Hand on this Courtroom and that with your mighty outstretched arm you will protect the innocent, give justice to those who have been harmed and mercy to us all.
>
> Let truth be heard and wisdom be reflected in the light of your presence here with us today. Amen.[19]

The federal court will issue a ruling soon.

Jury Nullification. Likewise, entire juries and even one juror have disregarded the instructions of the trial judge and acquitted rescuers because they intuitively knew what was right. For example, in September 1989, four others and I were on trial in Los Angeles for twenty-seven charges stemming from rescues the previous March. To the amazement of the judge, the prosecutor, and the pro-death media, we were found not guilty on twenty-four of the charges and received a hung jury on the other three. It was a tremendously exciting victory—just in time for me to come to Atlanta and get hammered!

Calling a Spade a Spade

Let me say this in the clearest possible terms: the judges and prosecutors who promote and protect child-killing are criminals. They have participated in crimes against humanity, either by directly opening the way for children to be killed or by ruthlessly prosecuting (persecuting) those who defend the children. They are criminals; blood is on their hands.

God will hold them accountable when they stand before Him; and any faint protests that they were simply following the law will be meaningless. We must warn them of their impending judgment, and we must hold them accountable *now* to follow Biblical justice.

As Judge Hekman reminded us concerning German officials who participated in the legal crimes of Germany, these officials will some-day, must someday, be brought to justice concerning their part in this holocaust. These judges who fined rescuers and sentenced them to jail for protecting babies should perhaps be fined in the amounts they fined rescuers and be sentenced to jail for the amount of time they sentenced rescuers. Whether their sentences should run concurrent or consecutive would be decided by those pronouncing sentences.

Perhaps judges who have issued injunctions against rescuers and presided over these massive lawsuits should be sentenced to jail terms and fined in the amounts of the huge awards which they have ordered pro-lifers to pay to abortion mills.

All judges who have participated in this holocaust should be thrown off the bench and disbarred from practicing law.

If the justices, who unleashed this holocaust, are still alive, they should be tried for legitimizing the massive bloodshed of tens of millions of babies. These trials would be conducted under the Nuremberg Accords, of which America is a part; and the charge would be crimes against humanity.

You may think that this is extreme. Do you think that it was extreme that Nazi war criminals, including judges who had never actually killed anyone themselves, were executed? This is an issue of justice. The judges who voted for Roe and upheld it in subsequent decisions opened the door for the death of nearly thirty million babies to date! That's two and one-half times more babies than all the people murdered in Hitler's holocaust. I know that I may catch a lot of heat for saying these things, but it's time we began proclaiming truth and heralding justice because it's right and not because it's acceptable.

Take Warning

I'm sure you are angered by what you've read, but you should also be worried. These same godless tyrants and unjust prosecutors will be motivated by the same anti-Christian ethic to oppress churches in lawsuits and RICO proceedings, to interfere in church discipline, to intrude into Christian schools, and to steal our children in mock legal proceedings. Tyranny does not rest; oppression is never satisfied. The antagonism which the courts have shown to Christianity, Christian principles, and Biblical law will continue to encroach on our churches and our families until we find it at our front door.

One major problem in our system is that many judges—Supreme Court justices, all federal judges, and some state judges—are appointed for life. They therefore lose accountability to the American people. Very few judges are ever impeached; normally that happens only after some gross scandal of misconduct rather than a blatant betrayal of justice. We need to change our system.

Perhaps, Supreme Court justices should be appointed every twelve years (thus, outlasting presidents), or perhaps, they should require a majority vote of confidence from the Senate every four or eight years. Therefore, if they consistently betray justice, show themselves calloused to the Constitution and, more importantly, rebellious to God and His law, they could be removed. These same principles could apply to other judges as well.

Or perhaps all judges should face general elections, making them again accountable to the electorate. If they are soft on crime or hard on justice, they can be ousted.

These are only ideas—perhaps there are better ones—but America's judiciary definitely has problems that require serious changes.

POLICE, PRISON GUARDS, AND PAIN

S elma, Alabama, March 7, 1965.[1] The brutal beatings are indelibly imprinted on our collective memory as a nation. Scores of civil rights activists intending to peacefully march from Selma to Montgomery were seeking to cross the Edmund Pettus Bridge going out of town. They were met by a wall of mounted Alabama state troopers. There was a brief stand-off.

Then it happened—the billyclub (a policeman's nightstick), beatings, the stamping horses, the tear gas, and the frantic, running marchers. Television cameras and still cameras alike forever captured that violent fragment of American history.

The television media played the scene over and over again. The print media decried this unprovoked attack. The *New York Times* commented regarding the outrage, "The scene in Selma resembled that in a police state. Heavily armed men attacked the marchers. . . . If this is described as law enforcement, it is misnamed . . . It disgraces not only the state of Alabama but every citizen of the country in which it can happen."[2]

The nation saw it and was repulsed. Rightly so. The unfortunate scene was repeated with slight variations in other cities in that tumultuous, troubling decade.

Still with Us

But when we left the sixties and early seventies behind, most of us thought we had left police brutality behind with them. We didn't. Beatings, kickings, broken arms, dislocated shoulders, cuts, bruises, pain compliance come-along holds and, unbelievably, *sexual molestation of women*—all by uniformed police officers—have resurfaced in our nation en masse.

Surely you've seen Dan Rather and his competitors showing extended news clips, the investigative reporting with hard-hitting commentaries by indignant national correspondents, and the scathing editorials and exposés in the *New York Times* and *Los Angeles Times*, naming names and demanding federal investigations and the resignations of the guilty parties. You mean you haven't heard the media outcry?

Maybe it's because there hasn't been one.

The incredible truth is that police departments in one city after another have been brutalizing nonviolent rescuers: moms, dads, grandmas, grandpas, boys, and girls. Little or no deference has been given to women, the elderly, or clergy. A frail elderly woman is knocked to the ground with the same careless force as a young man might be. It's almost impossible to believe that this is happening in the late eighties and early nineties. But it is.

Passive and Nonviolent

Before examining the police misconduct in several cities, let me make one point crystal clear: the pro-lifers being abused are and have always been nonviolent. Rescuers must commit to nonviolence in word and deed before they participate in a rescue mission. Of the hundreds of rescues and tens of thousands of arrests that have happened in the past two years, amazingly, there has not been one report of violence from rescuers toward police.

Police departments nationwide are aware of this through their communications with one another. For instance, Sergeant Jerome Leskowski of the Civil Affairs Division of the Philadelphia Police Department has confirmed that he was contacted by Sergeant Pyrdum of the Atlanta Police Department prior to the long series of rescues in Atlanta.[3]

In fact, the *FBI Law Enforcement Bulletin* recently dedicated an entire issue to policing demonstrations which focused on rescues. The lead article by Chief Robert J. Johnston, Jr., and Captain Lawrence F. Loesch, Jr., of the New York City Police Department clearly shows that the police know that we are nonviolent.[4] This only makes the abuse in many departments more disgraceful.

Going Limp

The rub with many police departments is that rescuers go limp; that is, they will not walk willingly away from the site of the death chamber. This requires police to carry or to drag them to waiting vehicles.

Why do rescuers go limp? It's simple. We cannot willingly walk away from the scene of a murder. If I was standing between an assailant and his victim, and the assailant ordered me to move, I could not in good conscience comply. Rescues are neither demonstrations nor acts of civil disobedience in which we hope to get arrested in order to make a point.[5] In fact, from May 1988 to December 1989 over sixteen thousand rescuers placed their bodies on the line in front of a killing center without being arrested. We rejoice in those incidents. A secondary reason we go limp is that it often buys more time, and that time equals lives saved.[6]

One can understand how having to exert the energy to physically move dozens and perhaps hundreds of limp bodies would be irritating. But police in many cities have removed rescuers without any incidents or conflict. Police in New York City, Philadelphia, Cherry Hill (New Jersey), and Binghamton (New York), just to name a few, have used stretchers and wheelchairs to move passively limp rescuers to waiting buses. In other locations rescuers have been slowly dragged or carried with an officer on each limb.

The professionalism of these and other forces stands in stark contrast to the careless and arrogant disregard for rescuers' safety displayed in some American cities. Let's start at the beginning—Atlanta.

Atlanta

Everyone remembers Atlanta. Most people actually think Operation Rescue began there. It didn't. But the premeditated police brutality against nonviolent rescuers did.

The rescues throughout the month of August produced an expected level of strained relationships between the police and the rescue community. At the beginning of September we suspended rescues in preparation for a major push in early October.

Prior to October, Joseph Foreman and Michael McMonagle, leaders in the Rescue movement, met with Major Burnette, Chief of Police Redding, J.D. Hudson, the director of prisons, Commissioner of Public Safety Napper, Sergeant Pyrdum, and Major Pocock of the correctional system. Burnette threatened, "Mr. Foreman, we have not wanted you in the city, but you've come anyway; we've asked you to leave, we're tired of you, of treating you with kid gloves, we're going to be taking them off."[7] Later on, Major Burnette publicly stated,

> We're not going to allow Operation Rescue—as they say—to bring this city to its knees. Somebody's going to be brought to their knees all right, but it's not going to be the city of Atlanta. . . . What we've told them, in no uncertain terms, is that they are not welcome to come here and engage in unlawful activities. . . . [T]hey've had their genteel treatment. We're moving now toward treating them as the lawbreakers they are.[8]

Major Burnette and his troops were fed up with the rescuers, and he intended to let them know with a very clear message: pain. He made good on his threats.

I doubt most people were emotionally prepared for what happened. The rescuers had been warned and trained, but it's still a shock to see police officers acting like thugs, deliberately inflicting as much as pain as possible on fellow citizens.

On the morning of October 4, three rescues occurred simultaneously at the Atlanta Surgicenter, the Feminist's Women's Health Center, and the Hillcrest Clinic. As the rescuers arrived at the abortuaries, they literally crawled past the police to the doors of the killing centers. This crawling was part of their training. An individual crawling by a police officer cannot plausibly be accused of assault. (This is a tactic which is being used increasingly by certain police forces.) If any violence were to occur, it would be have to be initiated by the police rather than the rescuers.

As the rescuers reached the doors, the police assault—the systematic, pre-planned brutalization of rescuers—began. Words on a page can never communicate even half the shock of that day. The Red Dogs, a SWAT-type outfit that is dreaded by criminals and known for their use of force, was called in wearing full riot gear. They were frightening just to watch. Dozens of police academy trainees had also been commandeered for the day's activities. They, along with uniformed police officers, began pushing their thumbs and knuckles on vulnerable pressure points below the ears and jaw.

At times officers literally picked people up by the jaw. At other times two, three, and even four Red Dogs piled on passive rescuers, bending fingers and twisting wrists and arms to the very breaking point.

Susan Jones, a thirty-five-year-old pro-lifer who lives with her husband in Philadelphia, states,

> [The police] lost control of themselves in the situation and just started throwing people out of the way, picking us up by our waists, dragging us away by our heels, by bending our arms, and by picking us up by our ears. . . .
>
> [As I waited on the pavement near the police bus,] I felt a body slammed into my back and looked up and it was father . . . ; and after he slammed into me, the police picked him up by his collar— they were choking him. His eyes were bugged out and it looked like he couldn't breathe as they picked him up and threw him into the bus. There was a woman who has been dragged by her feet to the bus and her blouse was up over her neck and she had horrible scrapes up and down her back.[9]

Near Death

Pastor Bob Cary had travelled from Indiana to participate in the October rescues. He didn't know it would nearly cost him his life. He was initially dragged from the scene of the October 4 rescue onto the sidewalk by police officers who then threw him aside so that he struck his head against a fire hydrant. Pastor Cary, having suffered a concussion, began bleeding from his nose and ears. This was in addition to the bruises, cuts, and scrapes he had sustained while being dragged along the pavement.

The officers on the scene continued their business, tossing Pastor Cary onto the police bus bound for the pre-trial detention center. Eventually, someone became aware of the seriousness of Cary's condition and shuttled him off to Grady Hospital. Here, Pastor Cary, near death according to his own recollection, was left unattended in the hallway on a gurney for over an hour. Eventually, his injuries were attended to, although he still today suffers from some impairment.

The Major's Drop-Kick

With the exception of Reverend Cary's injuries, perhaps the low point of police behavior came from the man who originated the threats, Major Burnette. There were too many rescuers descending on the Hillcrest abortuary, doing the Atlanta crawl, for the police to keep all of them from slipping under the barricades and making their way to the door. As the rescuers approached the door on all fours, Major Burnette walked in front of one male rescuer and lifted his upper torso so that he sat erect on his knees. He then stepped back and kicked him. From the angle of the video, it is unclear whether Burnette's foot caught the man's face or upper chest. Nevertheless, the major's stand for justice sent the man tumbling backwards.

Major Burnette later commented, "I used my foot on occasion to stop someone who was illegally in the process of assaulting a legally operating business, I make no apologies for that."[10] John Stossel of ABC's "20/20" responded to Burnette's claims, "Wait, They weren't assaulting your police officers. They were crawling."[11] Good point, John. But Major Burnette ignored it and continued, "I said they assaulted our lines. They charged over the line or under the line. The people would not get up and be arrested, so we chose to drag them."[12]

Two points make his action all the more reprehensible and heartbreaking. One, as the commanding officer on the scene, his actions set the pace for his men. What kind of example is that for other police officers or young cadets in training? Is this open season on Christians? Is that the way police in America ought to treat nonviolent citizens? Second, and this makes it all the more tragic, Major Burnette publicly testifies that he is a follower of Jesus Christ and a born-again Christian. He, in fact, serves as a deacon in good standing at a Baptist church in the Atlanta area. God help us.

Oh yes, Public Safety Commissioner George Napper firmly supported his troops: ". . . overall I think we've done a hell of a job."[13]

The Backlash

The national media exposed a portion of this brutality, and the local news did more so. The reaction was what one could expect—anger.

Complaints poured into Mayor Young's office and the police department. On the following day another rescue occurred, and the police behaved quite differently. When asked about the change of tactics, Major Burnette replied, "I believe the public would rather us take our time and be more gentle."[14]

But that was the extent of it. Neither the major nor any other officers were disciplined in any way. The police never publicly apologized or admitted that they had acted wrongly. No internal investigation ever occurred. So much for justice.

Then Major Burnette took his show on the road. He traveled to Boston to discuss his tactics with the Brookline Police Department, who soon thereafter began using the same violent methods against nonviolent rescuers there. He did a fine job. During one rescue, Donna Farris had the joints in her jaw shattered, her shoulder dislocated, and required surgery for a prosthesis implant. As Mrs. Farris comments, "Following the visit of Major Burnette, the Brookline police became absolutely brutal."[15]

Los Angeles

Holy Week, 1989. During the week of March 22–25, 1989, Operation Rescue held Holy Week rescues in the Los Angeles area. In the end over four hundred of us spent Easter Sunday in jail. The week began quietly. On March 23, three hundred and fifty were arrested in Cypress without incident; and on March 24, no one was arrested at a Long Beach abortuary.[16]

On March 25, 1989, however, all that was to change. Seven hundred eighty rescuers gathered in front of Family Planning Associates abortuary at 6th Street and Westmoreland at about 7:00 in the morning. (In addition to the thousands of babies that have been killed, at least two mothers have died in these mills, undergoing safe, legal abortions.)

The scene that day was truly frightening. It was a rainy, dreary day. There were at least five hundred proaborts present, screaming, blaspheming, blowing whistles, shouting, chanting, pushing our people, and trying to provoke an incident. Each time one of the leaders attempted to give an instruction, offer a prayer, or lead a song, the proaborts would begin howling like a pack of wolves.

The police began to arrive in droves. It looked like a Cecil B. DeMille movie. There was the ominous sight of hundreds of police pouring in, marching in military fashion, some riding on huge horses, many clad in full riot gear. A total of approximately five hundred police officers were deployed at this rescue, and it soon became evident that they weren't there to play games.

Why So Many?

The ACLU and local killing centers had put intense pressure on the police to get tough. They wanted us arrested and removed come hell or high water. On February 11, 1989, two rescues had been held in Los Angeles at which no one was arrested. This outraged the death industry there, and pro-abortionists increased pressure on the police.

Even prior to this, in October 1989, Councilman Woo had offered a resolution to the city council, saying that Operation Rescue was a public nuisance and calling on the police to vigorously enforce the law. (How does one vigorously enforce the law—by beating up those arrested?) The resolution passed 9–5. No other resolution of this nature was ever offered to deal with any of the many protest groups in Los Angeles (including animal rights, homosexual, antinuclear, and anti-apartheid protesters). It was unprecedented and was strictly political. But it did not end there. Woo and Councilman Yarolslavsky met personally with the Deputy Chief Vernon immediately prior to the March rescues to ensure that the law, again, would be vigorously enforced.[17] As Woo stated, "I thought I heard in our meeting that when push comes to shove—literally—that the police department would step in and clear the path."[18]

The police bowed their knees to their political masters. Chief of Police Gates himself was at the rescue, as was Department Chief Vernon. Both Councilmen Woo and Yarolslavsky were also present for the rescue. This was strong-arm politics at its worst.

So under the watchful political eye of the powers that be, the police went to work, freshly trained in pain compliance techniques and ready to teach the rescuers a lesson. The day was a basic free-for-all against Christians. No deference was paid to women, the elderly, the clergy, or the young.

Father Len Kowalski was among those injured. Police officers recklessly dragged him over a curb and then literally suspended his body weight from his nose. Try it sometime. You won't like it. Yes, he was literally picked up by his nose. As he sat in the street, an officer stood behind him, reached over his head, put two fingers up his nose, and lifted him as other officers twisted his arms and applied pressure below his jaw.

A little twelve-year-old girl was among those intervening for the children. Listen to the testimony of this young freckle-faced rescuer. "I was sitting on the pavement and a police officer came over and demanded, 'Get up or I'll break your arm.'"

The police manhandled and abused one rescuer after another. Cries of pain were common. Seeing your brothers and sisters being needlessly hurt by uniformed policeman is a gut-wrenching experience; it doesn't do much for your respect of the men in blue.

One woman stated,

> I have never been more frightened in my whole life. It was a systematic one-on-one torture. We stood there and watched as they would take the first person, twist him all around, twist his arms up, lift him up by the nose, and drag him across the street, two or three policemen on each rescuer, while hundreds stood in a row. They seemed to work one person over at a time.[19]

Captain McKinley, the captain in charge of the metro division, had the arrogance and gall in a sworn statement to say, "Pain for many of the demonstrators is a catharsis for past failure to take action against abortion."[20] In other words, they were doing us a favor by working us over! Thanks, Captain McKinley, but we would rather you didn't help us with our spiritual growth.

What makes that day so outrageous is that the police insist they did nothing wrong. Department Chief Vernon, a professing Christian, insists that he saw no excessive force by police and that very few people, if any, were injured. I have to question either his integrity or his eyesight.

The *Los Angeles Times*

Adding sin to sin, the *Los Angeles Times* the next day gave not a clue as to the extent of the police violence. The article's only mention of brutality was a brief reference to a press conference that was held by Operation Rescue to protest the outrageous police behavior. The *Times* did quote Operation Rescue leader Russ Neal charging, "One man's face was rubbed into the pavement and a pastor was stepped on by a horse."[21]

Fortunately, the *Orange County Register* more truthfully portrayed the day's events.

> Police tossed two of the men into the arms of other officers. As one of the men stumbled, a third officer dove at his knees, tackled him and thrust his head into the hood of a parked car. When the protester tried to stand up, the officer drilled his knees into the protester's calves and twisted the man's arms, forcing him to the ground.[22]

It's frightening when a paper like the *Los Angeles Times* is so committed to aiding abortion mills that it turns a blind eye to this type of police violence against those trying to protect children. Can you imagine the outcry if those being brutalized were protesting apartheid in South Africa? Sorry, rescuers, you're on the wrong side of the issue.

The Los Angeles Trial

My trial on the charges stemming from the Los Angeles brutality did much to expose the awful reality. Although the official police videotapes of the rescue failed to record the worst of the brutality, they did reveal enough to sicken and outrage the jury. The lies of the Los Angeles Police Department were refuted without question.

Much of the trial, however, was a sham, an absolute mockery of justice. Even prior to jury selection, Judge Paez had granted the prosecutor's motion to deny us the use of the necessity defense. We were forbidden from the very beginning to present evidence that we had acted to save the lives of the babies. The travesty continued. During the jury selection the prosecutor demanded that we put away our Bibles. What an outrage! It was only after we steadfastly refused to do so that the judge relented, warning us nevertheless not to flash them around.

The trial was a struggle of wills. We and our witnesses were continually badgered regarding our use of the words death camp and abortion mill by judge and prosecutor alike. Throughout the month-long proceedings, the court suppressed the truth of child-killing; but through persistence the truth was demonstrated.

I represented myself on trial and had opportunity to question Lieutenant Hillman about the events of March 25. The callousness of his testimony was as incredible as it was frightening.

Lieutenant Hillman coldly testified that "many bones had been broken, joints and tendons injured, scrapes and bruises suffered." I asked him if anything he saw on the six hours of police videotapes of this brutality made him wince or feel ashamed of the police department or if he thought maybe they went a little too far. He said no. In fact, he amazingly stated that it was safer for the rescuers to endure pain compliance than to be carried to a bus! I asked him plainly, "Lieutenant Hillman, is your heart made of stone?" The prosecutor objected. Defense attorney Doug McCann wryly stated under his breath, "It calls for speculation."

One would think that, after systematically injuring scores and perhaps hundreds of people, the Los Angeles Police Department would reconsider their techniques. They did. They decided to be *more* brutal, concluding that, since we "had an unusual capacity to withstand pain," they would have to introduce a new weapon against us . . . nunchakus.[23]

June 10

Snap! The sound of John Shorter's arm being broken could be heard forty feet away. Was he mugged? Was he jumped by a Los Angeles street gang? Was he beaten for his money?

No. The thugs who broke his arm were policemen. In uniform. Cold and calculated.

Before I go any further, let me explain what nunchakus are. Nunchakus are a martial arts weapon consisting of two pieces of wood or metal about twelve inches long and two inches wide connected by a twelve- or eighteen-inch piece of rope or chain. You may have seen them in a karate movie in which someone was swinging this weapon at incredible speeds. In California nunchakus or numchuks, as they are often called, are illegal. To own them is a crime. They are a dangerous weapon.

But the police used them on nonviolent rescuers. Lieutenant Hillman euphemistically refers to them as the Orcutt pain device. Cute, isn't it? Anyway, back to John.

John sat on the pavement outside the Los Angeles Midland Medical Clinic trying to intervene for the children scheduled to be killed that day. He was peaceful, prayerful, and nonviolent. The officers cuffed him behind his back. They then took the nunchukas and wrapped them around his left arm.

John was cuffed behind his back and was neither rude nor resisting in any manner. He rose to his feet as he was lifted by the police officer. Despite his cooperation, however, the officer wrapped the rope of the Arcot pain device around the upper part of his left arm and began to twist.

I could not believe my eyes as I watched a video of the attack. The policeman tightened the nunchakus like a nutcracker around his arm until it snapped like a stick. The audible snap occurred just as the bone of his upper arm suddenly bent. It appeared as if Michael had a second elbow—I felt nauseous as I saw it. Forgive me, beloved; but for the first time in my life I understand why others have called police officers derogatory names. Lieutenant Hillman testified in our trial that he and his men had never used nunchakus before and had absolutely no training in using them. That was quite evident on June 10.

Attorney Samuel B. Casey formerly of the Rutherford Institute has stated, "[nunchakus] have never, underscore never, been used on peaceful nonviolent demonstrators in the United States until June 10, 1989. . . . The use of a nunchaku is assault with a deadly weapon in this state. The mere possession of nunchakus is a felony."[24]

What is happening here? Police use illegal martial arts weapons with no training against nonviolent United States citizens, and they get away with it. Can any of you proaborts reading this honestly tell me that you believe a group of homeless black single mothers sitting in at the Bank of America would be treated this way? Why are prolifers' rights being trampled upon?

Joseph Foreman lends this insight.

> We shouldn't get surprised if police get violent with us. They are defending the most violent act known to man, namely the ripping apart of children in the mother's womb. There is a real spirit of murder; there is a spirit of infant sacrifice. I don't care how pious a Christian they [the police] are, they will wind up in the long run partaking of that spirit of violence. When violence breaks out it is nothing more than a dim reflection of the violence that would take place if we weren't there.

Joseph Foreman was arrested at both the March 25 and June 10 rescues in Los Angeles. Try to picture yourself in this position:

I can't tell you what it is like to be lying on the ground, police officers on top of you, using all sorts of torture holds on you. You can't
walk even if you wanted to walk and their sole intent is to torture
you. And then listening to the screams of the people (proaborts) as
somebody gets a bloody nose. And as I would look up there were . . .
throngs of pro-death people screaming for our blood. And if a person got a bloody nose they'd scream even louder, chanting blasphe-
mous chants.[25]

Sadly, the police brutality was not limited to the born. As one
woman describes her arrest,

The nunchakus apparently did something to my legs . . . at that
point my legs were curled in, paralyzed, and I couldn't move on to
the first step and an officer was screaming at me to get on the step
and I said yes and I was finally able with my thigh muscles to get on
the first step but I couldn't get any further. An officer on the bus
said, "Here I'll help you." I looked up and was so grateful and I said
thanks and then he grabbed my cuffed wrists which were behind my
back and lifted me from the first step by my wrists, my legs were
paralyzed so all my weight was on my wrists, and dragged me up the
steps and down the aisle and threw me onto, into my seat . . . A few
weeks after this, my treatment I received at the hands of the LAPD, I
miscarried my ninth child and I have no history of miscarriage and
the opinion is that the probable cause was the excessive and violent
use of nunchakus. . . .[26]

This child was killed in his mother's selfless effort to save other
children; was it killed by the Los Angeles Police Department?

West Hartford

They [The police] started to hyperflex my hands so far that my
hands touched my wrists. They carried me like that and I heard
everything crack and go. And I knew at that point that something
had been broken.[27]

Somebody took me to Saint Francis Hospital and I was in such a
state of shock, so battered and my clothes were so torn that when
they brought me in, in a wheelchair, the nurse at the triage desk
looked at me and she goes, "My God, has she been in a motorcycle
accident?" And we said no, that I had been basically brutalized and
tortured for the past three days and was now having difficulty

breathing. She asked if we had reported this to the police . . . we told her that it was the police who did this.[28]

Welcome to West Hartford, a city incorporated in 1854 with a current population of sixty-one thousand. This is a proud, affluent city where the law is the law; and if you're a pro-lifer who dares to try to rescue children from murder, you're going to get hurt, seriously hurt by the police. The city council doesn't care; the media will avert its eyes; the city fathers will denounce you and defend the police; the judge will pretend he doesn't hear or see as people scream in agony in his courtroom; the prison officials will deny medical treatment to the injured and you the right to see an attorney.

In mid-June 1989, while the national media and most of our nation had its attention riveted to the atrocities of Tienanmen Square in Beijing, China, a little bit of those might-makes-right rules crossed the ocean and slipped virtually unnoticed into the town of West Hartford.

Rev. Jesse Lee is a veteran rescuer and no stranger to police brutality, having participated on March 25 in Los Angeles and October 4 in Atlanta. Rev. Lee confided to me that "screams became so common place you felt you were in an insane asylum, you actually grew hard to it."

June 17, 1989

The Saturday morning, June 17, 1989, rescue had been planned for weeks, and rescuers were coming from the West Hartford area and the entire Northeast.

The police were aware that the rescue would probably take place, and a number of them were waiting at the abortuary, although far too few to stop the hundreds of rescuers that came. When the rescuers arrived, they streamed into the mall-like building that housed the Summit Women's Center abortuary and entered into the abortuary itself, filling the stairwell, the halls of the abortuary and three of the killing rooms.

When the police arrived en masse, Bob Clark, a rescue leader and a former police commissioner, saw this: "When the police arrived . . . they began to make preparations for their arrests. . . . They brought a patrol car in and all the policemen went to the back of the patrol car and they all threw their identification and badges into the trunk."[29] Another rescuer commented, "They knew they were about to assault people, and they wanted to make identification as difficult as possible.

Repeated requests by rescuers for the police to identify themselves went unheeded."[30]

One of the rescuers' attorneys, Joe Taylor, later said,

Of course they didn't wear their badges, they didn't wear name tags. Because I was coming to court on a daily basis for the first four or five days after that rescue, the police in West Hartford did not resume wearing their name tags until at least Friday of the week after the rescue lest they would be identified . . . I've never seen anything like that in my life.[31]

Commissioner Clark continues with the ominous sight.

[They] took out riot sticks, which was totally unprofessional behavior. When you bring out riot sticks, it is usually because you expect to see some opposition. You put on helmets and you put on face masks and you carry shields. These policemen were bareheaded; they knew they weren't going to get any resistance from the other side.[32]

They moved in for a full day of punishing the rescuers. It took twelve hours to arrest and remove 261 rescuers. This is unusually long. For example, it took only six hours to arrest nearly 800 rescuers in Los Angeles. The unusual time can only be explained by the fact that they were slowly and deliberately torturing people. Bones were broken, shoulders separated, nerves damaged, massive hunks of flesh scraped off as rescuers were dragged over pavement.

As they began to arrest the rescuers, it was clear that they were into torture. They would bring people out handcuffed behind their back and be suspending them by their wrists . . . obviously cutting off their nerves to their fingers and wrists and tearing people's shoulders out of their sockets. . . . There was no reason for having people's arms broken and shoulder separated. . . . It was clearly an effort to torture people.[33]

As the day wore on, so did the pain. One police officer mocked a praying rescuer, saying, "Jesus isn't helping you; pray to Satan."[34] Miraculously, not one rescuer struck out at the police or even shouted angry words. They bore the suffering patiently, although at times with screams and pleas for mercy. But the police ignored those pleas. Father Larry Drew concurs,

It was excruciating pain . . . calculated torture, and the policemen were enjoying the pain. They laughed at the people screaming—and all of them screamed—grown men, men, mature men; you couldn't help but scream." [Listen to his description of a pain technique similar to Nazi torture strappado.] What happened was when the two night sticks squeezed on the wrists, they cut off the nerve ends and the flow of blood and your hands swelled up to almost twice the size and turned black . . . those scissor effects—the two wires on your wrists—it's excruciating.[35]

Might Makes Right

Many rescuers that day saw and heard things that convinced them that the police were enjoying what they did to the rescuers. Jim Barry of New Hartford, Connecticut, shared this disbelief, "It was an amazing thing to realize that human beings took pleasure in inflicting pain on other human beings. And I'm absolutely convinced that a murderer is not treated that way, that a bank robber, or a drug addict or a pimp is not treated that way!"[36]

John Miller, a retired police officer from New York City, voiced his disgust and shock over the West Hartford police officers' actions. "It's never appropriate to torture anyone no matter what crime they committed, least of all people who are nonviolent. I'm really, frankly, ashamed of the way the West Hartford Police acted. It was barbaric."[37]

Ladies and gentlemen, this wasn't just a couple of cops losing their temper. This was an entire police force conspiring to trample the civil rights of American citizens, and then acting in concert to achieve those ends. That, my friends, is a crime.

Attorney Joe Taylor points out that under Connecticut law only legitimate force may be used to achieve legitimate police objectives. He then further states, "When he [a police officer] crosses over the line to use illegitimate force then he himself becomes a criminal. A police officer, because he wears a badge, is not insulated from being guilty of assault and battery."[38] Maybe that's why they took their badges off.

And so, you would expect the district attorney to bring charges against the police or, at least, perform an investigation, right? Wrong.

I was told by one prosecutor that I will not harm the reputation of West Hartford's finest police department so long as he draws breath. I've never heard that kind of discussion and of a prosecutor. His job is merely to pursue within the limits of truth charges against people charged with a crime.[39]

However, in case you haven't guessed, this isn't about justice or something as fundamental as right and wrong; it's about oppression, tyranny, might makes right, and, "If you don't like it, get your butt out of town and don't come back, you got it?"

The brutality continued for the entire day. Joan Kelly, a sixty-year-old grandmother who was picketing but not participating in the rescue, was knocked to the ground by the police and had her wrist broken.[40] One actual rescuer had his bare chest dragged across the pavement; his stomach bled profusely and later oozed pus for days.

Mark Miller was arrested and intended to cooperate but was denied the opportunity. He described his treatment, "I voluntarily stood up, I folded my hand behind my back, they put their plastic cuffs on, and as I was just standing there, they just starting pulling my thumbs. Finally, they popped the tendons in my right hand in my thumb and damaged two of my nerves. . . ."[41]

Since most of the rescuers were inside the building, out of the sight of the general public and the media, the police were able to abuse them with no third-party witnesses.

One reporter who entered with rescuers, Sheila Chase from the *Staten Island Advance* was arrested—in spite of her press credentials. Her notes were taken and destroyed. Listening to her protests, one of the officers mocked, "Ah, her First Amendments rights have been trampled."[42]

Something frighteningly similar to the tactics employed by Russian and Chinese soldiers also took place. Police officers siezed the still and video cameras of several free-lance reporters who had filmed the brutality from both inside and outside of the building. Only after the film had been destroyed were the cameras returned. Chief McCue called this regrettable, admitting that it shouldn't have happened, but attributed the action to the heat of the moment.[43]

That's it. No outrage, only insincere references to regret and the heat of the moment. Can you imagine if a CBS camera had been confiscated in Tienanmen Square, preventing the live coverage of the massacre?

Despite the abundant proof of the police brutality, West Hartford Police Chief Robert McCue stated, "I'm proud of the professionalism shown by my officers during the incident."[44] When questioned or challenged about police brutality, he dismissed the claims as "ridiculous [that he accepted] full responsibility for the action of all police [on the scene that Saturday, and that officers acted in a] highly professional manner." He later announced, "No internal investigation is planned by the department."[45] No surprise there. Fortunately, the FBI is investigating (although I have little hope of that producing much more).

Protecting Their Image

At various points during the day, different media were allowed inside to view the police, as were various town officials, including Mayor Christopher Drowney, Town Manager Barry Feldman, and State Representative Miles Rapoport.[46]

First of all, one has to ask, what in the world were all those politicians doing there? Clearly, this was one more of the political power plays exhibited in Los Angeles.

Second, the media has insinuated that, since they and these officials were present at times and didn't see any brutality, none occurred. Be real! What do they expect? "Oh, hello, Mayor Drowney! Come here, I want to show you this torture hold. It was developed by the Chinese communists. It's very efficient and effective." Wake up, would you, West Hartford?

What troubles me to this day is the manner in which the media and local politicians blindly recited the party line. It was like some dime store novel of an entire town that knows the truth but lies to protect its own vested interests. I wish I could have been a fly on the wall to hear some of the conversations planning the brutality and those designed to cover it up.

The local politicians rushed headlong to protect the image (and perhaps the liability) of their local legal thugs. Thus, on June 27 the town council unanimously adopted a resolution commending West Hartford police.

> WHEREAS the activities of the protesters have deprived merchants and service providers of their rights to earn an honest living [*how's that for a pro-death statement—the blood money of murdered children is an "honest living"*] and WHEREAS, the Police Department has acted in a highly professional manner . . . [*keep your eyes open for the buzzwords "highly professional"*] NOW THEREFORE BE IT RESOLVED THAT THE TOWN COUNCIL commends the West Hartford Police Depart-

ment for its professional and sensitive handling of these difficult situations . . . and supports the efforts of the West Hartford Police in enforcing the laws of the state of Connecticut.[47]

No, this isn't a novel. No this isn't the Politburo commending the KGB for a dissident crackdown. Yes, this really happened in America. But it gets worse. Where would Soviet propaganda be without Pravda to spout the party line? The West Hartford media dutifully fulfilled this role.

The manner in which they covered the abuse is disgraceful. Yes, they put a quote here or there from a rescuer who claimed brutality; but they quickly dismissed it by inserting a quote from a police spokesman (or two) who said they "saw no excessive force." One story by Debra Adams in the *Hartford Courant* failed to even quote the rescuers' claims of brutality. The only references to police violence were denials from police spokesman Sergeant Richard Leavitt.[48] What do they expect the police to say? "We were really surprised that Chief McCue gave us the go ahead to teach these people a lesson," or perhaps, "We were appalled at the lack of professionalism shown by some of our fellow officers."

It soon became evident why the newspapers had reported the brutality so poorly. It was, in fact, the *editorial position* of the two local papers that the police had done nothing wrong.

On Wednesday, June 21st, the *Hartford Courant* published and editorial entitled "Breaking the Law in West Hartford." The lead sentence exposes position, "It's doubtful that the West Hartford Police Department could have handled the anti-abortion protest Saturday much better than they did. . . ."

The editorial makes no mention of broken bones, lacerations, ripped tendons, or injuries of any sort. It's just a "nice job, boys" and a pat on the back. They comment that it's "not surprising" rescuers "complained about police brutality although the complaints in most cases probably lack substance." In other words, the rescuers are lying. Or at least they're whining a lot from a little discomfort. Because, after all, "Being carried around against one's will is not like a day at the beach."

So, "most cases probably lack substance." How's that for good journalism? Is there a little doubt coming through from the reporter? Well, ladies and gentlemen at the *Courant,* what if *some* cases didn't lack substance? What if an elderly woman was recklessly knocked to the ground, and had her wrist broken? What if a few men and women did get broken bones? Is that kind of police behavior acceptable to you? Where is your mighty sword calling for truth and justice? Are you so sold out to child-killing that you refuse to denounce brutality when it's related to those trying to stop the killing? Why the silence?

Well, the *Courant* must have gotten some heat over their lack of integrity—at least they got some scathing letters to the editor. On Friday June 30th, they published another pro-police anti-rescuer editorial entitled "Flamethrower rhetoric."

They comment that the rescuers' "overdone appeals to the heart are seemingly so out of proportion to events, so apparently untruthful, that you wonder why they are doing it." There you have it again— the rescuers are lying.

They went on to quote a letter from prisoner Baby John Doe 54, who testified, "Police Chief Robert McCue laughed as he watched elderly men and women, young mothers, priests, and ministers screaming in pain inflicted by officers using compliance holds." They scoffed at this and the other rescuers' claims that they were tortured, deriding them for making any comparison of West Hartford police tactics with those employed by Nazi stormtroopers. The editorial read in part,

> The point here is exaggeration that approaches ridiculous. Cruel laughter at human suffering? Torture for anyone? Sanctioning treadmarks on the backs of protesters? We don't think so.

> Not that the police are always pleasant. Perhaps some bones were broken—the police arrested more than 250 people, after all.

If cops have to arrest that many people, you've got to give them the room to break a few arms, right? What outrages me is the callousness of the editors. They say "perhaps some bones were broken. Did they go into jail to personally see the injuries? No. Did they interview the people who saw Chief McCue laughing? No. Why did they find it impossible to believe that in twelve hours of arrests, McCue didn't crack one joke? Did they do any professional, investigative reporting, trying to substantiate any of these claims? No. They just brazenly dismissed them out of hand.

Their bias against pro-lifers is simply outrageous! They assert, "But there is no evidence!" Who are they kidding! What about the cameras seized and film destroyed; numerous broken bones, lacerations, injured nerves—one man almost dying. That level of force is necessary? What's next? Repeated bludgeoning? Shooting rescuers? Are these people for real? What will it take for them to denounce the police—a dead rescuer?

They continue, saying, "In fact their [the police officers] conduct was commendable, given the circumstances."

They end their second editorial stating, "One wishes that anti-abortion protesters . . . if they choose a strategy of civil disobedience—should go to jail with smiles on their faces."

The other local paper, the *West Hartford News,* was no less ardent in its defense of the police. On June 22 they printed an editorial entitled, "The Dilemma of Abortion," which among other things reaffirmed the papers pro-abortion position. Like the *Courant,* there was no mention of the injuries.

They stated, "There are those who will argue that the police were unnecessarily brutal with those arrested, but this is not so." They weren't necessarily brutal, just acceptably brutal. You see the difference, right?

They continued, "The police operated not only under the supervision of their chief and two assistant chiefs, but under the watchful eyes of the print and broadcast media, mayor, town manager, and an assistant corporation counsel." The watchful eye of the media! Huh? Edward Carpenter—his stomach, scratched and bleeding—was under the "watchful eye" of the media. He tells his tale.

> I saw when they were interviewing people and I thought that if I could get out there, I could show them some of the brutality [on my body] . . . so I ran out in front of the tv [camera], raised my shirt and yelled, "Do you want to take my picture?" but the tv [camera] just pointed straight down to the ground; they obviously did not want to show it.[49]

The watchful eye of the television camera had looked the other way.

The *West Hartford News* also forgot about the confiscated camera. They too failed to point out that the arrests took twelve hours and that these "watchful eyes" were not watching the whole time. They also refused to acknowledge how tortuously painful it is to be handcuffed behind your back and two nightsticks inserted under the cuffs with your entire body weight hanging by a plastic strip tied around your wrists.

On June 29 they printed another staff editorial: "Don't Blame the Police." This was the first editorial that admitted that bones were broken, but that was quickly excused. They spoke of "come-along holds," saying, "These holds can, and did, result in bruises and even broken bones. They stood out not only because they are physical coercion, but because they are seldom needed and even less seldom seen by the general public."

Last week, they said that the police weren't brutal. Now they say that the police did break bones by physical coercion and that these injuries "stand out" because we so rarely see them. What happened that their eyes were opened to the injuries? Whatever it was, it wasn't enough to cause them to call the police on the carpet for their behavior. They finished their column with this clincher:

> The police are not perfect. but they handled the mass protest at Bishop's Corner on the 17th as well as could reasonably be expected. The people of this town who value law and order need not worry about the professionalism of their police department.

Pittsburgh, March 11, 1989

In October 1988, Pittsburgh was voted America's most liveable city by Rand McNally. That is, of course, unless you're a baby scheduled to be killed in one of Pittsburgh's abortuaries or a rescuer under the thumb of the police and prison officials.

On many occasions, the Pittsburgh police have shown little tolerance for nonviolent rescuers. Pro-lifers have had their arms twisted and their hair pulled. They have been punched and kicked. On May 13, 1989, Reverend Keith Tucci received a concussion and bruised ribs at the hands of these officers of the law. Furthermore, he was actually kicked in the groin so hard that he had no feeling in that area for several days and urinating was a painful experience for many more. That particular police escapade landed him in the hospital for two days. Tucci recalls that these police actions appeared to be premeditated. "One of the officers earlier in the day [prior to his being injured] told me, 'We'll get you.'"[50]

On March 11, 1989, however, the Pittsburgh police were far outstripped by their associates, the guards in the Allegheny County prison system.

The rescuers arrived at the Allegheny Reproductive Health Center abortuary at about six in the morning. As usual, the police arrived and were physically abusive to the rescuers. Additionally, they charged one rescuer with assault and battery because he allegedly struck a cop. When the rescuers learned this, they immediately went into noncooperation mode to protect through their solidarity the rescuer who had been unjustly singled out. (Noncooperation occurs when rescuers refuse to walk, give their names, or cooperate with the authorities in any way until the unjust treatment of certain rescuers is stopped.)

This was not the first time such a confrontation had occurred over a false charge. According to Reverend Tucci, this has occurred in nearly a dozen rescues; and never once have the police been able to prove the charges in court.

Well, on March 11, the police saw things differently. They were sick and tired of Operation Rescue and were determined to play hard ball. After the police had made their false charges and the rescuers entered into noncooperation, the police moved to place the pro-lifers into the system,—that is, the jail system itself, not the holding tanks at the police department.

First, the men and women were separated. The men were taken to the Northside Station; the women to the county jail. At this point, the police turned the nearly sixty female rescuers over to the Allegheny County Jail guards, and the nightmare began.

It must be made perfectly clear that, although the women still were not cooperating with the guards and remained limp, they provoked the police neither physically nor verbally. In fact, many tried to apologetically explain why they were doing this. No matter, the guards snapped.

As in West Hartford, the guards removed their identification. A group of women would be taken into the processing area, and then one or two at a time would be carried upstairs through a portion of the jail in which criminally insane male inmates were housed. Most of these women were verbally harassed; about half of them were physically abused in one way or another; and some of them were sexually harassed or molested.

All this took place under the watchful eye of the warden, Charles Kozakiewicz, who was participating.[51] He had previously been sued on other brutality charges by nonrescue prisoners and lost.[52] Evidently, he had not repented of this type of behavior. He's now facing another brutality lawsuit brought by the women that he and his officers abused that day.

The attorney of record for the women is Susan Lucas. She gave this general overview of the day's and night's events:

> They [the female rescuers] were verbally abused by the officers—not just profanity but comments on the size of their breasts and their condition and what they were going to do with them. They were variously threatened with rape by the guards, with sodomy, with being thrown naked into the prison cells. The women told me they could actually hear the prisoners, [but] they couldn't tell what they were saying [for all the] . . . hooting and howling.
>
> One woman, a grandmother, has three children who have served in the service and can't believe that this happened to her. She was threatened with rape by the guards if she didn't walk up the stairs. They were in mortal fear at this point. Here they are at night in a men's prison being dragged up stairs in this horrific scene. They were taken up one at a time; they really had no sort of communication with someone else who could support them to let them know that they weren't going to be raped or further abused.[53]

Betty Jones, one of the rescuers, tells what happened to a friend of hers:

> She was carried by her breasts, and she has ten large finger marks left, . . . two months after the rescue. . . . She had large chunks of hair pulled out of her head. She was kicked in her stomach and . . . also . . . in the genital area. Officers were holding either leg and they kicked her between her legs. And she was also punched in the breasts. She has asthma; they blew cigar smoke in her face, [and] she went into an asthma attack.[54]

Her friend Mary Kelleher not only had smoke blown in her face but was maliciously denied emergency medical care. Several guards actually prevented a nurse from giving her oxygen in the midst of her acute asthma attack. Mary recalls one guard telling her, "I'm sorry, we can't give you anything. We can't give you oxygen until you give your name." In other words, "I'm sorry, but we'll have to let you asphyxiate; perhaps, though, some end smoke from my cigarette might liven you up."[55]

These women were horribly abused by the prison officials: physically, psychologically and sexually. Here are two detailed testimonies.

After being detained at the police lockup, we were transported to the Allegheny County Jail. There we were dumped at the door by the Pittsburgh police. I found myself lying face up on the floor, my clothing pulled up around my neck. The warden, Charles Kozakiewicz, was holding my hand and squeezing my left ring finger forward in a C shape and backward in and out at the same time. He was screaming, "Get up!" over and over. I said, "I'll get up if you let me pull my shirt down." He continued to scream and say no. At that time two other guards grabbed me and yanked me into the large holding tank to the right. . . . He [the warden] asked us to move, and we refused. He left, and the guards grabbed me. . . . They threw me against the podium with a force to cause bruising of my breasts. They leaned against me, holding me up, and searched my pockets and patted me down. They threw me into the room for photos, holding me up by a hand around my neck. I was then drug up the steps five flights by my clothing and all upper clothing was off except my bra. I was dumped on the floor in the shower room.[56]

On March 11, 1989, I was sexually assaulted at a building on Ross Street. . . . The assault was when I was being taken up the stairs in the jail. One guy was gonna carry me up the stairs but the other guy said not to and to make it hard on me. So a tall black guy said, "Let's just put her arms behind her back," and they tried, but it didn't work. This is when the guy who assaulted me comes in. He said, "No, this is what you do." He grabbed me between my breasts and dragged me up the stairs by my wire-rimmed bra. My breasts were fully exposed as I was being dragged up the stairs. My hands were still behind my back and I couldn't pull my top down. Then I was taken to another room and thrown to the floor. I was pulled up by my ponytail and slammed to the table. I was frisked and had a Jane Doe number put on my wrist. Then they dragged me to a chair to get my picture taken. (They held my head up for the picture.) I was then dragged to a room where I was searched again. To get me off the floor a black woman pulled my nose and I didn't know what to do so I got up. Someone said, "This one is getting it different;" and they took my shoes and socks off and led me to my cot.[57]

Many women were sexually molested:

- "And one of them, he reached down my pants to carry me and told the other guy, 'Hey, just reach down her pants.'"[58]

- "He [An officer] had me by my chest, he was pulling really hard on my chest."[59]

- " . . . one of the guards [took] me by my breast . . . and I have bruises all around where he squeezed with his fingers. . . . Then the male officer started to undo my coat and . . . my pants . . . One black woman went underneath, pulled my shirt up all the way, and started feeling . . . my breasts all around."[60]

- "And as he was dragging me, my hands were constantly in his crotch; and I could tell that he was sexually aroused. . . . I tried to move my hands, but they were cuffed, and the way he was holding my arms I couldn't move them."[61]

Others were threatened with rape. One rescuer reports of officers asking, "How would you like to be raped?"[62] Another tells of a female prison guard threatening to take off her clothes and molest her "in front of the male guards."[63] The guards also subjected the women to perverted verbal abuse.[64]

These women were also physically harmed.

- "Then they went on to drag me up the steps by my hair and one officer kicked me in between the legs. . . . [Another time] they took my legs and opened them and she [the guard] kicked me in between my legs. . . [Again, later] I felt very traumatized and the woman again kicked me in my back." [65]

- "One [officer] said, 'I'm gonna bounce you off these steps.'. . . Then he said, 'You like sore ankles, don't you?' You know, from being dragged up. I had boots on, too. My ribs got bruised from being bounced up the stairs and around by the side. . . . [Later] they picked me up by the back of my coat and the other lady picked my arm up and slammed me into the wall." [66]

- "She [a guard] purposefully kicked me in the head many times." [67]

God help us. No one could endure this type of abuse without a toll being taken. One rescuer tells the effect it had on her. "After this, I had nightmares pretty often; it was different police officers in my dreams, and they were really scary. I was really afraid whenever I would see a police officer or a police car . . . it still does make me really afraid."[68]

What an outrage! This happened in the United States. As the *New York Times* said twenty-five years ago, we ought to be ashamed to live in a nation where such a travesty has occurred.

Please understand: What the prison officials did was blatantly illegal. They committed misdemeanors and felonies against some of these ladies. Wearing a badge does not confer upon officials the right to abuse women. With this many independent testimonies of abuse, you would think that the prosecutor's office would have brought charges or that, at least, Mayor Sophie Masloff would have launched a full-scale investigation to determine if criminal charges were warranted. No way.

Listen to Tina Cole's frustration in her attempts to get some legal action from the District Attorney's office.

> As soon as the rescue was over, we went down to file a complaint, and they were taking their good ol' time trying to get things going, because they said that we didn't have any identification [of the guards] for them. And when we told them that we would like to see a lineup so that we could identify them, they [refused]. We want to have some justice done here and we've been going to the district attorney and we've been going to the warden. Nobody is doing anything.[69]

I wonder why? The political and judicial systems in Pittsburgh have joined forces to stonewall any attempt to achieve justice for these women. To this date, the district attorney has done nothing. I doubt they ever will pursue an investigation. A federal lawsuit is now being prepared.

Unfortunately, this type of abuse is on the rise. Space prohibits me from detailing the events in other cities: the nunchakus used in San Diego; the mace sprayed in the faces of rescuers—including a mother and her two-year-old baby—by the police in Sacramento; the litany of pain compliance and come-along holds; the lost tempers of police in Milwaukee, Austin, Detroit, and numerous other cities.

The New York and Philadelphia police departments are examples of professionalism, which, again, stands in stark contrast to the callousness and, at points, thuggery of other police departments.

Conclusion

The silence of the national media is a damning indictment of their utter disregard for the rights of citizens who are involved in political causes which they don't support.

Dr. William B. Allen serves on the United States Commission on Civil Rights and, at the time these events took place, was the chairman of that commission. On August 18, 1989, the *Wall Street Journal* printed a column by Dr. Allen entitled "Police Brutality—but No Outrage."[70]

The main thrust of Allen's column was his frustration at the lack of response by both the media and government officials to the reports of police brutality against rescuers. Allen derided the fact that to date, "No national news organization has deemed the allegations [of brutality] worthy of coverage." He further bemoaned the fact that up until that time the United States Department of Justice had not responded to the allegations he had passed on to them. Allen stated, "The head of the section in charge of investigations stated that the group was violating a court injunction, as if such a violation made perfectly reasonable the kind of treatment to which the antiabortion protesters have been subject."

He then exposed the bias against rescuers on the Commission of Civil Rights itself.

> In July, I placed on the agenda of the U.S. Commission on Civil Rights a resolution to recommend to the President that he direct the Department of Justice to undertake an investigation of these allegations at the earliest possible moment. My resolution did not condone the illegality of Operation Rescue's actions. Nor did I associate myself with their cause. Rather, I sought to affirm the continued support of the government and the people of the U.S. for the rights of protesters. After lengthy and sometimes hostile scrutiny, my resolution was dropped from the agenda.
>
> My colleagues argued that the resolution was a back door way to discuss abortion, as if the subject matter of the protest determined the legitimate police response. Rep. Don Edwards [D, CA], chairman of the commission's oversight committee in the House of Representatives, joined in—not coincidentally during the middle of the debate over reauthorization of the commission—with a direct threat: "Consideration of this issue," which "appears to violate the Commissioner's authorizing statute" prohibiting "the Commission from studying issues relating to abortion," would "seriously erode Congressional confidence in the Commission."[71]

Fortunately, on September 15, 1989, the commission changed its mind, voting unanimously to request that the Justice Department perform a formal investigation into the brutality. Perhaps the Justice

Department's Civil Rights Division will now respond to the over two thousand complaints of brutality against rescuers it has received.[72]

At the time of this writing, the FBI, under the guidance of the Justice Department, is continuing its investigation into allegations of brutality in West Hartford, Los Angeles, Pittsburgh, and other localities. To be honest, with all I've seen in the area of law and order, I have little hope of much happening.

Voices in the Wilderness

I thank God for the Christian media. While they don't have the huge audiences of ABC, CBS, CNN, NBC, the *USA Today,* and the *New York Times,* their combined voices have been able to reach millions of people and to bring some of this dark oppression to light. I'm speaking of James Dobson, Marlin Maddoux, Pat Robertson, Jerry Falwell, Don Wildmon, Paul Crouch, Moody Broadcasting, the *Wanderer,* the *National Catholic Register, Charisma,* and many other publications, TV shows and radio broadcasts.

If it were not for the integrity of these men and women, this suffering would have gone almost unnoticed.

A few national columnists have also sought to expose this sickness, including Nat Hentoff, Cal Thomas, Pat Buchanan, Don Feder, and William Buckley.

Buckley blasted the West Hartford police. "[T]he policemen tried to get the crowd to disperse, failed to do so—whereupon they illegally removed their badges. As though this gave them immunity to act like thugs rather than to pursue their profession, which is, among other things, to prevent thuggery."[73]

Nat Hentoff launched his attack against the so-called liberals who are silent while we are abused. " To the liberals, Operation Rescue are pariahs and you can't beat them too hard."[74]

Don Feder trains his sights squarely on the media, pointing out that the media did extensive coverage of civil rights abuses in the sixties.

Had television news not done such an enlightening job of bringing these images into our living rooms each evening, it's doubtful Congress would have enacted the civil rights legislation of the 60s. [*Then he lowers the boom.*] But what if the media doesn't sympathize with protesters? What if it does its best to conceal official acts of violence? With no one there to tell the story, the public is oblivious as decent men and women are subjected to infamies worthy of a fascist regime.[75]

This is what is so disturbing about this blackout. In China, the media is forcibly held in tow by the iron-fisted government. "Nothing happened in Tienanmen Square. No one died there." In America, *the media has willingly become a co-conspirator* through their ideologically-induced silence.

Feder ends his column, caustically asking: "Does a billy club cracking a skull make a sound, if the media choose to ignore it?" Ask Dan Rather.

A Little Help from Congress

The brutality has not gone unnoticed in Congress, however. One at a time, several congressmen have became aware of the atrocities and begun to speak out. Congressman Molinari (D-NY) learned of West Hartford and flew there to hold a press conference. It received little attention. When Bob Dornan (R-CA) learned of Pittsburgh, he was outraged. He requested several of the women to come to Washington to tell him their story.

Following this meeting, Congressmen Robert Dornan, Robert Walker, Chris Smith, and Clyde Holloway sent letters to FBI agent Robert Reutter and the acting U.S. attorney in Pittsburgh, Charles D. Sheehy, requesting that a thorough investigation be launched immediately into the allegations of physical abuse and sexual crimes in Pittsburgh. They stressed the slow response of Mr. Sheehy's office and the apparent disinterest in performing a proper investigation. Referring to their meeting with one of the victims, one of the women assaulted, they commented, "She stated that he [FBI field agent Mr. McLaughlin who did the interview] was more interested in those participating in Operation Rescue than in her mistreatment at the jail. We have no reason to doubt [her] account."[76] In spite of the interest and concern of these congressmen and a few voters, little was happening.

Some lawmakers had the idea if they could hit a city where it counts—the pocketbook—they might get the police to back off.

On July 20, 1989, Congressman Bob Walker introduced an amendment to the HUD Appropriations Bill that would eliminate any community development block grant funding to any city in which any municipal employees are convicted of using force against nonviolent civil rights demonstrators three or more times. "I just want to make the point that the intent behind this amendment is to try to assure that the communities across the Nation are not using violent means against nonviolent demonstrators." It passed by a voice vote.[77]

On September, 19, 1989, Senator William Armstrong introduced the Senate version, although with slightly different language.

None of the funds appropriated under Title II of this Act under the heading entitled Community Planning and Development, Community Development Grants, to any department, agency, or instrumentality of the United States may be obligated or expanded to any municipality that fails to adopt and enforce a policy prohibiting the use of excessive force by law enforcement agencies within the jurisdiction of said municipality against any individuals engaged in nonviolent civil rights demonstrations.[78]

During deliberations on the floor of the Senate, he summarized the measure's intent, "Our desire is to send an unmistakable message to the municipalities and other jurisdictions in this country that we are not going to stand still and watch as non-violent protesters are manhandled, brutalized and mistreated in the way described."[79] The amendment also passed by voice vote.

The language differences were worked out in a conference committee meeting and the amendment was retained in the HUD bill. On November 9, 1989, President Bush signed into law PL 101–144. It's too early to see what effect this law will have, but it is a step in the right direction.

What a portion of this debate is boiling down to is whether or not police should be permitted to brutalize nonviolent and passively limp individuals by using pain compliance, come alongs, and nunchakus.

Of course, the police object bitterly to it being called brutality or torture. Nat Hentoff, however, points out the obvious: "And what is torture but making pain so excruciating that the prisoner succumbs?"[80]

Two police experts testified before the Commission on Civil Rights against these strong-arm tactics. The *Congressional Quarterly* reported on their input.

"I don't think it's appropriate as a first resort," says Hubert Williams, a former police chief of Newark, New Jersey, and now president of the Police Foundation, a research group. The accepted standard, he says, is for police to use "only that amount of force that's being used against them, as much additional force as is needed to effect the arrest." Frederick Pearson, of the National Association of Chiefs of Police, says inflicting pain is usually acceptable "only if its [sic] necessary to remove somebody who's causing a hazard to himself or somebody else."[81]

My position is this: no nonviolent group should be tortured in order to remove them from the scene of a protest. I don't care if they're animal rights protesters or homosexuals sitting inside St. Patrick's Cathedral. They should not be brutalized. This is America, not China. They can be put on stretchers, in wheelchairs, carried by hand, or even dragged by an officer under each arm; but these various torture techniques and the resulting injuries are wrong. The police are not jury, judge, and executioner.

We are not saying police should not protect themselves; nor are we saying that the police shouldn't use pain compliance to subdue a violent arrestee. But to use pain compliance simply to force a nonviolent protester to walk, is wrong; it flies in the face of one of the prized achievements of the Civil Rights Movement.

Dr. Allen concluded his essay,

> In the aftermath of the Supreme Court's Webster decision—which substantially returns the abortion debate to the states—we can expect more antiabortion demonstrations. We ought to guarantee that we will not also see more police violence in the handling of them. It is imperative that we as a nation assert our commitment to equal treatment before the law. Nonviolent protesters should all be accorded the same treatment no matter what the subject of protest. To do less is to destroy the most prized achievement of the civil rights movement—the recognition of the rights of everyone. And we will have destroyed that achievement, not just for Operation Rescue, but for all.[82]

PART FOUR

THE ACCOMPLICES

11

WOLVES IN
SHEEP'S CLOTHING

T he day of Pentecost came, and the church was born. Thousands
    began coming into the fold of God, their sins washed away by
the shed blood of Christ. Their newfound faith transformed their
lives, the Roman Empire and, ultimately, the whole world. Those of
us who are Christians are walking in a heritage two millennia old.
Blessed be God. Amen.

The Church's Historical Stance

The early church was vibrant, courageous, and determined. Christian
lives and ministries were peppered with miraculous displays of divine
power. Individuals were dramatically healed and even raised from the
dead; Philip was actually transported by the Spirit from one location
to another. Those days must undoubtedly have been among the most
exciting in the history of the world.

Yet for all the drama, the sense of destiny, and providential miracles, the early church had major problems. The early church had, in
fact, barely begun to walk when damnable heresies crept in, working
to trip her up.

Some factions arose declaring that a Gentile could not be saved
without circumcision; others introduced asceticism; still others argued
that the Resurrection had passed. The early church was rife with such

171

heretical cliques. One group proclaimed that Christ was not God; another, that He had not actually died; and still others, that Christ had not come in the flesh but had been a phantom. Much of the New Testament was written to combat and correct such heresies, and many of the church councils and creeds in subsequent centuries dealt with specific heresies as well.

Yet in the midst of these doctrinal battles there was at least one area of theology on which the church never wavered or divided: their unyielding opposition to child-killing in the womb. Without reservation or exception, abortion was considered to be murder.

George Grant has compiled just a few of the plethora of statements made by the early church fathers on the topic of child-killing.[1]

> Do not murder a child by abortion or kill a new-born infant (*Didache* 2.2).

> You shall love your neighbor more than your own life. You shall not slay a child by abortion. You shall not kill that which has already been generated (*Epistle of Barnabas, 19.5*).

> We say that women who induce abortions are murderers, and will have to give account of it to God. . . . The fetus in the womb is a living being and therefore the object of God's care (Athenagaoras, *A Plea for the Christians, 35.6*).

> [O]ur whole life can proceed according to God's perfect plan only if we gain dominion over our desires, practicing continence from the beginning instead of destroying through perverse and pernicious arts human offspring, who are given birth by Divine Providence. Those who use abortificient medicines to hide their fornication cause not only the outright murder of the fetus, but of the whole human race as well (Clement of Alexandria, *Paedogus, 2:10.96.1*).

> [M]urder is forbidden once and for all. We may not destroy even the fetus in the womb. . . . To hinder a birth is merely a speedier man-killing. Thus, it does not matter whether you take away a life that is born, or destroy one that is coming to the birth. In both instances, destruction is murder (Tertullian, *Apology, 9.4*).

> She who has deliberately destroyed a fetus must bear the penalty for murder. . . . Moreover, those who give abortificients for the destruction of a child conceived in the womb are murderers themselves, along with those receiving the poisons (Basil, *Canons, 188.2*).

There are many more such admonitions and proclamations from our fathers in the faith, including Origen, Hippolytus, St. John Chrysostom, who have added their hearty amen.

Their belief that abortion is murder was well founded; it was based upon a thorough understanding of the Bible. Both the Old and New Testaments use language which describes children as fully human and made in the image of God. "And they were bringing even their *babies* to Him so that He might touch them, but when the disciples saw it, they began rebuking them" (Luke 18:15, emphasis added). The Greek word for baby is *brephos*. It is the same Greek word used to describe John the Baptist while he was still in his mother's womb. "And it came about that when Elizabeth heard Mary's greeting, the *baby* leapt in her womb" (Luke 1:41, emphasis added).

The Holy Spirit who inspired the Scriptures chose to use the same Greek word to identify a born baby and an unborn baby. Why? Because in the mind of God, they are both fully human; the only difference is their location and how they receive their nourishment.

The same holds true in the Old Testament. The Hebrew word *ben* is used interchangeably to describe individuals inside or outside the womb and even the elderly (see Genesis 25:22; Psalm 72:20). Hence, to destroy the life of a judicially innocent baby, whether in the womb or out, is murder. (For further study, see Psalm 139:13–16, Luke 1:42–3; Psalm 51:5, NIV).

In short, "The idea that infanticide and abortion is wrong . . . is a distinctly Christian idea . . . that the church has *always* held to." [2]

Defying Our Heritage

The twentieth century is the first period in the history of the church in which anyone who claims to follow Christ has betrayed this orthodox Biblical teaching. Yet, tragically, the betrayal is rampant.

Religious Coalition for Abortion Rights

The seductive element of heretics is their appearance. Jesus described them as wolves in sheep's clothing (see Matthew 7:15). They look like sheep and may even sound like sheep!

Let me introduce to you the leader of the wolf pack: the Religious Coalition on Abortion Rights (RCAR). According to their own fact sheet, RCAR is "composed of 34 national protestant, Jewish and other faith groups, which have joined together to preserve the legal option of abortion."³

Much of their literature couches their position in religious lingo. They often refer to the love of God, the love of Christ, the freedom of Jesus Christ, the grace of God, and other Christian truths which they have perverted. (References to Christ obviously are found in the Christian pro-death literature on which I will focus. I will leave the Jewish heretics for their Orthodox brethren to fry.) The authors of RCAR materials often have impressive credentials and degrees hanging on their walls; some even wear respectful clerical garb. Hence, they are all the more seductive and deceptive. Their appearance lends an authority and legitimacy to what has always been considered an anti-Biblical, antichrist heresy. As Paul said, Satan will transform himself into an angel of light in order to deceive us (2 Corinthians 11:14).

Truth is truth, however, no matter how backward or close-minded those who proclaim it may appear. Likewise, lies are lies, no matter how slick their packaging. And let me tell you, RCAR and company have some slick-packaged lies.

One of RCAR's publications is a twenty-seven-page booklet entitled *Personhood, the Bible and the Abortion Debate* by Dr. Paul D. Simmons.

> The abortion question focuses on the personhood of the woman, who in turn considers the potential personhood of the fetus in terms of the multiple dimensions of her own history and the future.
> This [abortion] is god-like decision. Like the Creator, she reflects upon what is good for the creation of which she is an agent. As steward of those powers, she uses them for good and not ill—both for herself, the fetus and the future of humankind itself. She is aware that God wills health and happiness for herself, for those who [she] may bring into the world and the future of the human race.⁴

So, for the happiness of the human race, for the good of the fetus, and for the future of humankind itself, a woman has the Biblical right to make the god-like decision to have her child's life brutally ended. After all, she knows that God wants her and her baby to be happy; and if she won't be happy, then certainly the baby won't be. This is sufficient reason then, according to Dr. Simmons, to warrant the death penalty for the child.

He goes on to discuss handicapped children and the burden that they may be as "those evils sure to afflict the human family." He continues, "Aborting a fetus that is radically deformed may well be a morally responsible action to prevent the greater evil of a child's being born with an incurable illness. . . ."[5] Since when is being radically deformed or even incurably ill an evil thing?

For the child conceived through rape or incest (a rhetorical red herring since such cases comprise less than 1 percent of all child-killing), Dr. Simmons compassionately says, "Terminating such a pregnancy is to act with God to prevent further threat to the health and well-being of the woman."[6] Now he has God soliciting our help in killing an innocent child!

So, when is an abortion *not* appropriate? He doesn't say. One has to presume from his silence that there is *no* inappropriately dead child. One would expect that someone who professes to be a Christian would throw at least a sop to the child, perhaps offering clemency for viable children (third trimester). No such pardon is forthcoming. In fact, he agreeably quotes Charles Hartshorne. "An embryo is not a person but the possibility of there being a person many months or even years in the future."[7] A baby is not a person (hence, unprotected under civil law) for *years?* Is this an invitation to post-pregnancy abortion?

What makes Dr. Simmons's remarks as tragic as they are deplorable are his credentials. He has a Th.M. from Southeastern Baptist Seminary and a Ph.D. from Southern Baptist Seminary; he is a member of the Society of Christian Ethics, the American Academy of Religion, and the Association of Baptist Professors of Religion. Most alarmingly, he has been a professor of Christian ethics at the Southern Baptist Theological Seminary in Louisville, Kentucky, since 1970. With men such as this training pastors, is it any wonder that so many of them have the convictions of a chameleon? *How can we hope to defeat the enemy when their agents are training our leaders?*

The Big Lie. It was Goebbels, Hitler's propaganda specialist, who observed that if you tell a lie often enough, people will eventually believe it.

RCAR has faithfully followed in the footsteps of these great liars, droning its own monotonous fabrication. It goes (and goes and goes) like this:

WOULD THE PASSAGE OF A "RIGHT TO LIFE" AMENDMENT ENDANGER OUR RELIGIOUS FREEDOM? Yes. The First Amendment states that "Congress shall make no law respecting an establishment of religion, or prohibiting the free exercise thereof." To place

into the Constitution the theology of one particular religion concerning the beginning of life compels every citizen to accept that
doctrine, even when it conflicts with his or her own religious beliefs.
If abortion were banned these individuals whose religions teach that
abortion may sometimes be a moral solution to a problem pregnancy would be unable to practice the tenets of their faith.[8]

Thus says RCAR's *Religious Freedom and the Abortion Controversy*
tract. (What kind of faith has child-killing as one of its tenets?) By
insisting that this is *solely* a religious issue, RCAR hopes to preclude
legislation outlawing child-killing. One wonders what they would say
to those who insist that infanticide in the first three months after
birth is also a strictly religious issue. Perhaps Dr. Simmons ought to
initiate a dialogue since he seemed to suggest that newborns might
not be persons at all.

The denominations and their outreaches (I cannot bear to refer
to them as ministries) which are official members of RCAR include:

- Division of Homeland Ministries / Christian Church (Disciples of
  Christ)

- Women's Caucus / Church of the Brethren

- Women in Mission and Ministry / The Episcopal Church

- Episcopal Urban Caucus

- Episcopal Women's Caucus

- Federation for Reconstructionist Congregations and Havurot

- Northern Province / The Moravian Church in America

- Social Justice and Peacemaking Ministry Unit / Presbyterian
  Church (USA)

- Women's Ministry Unit / Presbyterian Church (USA)

- Board for Homeland Ministries / United Church of Christ

- Coordinating Center for Women / United Church of Christ

- Board of Church and Society / United Methodist Church

- Women's Division, Board of Global Ministries / United Methodist
  Church

- YWCA National Board[9]

Each of these groups officially supports Roe v. Wade, hence, child-killing through all nine months of pregnancy.

It is simply unfathomable that the Methodist church which John Wesley founded, once alive with zeal for souls and for justice for the oppressed, would endorse the brutal destruction of innocent children. Their official position booklet, entitled "Social Principles, The United Methodist Church," comments on abortion:

> The beginning of life and the ending of life are the God-given boundaries of human existence. While individuals have always had some degree of control over when they would die, they now have the awesome power to determine when and even if new individuals will be born. Our belief in the sanctity of unborn human life makes us reluctant to approve abortion. But we are equally bound to respect the sacredness of the life and well-being of the mother, for whom devastating damage may result from an unacceptable pregnancy. In continuity with past Christian teaching, we recognize tragic conflicts of life with life that may justify abortion, and in such cases support the legal option of abortion under proper medical procedures.[10]

What a pillar of strength. If a woman has an unacceptable pregnancy, she has the awesome power to determine that the child should never see the light of day (unless the dreaded complication occurs). This act of murder, of course, ought to occur only "after thoughtful and prayerful consideration by the parties involved with medical, pastoral and other appropriate counsel."[11] I wonder what the abortionist's opinion would be. Or the unborn baby's.

The Scare Tactic. RCAR and their allies have managed to stretch the above lie beyond belief by arguing that if child-killing is outlawed, then *all* our rights would be in jeopardy. Sure, granting the right to life to the unborn child will be the first step towards the establishment of an oppressive and tyrannical regime in the United States. Listen to their logic.

> COULD A CONSTITUTIONAL AMENDMENT TO BAN ABORTIONS AFFECT OUR OTHER CIVIL LIBERTIES? Legal scholars think this is possible. American liberties have been secure in large measure because they have been guaranteed by a Bill of Rights which the American people have considered to be virtually unamendable. If the first clause of the Bill of Rights, which protects

religious freedom, should prove so easily susceptible to amendment, none of the succeeding clauses would be secure.[12]

The utter folly of this statement is revealed by a brief view at recent United States history. It has, in fact, been since the advent of legalized child-killing that we have had *more* government control, *more* government harassment, *more* government regulations concerning our religious, family, and individual freedoms. Why? When we reject the moral absolutes of God's Word as the fundamental basis for our laws, we embrace moral anarchy. There are no rights and wrongs and no constraints upon the actions of the government. Those in power determine what is right. This ultimately leads to tyranny. The examples of atheistic China and Russia (which both have incredibly high abortion rates) ought to be enough to prove the point.

Withheld Endorsement. On October 24, 1988, RCAR held a press conference denouncing Operation Rescue. (We were flabbergasted. We had hoped to gain their endorsement!) The press conference offered a rehash of the standard pro-death rhetoric: "It's a woman's right; it's a religious freedom issue." It did, however, introduce a little fresh frothing of the mouth from some of RCAR's members. Moderator Natalie Gubrandson had these comments:

> How dare they call themselves pro-lifers! I am pro-life! Everyone I know is pro-life. Their misguided view focuses only on abortion and omits the concern for the woman who is pregnant because of rape or incest, the woman who is already struggling with the family she has, the pregnant teenager, a child herself, the unwanted child, the abused child or the children who cannot care for themselves and end up as victims of the street, downed by drugs and charlatans, ravaged by disease, soon to become the responsibility of tax-supported health clinics, social agencies and prisons. [In other words, kill them all before they become a burden or an eyesore to us.]
>
> Theirs is not the message of love, compassion and concern that a Jesus of Nazareth would condone. [I'm not kidding. She really said this.] Their's is a message of lies, of hate, of cruelty and of punishment reflective of witch burners and torturers, disguised in the name of religion. Flashing their God placards, they seek to press their will on the majority; destroy the rights of the living and threaten the basic tenet of democracy—the Freedom of Choice.

The freedom to kill those plentiful poor people, is that what you really mean? I'm sorry, but I have a hard time hearing the message of Jesus of Nazareth in your cries of "Crucify them! Crucify them!"

Catholic Troubles

Defections from Christian principles have not been limited to Protestants. Our dear Roman Catholic friends have had their share of heartache.

For example, Father Curran was a professor at the Catholic University of America, the only American Catholic university with Pontifical endorsement. This school, above all others, should be a bastion of Catholic orthodoxy.

However, it was not. Father Curran, a rebellious priest, was determined to instruct his students contrary to Catholic teachings in the area of birth control, divorce, and abortion. Fortunately, he was finally removed and barred from teaching. Church officials received a great deal of criticism for their courageous action, especially from the media who exalted Curran's rebellion as an act of virtue.

Catholics for Free Choice. Catholics for Free Choice is another fly in the ointment of Catholic orthodoxy. This is hardly a mainstream Catholic think-tank. Its president, Frances Kissling, is a former director of the National Abortion Federation and previously operated three abortion mills, of which two were illegal.[13] She now shamelessly parades herself as a Catholic church leader in the United States and abroad. What a deep offense to true Catholics!

In late 1989, she traveled to Brazil flying her Catholics for Free Choice banner and eager to help the Brazilian killers legalize childkilling in their nation. Father Marx and other Roman Catholic leaders are calling for her excommunication. I sincerely hope that they prevail.

In all reality, however, Catholics for Free Choice is small potatoes. They virtually do not exist other than in the public relations materials cooked up by Kissling. The illusion of their size, however, is generated by the sympathetic coverage they receive from the pro-death (and anti-Catholic) media. They have been an irritation and embarrassment in the Catholic community, and I join the faithful in hoping for their quick demise or, at least, their excommunication!

Notable Courage. It is appropriate now to mention the courage of Bishop Leo Maher in San Diego, California, who forbade Lucy Killea from receiving communion as long as she promoted child-killing. God bless him for acting upon his convictions.

Another such confrontation between a Catholic Church leader and a pro-death Catholic politician occurred in New York State. Auxiliary Bishop Austin Vaughn, in the midst of a fifteen-day jail sentence for rescuing, warned New York's Governor Cuomo that his pro-death stance was paving his way to hell. (We evangelical New Yorkers, as well as faithful Catholics, enthusiastically applauded Vaughn's courage.) Moreover, before the ink had dried on that story, Bishop Daley, having just been installed in the diocese in which Governor Cuomo lives, forbade the Governor from speaking at any Catholic church or function in the diocese. Cardinal O'Connor backed the bishops completely, even comparing Bishop Vaughn to Thomas More.

Oh that such zeal to cleanse the temple of God would spread throughout the Catholic, Orthodox, and Protestant communities. If it did, chapters like this might become unnecessary.

The Evangelical Church

The charismatic, evangelical world is not without its own renegades. On September 11, 1988, Bishop Earl Paulk, pastor of Chapel Hill Harvester church in Decatur, Georgia, issued a statement against Operation Rescue. The statement, released at the height of rescue activity in Atlanta, appeared as a guest opinion in the Sunday edition of the *Atlanta Journal and Constitution.* My friend Mark Lucas saw the piece before I did and began reading it silently. He began exclaiming, "This is pro-abortion! This *is* pro-abortion!" I at first assumed that Mark was overreacting to an antirescue statement. He was not.

I could not believe my eyes. It was an absolutely pro-abortion argument. As I read, my heart sank with grief for the church. I repeatedly murmured under my breath, "My God, what have we become?" The question still haunts me.

His column begins innocuously, "Many of us believe very much in the right to life." Not bad. Paulk continues, however, drifting slowly into pro-abortion rhetoric, "We believe abortion is wrong in cases other than where the physical life or mental well-being of the mother is at stake." Wait a minute. Who defines mental well-being? Justice

Blackmun? Faye Wattleton? An abortion counselor? Bishop Paulk himself? The mother herself?

Paulk continues, "To confront an already distraught woman at the door of an abortion clinic and attempt to put her on a guilt trip for what she is about to do is not the solution. Nor is the solution concerned citizens allowing themselves to be arrested." We're putting a guilt trip on the girl! Did the bishop ever consider that *God* might be putting a guilt trip on her? Or that she actually *is* guilty?

It is critical to note that all of Paulk's sympathies lie with the mother. What about the baby who is about to murdered! He *never once* mentions children or babies in the entire article.

He goes on, "We abdicate our responsibilities as Christians and as parents when we turn to civil authorities to legislate moral issues." Paulk now aligns himself with such people as Norman Lear, the founder of People for the American Way, and the entire cadre of ACLU attorneys:

In the September 11, 1988, *Atlanta Constitution,* he mentions:

The only right civil government has in our lives is to provide us with the freedom of choice. . . .

If the civil authority is called upon to make moral judgments and does so, where will the line eventually be drawn? Will we not jeopardize our religious freedom by their intrusion into our domain? Could it be possible when the civil government begins to make moral decrees that it will also make other arbitrary statutes that could greatly affect our religious freedoms?

Paulk, equating the right to kill children (freedom of choice) with religious freedoms, echos the RCAR party line:

Many of Atlanta's religious leaders do not support public funds being used for abortions. We do strongly support the right of the individual, the family and the church in making these moral judgments without any interference or intervention by the civil government.

If that's not enough, Paulk concludes

Some have compared these demonstrations to the civil rights demonstrations. It's not a valid comparison. The civil rights demonstrations were to gain freedom. These demonstrations call for the restriction of rights. Though many of use [sic] don't agree morally with abortion, we do agree with the concept of freedom of choice. Moral law and civil law are not synonymous. The individual, the family and the church legislate moral law. Civil law legislates secular law. This is true separation of church and state.

His statements mirror perfectly the rhetoric of the proaborts. Whom is he trying to impress or whose favor is he trying to win with such statements? If Eleanor Smeal and her Fund for the Feminist Majority cuddle up to him because of his compromise, what has he gained?

Yes, Bishop, we are trying to restrict something, but not freedom. No one has the freedom to murder their offspring. We are laboring to restrict—in fact, eliminate—the systematic, premeditated slaughter of defenseless babies—a slaughter which is an abomination before God.

With all due respect, sir, your statement was issued publicly; therefore, you must issue a public retraction and apology. Your words were a betrayal of the children, a blight on the church, and an offense before heaven. You need to repent and to radically alter your thinking.

Conclusion

It is interesting to note that the denominations that have sold out to the death industry are dying out numerically. God has indeed written *Ichabod* (The glory has departed) over their doorposts. His blessing has departed.

Those who belong to denominations who betrayed the children may still be faithful Christians. In fact, certain congregations within heretical denominations have remained faithful to God and His Word and do not submit to the "party line." To these brothers and sisters, I ask, "Why do you stay?"

" To have a godly influence," you may respond. Haven't you, however, tried for years, with little or no fruit? Why give your tithes to churches and denominations that support child-killing and may actually use a portion of *your money* to support the likes of Planned Parenthood?

To those who are in denominations who are yet faithful but have renegades in your midst, I exhort you. Purge the temple! Bishops, discipline or remove clergy that betray the children. Would you not defrock a priest or minister who called for blacks to be reenslaved? Then how can you tolerate men (and women) who clamor for the "safe and legal" extermination of our children?

To those faithful Christians who attend a church at which the pastor is not pro-life, I admonish you. Call on him to repent. If he fails to do so, then labor to get him removed as pastor. If you are unable, then you should leave the church. Realistically, what quality of spiritual food and care can you expect to receive from a man who defends child-killing?

To the seminaries, I adjure you. Clean your ranks! Have you inventoried your ethics department lately? Young people, carefully investigate before enrolling at a supposedly "Christian college." Some are Christian in name only, having long ago abandoned the faith. Parents, beware of sending your children to schools at which men like Dr. Simmons will fill their minds with poison, subtly undermining rather than undergirding the faith you have instilled in them as little ones.

Until the church cleans up its own act and purges our ranks of the enemy's emissaries, how can we ever hope to defeat a movement fueled by hell and the blood of the innocents?

Let's wake up, make a scourge, overturn some tables, and drive out the thieves. Undoubtedly, this kind of action would be unpopular. Well, I'm sure a standing ovation didn't greet Jesus after He cleansed the Temple. Likewise, we would be far better off pleasing God rather than the proaborts. The church was meant to be a house of prayer and righteous action, not a den of thieves who have stolen the lives of innocent children and become rich with the cursed blood money.

12

REEDS IN THE WIND

The birth and growth of the Rescue Movement have been nothing short of miraculous. The encouragement and endorsement which the movement has received from Christian leaders of stature has undoubtedly accelerated that growth. Rescues, however, have not been without their critics in the Christian community. Along with the praise and commendations of James Dobson, Pat Robertson, and John Cardinal O'Connor (and many other godly men and women) has been severe criticism from a few godly men. Fortunately, the voices against the Rescue Movement have not equalled in stature, volume, or number those who have endorsed our activities. Nevertheless, it distresses me to read a document penned by a brother in the Lord who ardently speaks out against our efforts to save children from death.

Writing this chapter has caused me much distress. Picking up a pen to respond to these brothers is difficult and, at times, heart wrenching. The men whom I address here have been a great blessing to thousands of Christians in their respective spheres of influence. They are surely beloved brothers in the Lord. This makes it all the more difficult to write.

It must be clear that I am in no way calling into question their commitment to the Lord or their integrity as men. Moreover, their tragic error in this area does not negate the truths they teach in other areas.

Thus, it is neither with glee nor self-righteous lip-smacking that we expose the folly of their arguments against rescuing children. It is rather with great sorrow. We are in a desperate hour as a church. Division in our midst is tragic and often a tool of the enemy, who knows well the principle of divide and conquer.

Some may ask, "Why don't you just ignore these differences on rescue? Why respond at all, thus accentuating and possibly exacerbating the division?"

The answer is simple. *It is a matter of life and death.* We aren't discussing such issues as the frequency of communion or end-times prophecy. We aren't even debating something as divisive as infant baptism. My friend Joseph Foreman wryly points out, "We used to argue whether or not to baptize babies. Now we argue whether or not to save them from murder."

So, due to the critical—life and death—nature of the debate, I will not mince words. Children's lives are in the balance. That is the awesome, frightening reality.

This may trouble you; but, just as there is only one Biblically correct position on covetousness or adultery, there is only one such position on rescuing children. There is a right position; there is a wrong position. Rescues are right and pleasing to God, or they are wrong and displeasing to Him. Either this is an appropriate occasion to "obey God rather than men" or it is not (Acts 5:29). You may never participate in a rescue mission yourself; you may question their effectiveness in saving children; you may believe that they galvanize our enemies. These thoughts, however, are secondary. The primary question remains this: *Is it proper, moral, and Biblically correct for Christians to participate in Rescue missions, or does the Bible clearly forbid rescues?*

Therefore, the stakes are extremely high; and I must respond. For the sake of the children and the health of this movement, I must expose the folly of arguments against rescue and unashamedly label them as false teaching.

One pillar of the Rescue Movement is the Higher Law principle. It simply states that there are certain instances when the Bible mandates that Christians obey the laws of God regardless of the laws of men. The men I will address all believe in the Higher Law principle—the legitimate practice of civil disobedience at one time or another.[1] For example, if the government outlawed the preaching of the gospel, all would agree that we would have no choice but to disobey that law. This would be the case in Soviet Russia and Communist China. The pertinent question, then, is this: Is sitting or kneeling in front of an abortion mill to save children from certain death an appropriate application of this principle?

Bill Gothard

Bill Gothard is the president of the Institute in Basic Youth Conflicts and a respected teacher in the body of Christ who travels the nation conducting his Basic Seminar. Gothard also offers one-day seminars strictly for pastors. In his 1989 Pastors' Seminar, he began forcefully speaking out against rescues; and it is the material originally contained in the seminar's handouts that I will address.

Bill and I had actually communicated before this series of seminars began, even as he was preparing his material. I appealed to him on the basis of Acts 5:34 to receive Gamaliel's wisdom and asked him to wait and see, refraining from speaking out against Operation Rescue. If rescues were not of God, they would fail. If they were of God, they would flourish. He responded that my request was a completely inappropriate application of that Scripture and suggested that a more fitting one was 1 John 4:1–6, implying that I was a false prophet. He subsequently launched his rhetorical offensive.

The initial error in Gothard's material (and in nearly every attack upon the Rescue Movement) is his insistence on characterizing Operation Rescue as a movement of civil disobedience. He states, "Today some who are seeking to protect the unborn are urging Christians to practice civil disobedience in order to stop the tragic holocaust of abortions in America." He then lumps the Rescue Movement with such historical godless individuals as Robespierre[2] and the lawless period of the bloody French Revolution.

Allow me to set the record straight. The Rescue Movement is not one of civil disobedience but of *Biblical obedience*. We firmly believe that God has mandated in His Word that the church is to rescue innocent children and that these mandates supersede the law of man. In other words, the principle of higher laws unquestionably applies to rescue. Examine the Scriptures:

> Rescue those who are unjustly sentenced to death; Don't stand back
> and let them die. (Proverbs 24:11, TLB)

Defend the cause of the weak and fatherless; maintain the rights of the poor and oppressed. Rescue the weak and needy; deliver them from the hand of the wicked. (Psalm 82:3,4, NIV)

This is pure and undefiled religion in the sight of our Father, to visit orphans and widows in their distress, and to keep oneself unstained by the world. (James 1:27)

These commands, and many similar ones, are binding upon Christians regardless of the laws of men. Over the past twenty years, however, much of the church has chosen to ignore them. The message of the Rescue Movement is to repent and obey God's Word.

We, therefore, are not urging people to protest or to break the law. *Rather, we are urging people to repent and to bear the fruits of their repentance through rescue.* We emphasize again and again that repentance is the springboard of this entire movement. In my book, *Operation Rescue,* the word *repent* or *repentance* is used dozens of times, while the phrase *civil disobedience* is used only eleven times, usually in reference to past church history, not the Rescue Movement. Our brother, by placing the Rescue Movement in the context of protest and civil disobedience, has completely missed the message. Let me now examine his material point by point.

His first section is headed "Civil Disobedience [read the Rescue Movement] Fails to Separate Commands to Do Evil from Laws That Allow Evil." Its lead sentence reads, "If any Christian is commanded to do evil, he must disobey." We agree completely. However, what about when the government forbids us from doing good, such as rescuing children from murder?

Mr. Gothard fails to acknowledge that evil or sin has two forms: sins of commission—doing wrong—and sins of omission—not doing something right. James 4:17 says, "Therefore, to him who knows the right thing to do and does not do it, to him it is sin."

Peter and the apostles were commanded not to preach in the name of Jesus (see Acts 4:17,18). Daniel was told not to pray to any god but the king (see Daniel 6). To obey would have been a sin of omission. It is critical to understand this, because Christians *are* being commanded to do evil. The authorities have said, "Do not rescue! Let the children die! You can talk against it, preach against it, but don't physically intervene to prevent their murder!" To comply is to commit the sin of omission by failing to fulfill the mandates of Proverbs 24:11, James 1:27, Psalm 82:3–4, and other Scriptures.

Mr. Gothard says, "However, in civil disobedience people not directly commanded to do evil assume responsibility for the law itself." Notice how he ignores the children. What if he said, "In rescuing children about to be legally murdered, people not directly commanded to kill children assume responsibility for the law itself when they rescue these children?" Would anyone countenance such a statement?

As evidence for his position, Mr. Gothard cites Daniel, the three Hebrew children, Peter, and Moses' parents. He says of Moses' parents, "Consider the faith of Moses' parents in God's ability to work through human authorities. They complied with an evil law as far as they could by placing their baby in a basket on the river." This is a Biblically inaccurate portrayal of the attitude of Moses' parents. Hebrews 11:23 says, "By faith Moses, when he was born, was hidden three months by his parents, because they saw he was a beautiful child; and they were not afraid of the king's edict." To say they had faith in God's ability to work through human authorities is to force Scripture to fit a doctrine. It is probably better said that they *disobeyed* an evil law as much as they could by hiding their child for three months and then preserving him in a basket.

Mr. Gothard's next section is headed, "Civil Disobedience" [again read the Rescue Movement] Demonstrates Power from Beneath Which Is in Conflict with Power from Above." Gothard states, "Rulers are established by the hand of God rather than by the will of the people. The ruler is, therefore, directly answerable to God."

This is dangerously out of balance. It denies the Biblical principle of representative government. The American people elected officials in our country. It is heartily agreed that elected officials are answerable to God, but they are also answerable to us. Why? Because God has given us a constitutional republic in which to live. The Constitution is the "ruler". It is the law of the land under God's law. Romans 13:1 should encourage us to be political activists because the higher power God has established in America is a Constitution under which we are *part* of the government. Oftentimes we have godless officials because we are too busy to elect godly officials.

Mr. Gothard continues, "God has made provision for those directly affected by evil laws to make proper appeals, and He gives us powerful testimonies of those who were effective in their appeals, such as Esther." But what provision exists for a baby about to be slaughtered to make an appeal on his or her own behalf? This is absurd.. He has now forgotten the babies and is strictly defending an indefensible principle—a principle that insists we not defend the children about to be killed.

Esther, however, is an excellent Biblical image of a Rescue Mission. She illegally trespassed before the king—risking her very own life—in order to save the lives of innocent people who had no provision for a "proper appeal." She was not in danger herself, nor was she commanded to kill other Jews, yet she trespassed to rescue them. Thank you, Esther.

A centuries-old discussion exists as to when it is proper to obey God even if it means defying civil authority. It is a very serious matter and an action no one enters lightly. To wave Romans 13:1–5, as many, including Mr. Gothard, have done, in the face of those who would rescue children is to err.

> For rulers are not a terror to good works, but to evil. Do you want to be unafraid of the authority? Do what is good, and you will have praise from the same. For he is God's minister to you for good. But if you do evil, be afraid; for he does not bear the sword in vain; for he is God's minister, an avenger to execute wrath on him who practices evil. (Romans 13: 3, 4, NKJV)

Governing authorities are to praise the righteous and punish the unrighteous. What do we do when government defies God's Word and punishes those who do good, while protecting and rewarding those who do evil—such as those murdering children? Romans 13 doesn't address this. We must turn to other portions of Scripture that provide the answer. When God's law and man's law conflict, obey God!

Third, Mr. Gothard argues that "Civil disobedience [Rescue] violates Christ's command not to take up the sword." This section *radically distorts* our views. He accuses us of picking up the sword. He quotes the following Scripture:

> You shall also say to the sons of Israel, "Any man from the sons of Israel or from the aliens sojourning in Israel, who gives any of his offspring to Molech, shall surely be put to death; the people of the land shall stone him with stones. I will set also set My face against that man and will cut him off from among his people, because he has given some of his offspring to Molech, so as to defile My sanctu-

ary and to profane My holy name. If the people of the land, however, should ever disregard that man when he gives any of his offspring to Molech, so as not to put him to death, then I Myself will set my face against that man and against his family; and I will cut off from among their people both him and all those who play the harlot after him, by playing the harlot after Molech." (Leviticus 20: 2–5)

We often quote Leviticus 20:2–5 to show that God holds bystanders accountable for the murder of children during child sacrifice. Gothard accuses us of setting the stage for bloodshed because this passage calls for the death sentence on child-killers. This is a gross misrepresentation of our position. We hold that the blood pollutes the land, and hence we are all guilty. Moses wrote:

Do not pollute the land where you are. Bloodshed pollutes the land, and atonement cannot be made for the land on which blood has been shed, except by the blood of the one who shed it. (Numbers 35: 33 NIV)

Mr. Gothard chides the use of Leviticus 20, saying

This passage is misinterpreted to mean that God will turn His face against anyone who stands idly by and allows someone else to kill his child. Many scholars would strongly disagree with this interpretation.

I immediately referenced Matthew Henry to see how he interpreted this Scripture.

. . . all his aiders and abetters should be cut off likewise by the righteous hand of God. If his neighbors concealed him, and *would not come in as witnesses against him*—if the magistrates connived at him, and *would not pass sentence upon him, rather pitying his folly than hating his impiety*—*God Himself would reckon with them.* . . . If magistrates will not do justice upon offenders, God will do justice upon *them,* because there is danger that many will *go a whoring after those* who do but countenance sin by winking at it. And, if the sins of leaders be leading sins, it is fit that their punishments should be exemplary punishments. (emphasis added)[3]

I checked three other sources. Two made no comment, and the other agreed with Matthew Henry. I don't know what commentaries he was speaking of, although I'm sure some do exist. However, those I have read, and other clergy I have spoken with, all agree; those who stand by while children are murdered are guilty, and God will hold us accountable. Why is Mr. Gothard trying to deny the guilt the church is under?

Mr. Gothard's fourth section begins, "Civil disobedience [Rescue] replaces our spiritual weapons with the world's carnal weapons." Thank God we live in a day when God has restored to His body the reality of spiritual warfare. We acknowledge that child-killing has roots that go back centuries, which involved then (as now) demonic influences and power. Therefore, we must do battle on our knees if we expect to win the war against child-killing. However, the pendulum has swung too far. Prayer alone is not enough! We must pray *and act.*

Mr. Gothard states, "Spiritual weapons are, in fact, our only effective weapons with the world's carnal weapons." This is out of balance. Why should we involve ourselves in any physical pro-life activity at all? Why not just pray? Can you imagine if a preacher declared, "We aren't going to send missionaries any more, nor finance their work; we aren't going to print gospel literature or preach the gospel. We're just going to pray." Would we accept such nonsense?

We are not trying to replace our spiritual weapons with the world's carnal weapons. We are trying to bring healthy balance to the concepts of spiritual weapons and spiritual authority. God does not wave a magic wand. We are His body—His hands and feet. He uses people who work hard, get their hands dirty, and make great sacrifices; people who work as if it all depends on them, while praying as if it all depends on God!

James rebutted the "no works" philosophy nearly two thousand years ago.

> What good is it, my brothers, if a man claims to have faith but has no deeds? Can such faith save him? Suppose a brother or sister is without clothes and daily food. If one of you says to him, "Go, I wish you well; keep warm and well fed," but does nothing about his physical needs, what good is it? In the same way, faith by itself, if it is not accompanied by action, is dead. (James 2:14–17, NIV)

Rescue Missions *are* spiritual actions. They are the fruits of repentance of which Paul preached in Acts 26:20. They are loving our neighbor as ourselves.

In this section Mr. Gothard also quotes me addressing American politics. "Whether for good or for bad, political change comes after a group . . . brings enough tension in the nation and pressure on politicians that the laws are changed." He chides us that this is a worldly tactic and is dangerous thinking.

Several critics have employed these statements against me, a couple even suggesting that I am a Marxist advocating social upheaval. Again, let me set the record straight. This statement is simply my observation of America's political history. The birth of our nation, the ending of slavery, the adoption of women's voting rights, the Constitutional prohibition on alcohol, its repeal, the adoption of broad civil rights legislation, the feminist movement (which brought us child-killing), the "sexual revolution", the Berkeley "free speech" upheaval, and the anti-Vietnam War movement all testify that, whether for righteous or unrighteous change, "politicians see the light after they feel the heat." To deny this is to deny America's history.

Elsewhere in this section, in a gross misrepresentation of the truth, Mr. Gothard also states, "Those advocating social upheaval claim Proverbs 24:11 as their theme verse. It is usually quoted from The Living Bible: 'Rescue those who are unjustly sentenced to death; don't stand back and let them die. . . .'" We don't claim Proverbs 24:11 as a call to social upheaval. It's a call to rescue innocent people, including babies, from death!

He never states that children in the womb deserve full protection, that they are our neighbor, and that we are commanded to love them as we love ourselves. If *you* were about to be murdered, would you want us wrangling over whether or not it was theologically sound to rescue you? In fact, Mr. Gothard uses the word *child* or *baby* very few times in connection with abortion.

Mr. Gothard heads his final argument against rescue, "Civil Disobedience Fails to Deal with the Real Attackers." He states, "Abortion clinics are being singled out as the primary offenders by those who are advocating civil disobedience. Great animosity is being generated toward these 'Murder Mills' and toward the doctors who are performing the murders."

Well, who should we single out? Tell the dead babies that the "doctors" (we call them executioners) at the murder mills weren't their real attackers. Who was? A phantom?

He continues, "There is no question that those who run abortion clinics are committing sin." Yes. They're committing sin, murder to be exact: cold-blooded, violent murder for hire.

It is distressing is that Mr. Gothard refuses to confront those child-killers.

Norman Geisler

Dr. Norman Geisler is a nationally-recognized author and speaker and a former instructor at Dallas Theological Seminary. On January 21, 1989, First Baptist Church of Atlanta invited Dr. Geisler to its pulpit to speak about child-killing. Many of his remarks attacked Operation Rescue.

Before unraveling his arguments against rescue, let me point out a few areas of agreement in his remarks. First, Dr. Geisler praised the Declaration of Independence and taught how the Declaration embodied three Christian truths:

1. That there is a Creator;
2. That we are created and did not evolve from primal slime;
3. That there are inalienable rights given from God—moral absolutes.

Second, he presented how the Darwinian natural selection, the "survival of the fittest" ideology, led to humanism, which rejects the above three truths in the Declaration. Darwinism and humanism—the rejection of the Creator and moral absolutes—were, in turn, the ideological underpinnings for Hitler's holocaust of twelve million, Stalin's holocaust of eighteen million, and now America's holocaust of twenty-five million. We agree wholeheartedly.

Subtle Indictment

We, however, disagree vehemently on much of the remainder of his sermon. Dr. Geisler launched and maintained his attack against rescuing children with highly charged prejudicial language. "Unfortunately, there are some overzealous Christians who are going too far and doing some wrong things. And I would like to speak Biblically to the issue of civil disobedience in the abortion matter." He then went on to discuss rescue in the same context as clinic bombings, assassinations of abortionists, and tax protests! His listeners consequently were taught to treat each of these activities with similar disdain.

Dr. Geisler, in fact, discussed rescue last and in the worst possible terms—that of revolution. He states:

Do not start a revolution. Proverbs 24 is often quoted by those militant activists in the pro-life movement who are engaging in civil disobedience. And they use Proverbs 24 to say, 'We ought to rescue the perishing.' They don't read far enough down, because in the twenty-first verse of the chapter, it says, don't even hang around with people who are lawbreakers. Don't hang around with revolutionaries. Fear the king and God. And we ought to take to heart not just a verse out of context, verse 11, 'rescue the perishing,' but we ought to take to heart the entire chapter, which is against violence and lawbreakers and wicked people and revolutionaries.

Geisler has thus indicted us. We are not peaceful, prayerful, non-violent Christians, but "militant activists!" He has lumped us in with lawbreakers and wicked people and revolutionaries. Gothard used his version of history to link us with revolutionaries; Geisler used his version of Scripture. His arguments possess no more factual soundness; but they do make quick, emotional converts.

He then prefaced his prepared arguments against rescue, "Nowhere in the Bible did God ever give the sword to the citizens to use on the government. The sword was given to government to use on disobedient citizens." His implied accusation that we are taking up the sword is as dishonest as it is absurd. Nowhere have we advocated retribution against abortionists or violence against abortion mills. (Some punishment will, however, occur when this holocaust is ended, and the truth exposed to the American people.)

Then in a "God-save-the-king" line, he pointedly commented,

And there are some Christians about to find out how sharp that sword is in the very near future when they come before the judge for their sentence for their disobedience in the abortion issue. And the sword cuts sharply. And when Christians disobey the law; they deserve the punishment of the law, like any other lawbreaker in the country. Don't start a revolution and don't break the law.

Since I'm sitting in jail as I write this, this statement has particular interest to me! I deserve what I'm getting! How dare we try to save children without the king's permission!

In fact, as do others who argue against rescuing children, Geisler spoke throughout his talk only of the abortion issue and ignored the victim, the unborn child. He never used the words *child, baby,* or *people,* except to accuse us of being "humanists." He says, "And they tell us these sad stories and I know them, cause I'm there, about 4,300 people a day and the girls crying and so forth, but listen, don't let the emotional appeal obscure your rational and Biblical judgment."

Be rational! Be Biblical! Be careful when someone talks about 4,300 innocent children being murdered daily and our duty to rescue them! Don't let your common sense and a Biblical mandate to rescue the innocent get the best of you!

Reasons Against Rescuing

Geisler's attack upon Operation Rescue then centered on his six reasons why we shouldn't rescue children. Let me address those I did not address in my rebuttal of Bill Gothard. He says,

> Thirdly, it's counter-productive. This is the worst time in the history of the pro-life movement for Operation Rescue to come along, the very worst time. You know why? Because we are winning without that kind of activity. We're winning judicially on the Supreme Court. We're winning in public opinion. We're winning in terms of Christian involvement. We're winning on every front and now a group of radicals come along causing a counter-productive activity.

"We're winning!" he declared. Who's "we?" The pro-life movement? Certainly not the babies scheduled to die today or the babies who died in Atlanta while he confidently claimed "we're winning!"

Moreover, we *aren't* winning. The 1989 political battles reveal just how badly we are losing. If Roe were overturned today, child-killing would remain entrenched in certain states for decades. The current prospects for a constitutional amendment banning child-killing are bleak at best.

Dr. Geisler then argued that the Rescue Movement was "faithless." Was Esther faithless? Was she taking matters into her own hands when she intervened on behalf of the Jews? Why didn't she just pray and trust God? Was Rahab faithless? Or were the Hebrew midwives? When someone is about to die, you act! Have faith and pray, yes: but *do* something while you're praying!

Gross Inconsistencies

In closing this section, I want to point out two areas of gross inconsistency in Dr. Geisler's arguments. First, it is hypocritical for Dr. Geisler to laud the Declaration of Independence and then to condemn rescuers for taking "illegal" actions and falsely accuse us of being revolutionaries who have taken up the sword. Allow me to point out the obvious. The Declaration was an illegal document. The Declaration was revolutionary. The Declaration was a call to take up the sword. Finally, many thousands died in the Revolutionary War which bought America freedom. Let's be honest and consistent.

Second, he claims that we are humanistic. In reality, arguments against rescue are humanistic because they exalt the laws of men— "No Trespassing" and "Roe v. Wade"—above the laws of God—Thou shalt not murder, and rescue those unjustly sentenced to death.

We uphold the laws of God urging us to rescue children from death above the laws of men permitting them to be murdered; and we are accused of being humanists! God deliver us from such a theology!

John MacArthur

John MacArthur is the pastor of Grace Community Church in Panorama City, California. He is a distinguished author and hosts a daily radio show heard on five hundred stations nationwide. John could certainly be regarded as a well-known, respected leader in fundamentalist circles.

On April 2, 1989, MacArthur preached a message in his church against rescue missions. I will address the substance of his remarks that day. It is important to note initially, however, that at this writing, Robert Vernon, deputy police chief of the Los Angeles Police Department and the supervisor who has overseen much of the police brutality against rescuers, is a member of MacArthur's church.

I will focus on MacArthur's comments in four areas:

1. What he said concerning rescuers.

2. What he said concerning the government.

3. What he said about rescues.

4. What he believed to be the true solution.

The Rescuers

As with others who speak out against rescuing children, MacArthur first set out to question the character and reputations of the rescuers themselves, painting them as misguided, overzealous Christians.

> [T]here also are in Christianity today, people who are living in the world in such a way that even their function as citizens is causing a reproach to fall on the name of Christ. You can lose the credibility of your testimony by failing to live a supernatural life which is alien to this world which demonstrates the power of Christ. . . . [They] have violated the standards of citizenship, they have violated the law civilly, and they have not honored the authority over them.

From the very beginning, prior to the introduction of any Biblical arguments, his listeners are emotionally antagonistic to the rescuers. After all, rescuers are bringing reproach on Christ; they don't have a credible testimony; they're failing to live a supernatural life; and they've violated the standards of citizenship. (After hearing this, who *would* like them!) His character assassination is capped off later in his message when he referred to us as rebels and insurrectionists.

MacArthur made one statement which sheds much light on the type of life and testimony he thinks we ought to have: "He [God] wants us to demonstrate self-restraint, to demonstrate virtue, to demonstrate a concern about community, to do all we can to prevent trouble [I ask, is murder of an innocent baby trouble?], to live in such a way—in peace and good will—that we deprive our enemies of the grounds of all their false accusation."

We agree that our lives as Christians should be free of moral failure that would dishonor the Lord. It appears from these statements, however, that Reverend MacArthur simply doesn't want Christians to rock the boat. Yet the Lord and the early disciples stirred up trouble everywhere they went! Does he believe Christians ought to imitate the early church? If so, then the godless should be accusing us of turning the world upside down, of *causing* trouble (see Acts 17:6)!

The Government

Concerning the government, MacArthur commented,

> When a leader in the society says, "Do this!" you do it. When the police say, "Get up and move over here," you get up and move over there because that's what the Bible tells you to do. Why do you do it? Because of the Lord. Why? Because the Lord has called us to obey the authorities because the authorities are ordained by God and it's a matter of obedience. . . .
>
> What I want you to understand is that God controls and owns it all. And what we want to do is recognize that He has ordained gov-

ernment to keep the peace in society and He has commanded us to submit to that. And you do not accomplish the divine end by violating the divine law.

Is he saying that those Christians under Soviet rule who violate the law by teaching their children to pray are wrong? Is he saying that God instituted communist regimes that demand a confession of atheism from those citizens who wish to get ahead in society? His statements are perilously out of balance. He continues,

> Robert Haldane, many years ago, wrote that the people of God ought to consider resistance to the government under which they live as a very awful crime; a very awful crime. Because it detracts from the glory of Christ. It shows Christians in anger, hostility, rebellion. That's not honoring to God. To see us in peace, in graciousness, in kindness—does honor God. To see us in virtue, obedience, submissiveness, humility—that honors our Christ.

Is he, then, rejecting the Declaration of Independence and the American Revolution that brought us our incredible freedoms? Let me pose another question. What if, as the Nicolae Ceaucescu regime collapsed in Romania and his tyranny was being overthrown, Ceaucescu had called upon the Christians to prop up his crumbling dictatorship? Should they then have submitted? As I ponder his response to the police brutality in Los Angeles, I honestly wonder what he would have had a Romanian Christian do.

After the police wantonly brutalized pro-lifers on March 25, 1989, a hue and cry went up from much of the Christian community. The criticism was particularly targeted at Chief Daryl Gates and Deputy Chief Robert Vernon, a member of MacArthur's flock. MacArthur, however, reproves these critics, commenting, "I read that some people felt that the police should not have used pain compliance. They are ministers of God who bear not the sword in vain, says Paul (in Romans 13). And if you violate the law, then they have every right to bring about wrath, punishment."

Is MacArthur really saying that God's Word gives police the authority to inflict punishment on the spot to whoever they want? Does he want to throw away our Fourth, Fifth, Eighth, and Fourteenth Amendment rights that protect us from government abuse? That the police should ignore these portions of our Constitution which *prohibit* them from punishing citizens who have not been convicted of any crime? I fear he is.

The Rescues

MacArthur's attitude toward rescues themselves is revealed in this one paragraph:

> If the people who are doing this really wanted to aggressively rescue children from abortion, I'm convinced that this isn't how to do it, even on the physical human level, because all they're doing is hindering the police from doing their work. They're not hindering the abortionist from doing his. There's no rescue. If this is a rescue, what's it a rescue of? . . . But to lay around the outside, which winds up being harassment of the police, directs the whole attack at the wrong group. They're not doing it, and it isn't really rescuing. It seems to me to be a little more—and they will admit this—than a large-scale demonstration to try to manipulate the government to change this.

"All they're doing is hindering the police from doing their job." That's not true. *Their job* is to protect human life. They ought to be rescuing with us. Many policemen have done just that. One, in fact, Chet Gallagher, rescued in full uniform in Las Vegas, Nevada. Where does Officer Gallagher fit into Reverend MacArthur's theology? Short of joining with us, the police can just refuse to arrest us. At various times, the police in Los Angeles and other cities have chosen not to arrest.

"They're not hindering the abortionists from doing his work [killing children]." This statement ignores the obvious reality. Of course we are preventing him from slaughtering his victims! As long as we peacefully and prayerfully keep our positions, the abortionist can't kill children. Just read the anti-Operation Rescue pro-death literature which describes how we "disrupt services" (more truthfully, save children).

"There's no rescue. If this is a rescue, what's it a rescue of?" The object of our rescue is not *what* or *it*, Rev. MacArthur, but *who*. It's a rescue of unborn babies scheduled to die. Where is his compassion for the children?

MacArthur's True Solution

Reverend MacArthur's solution can be summarized in this manner:

> I believe that the instruction of the Word of God is that there's a better way. Recognize God as sovereign, pray and publish the Word. You know, if we can lead these people who are getting abortions to Christ, we can stop it. If we can lead the doctors to Christ, we can stop it. But in the end, only God can stop it. . . . And that's in His sovereign hands.

That's it. We are to pray, preach, and trust in the sovereignty of God. It sounds right. In fact, it appears to be so noble, so *spiritual.*

> We approach the massive institutions of men, we approach their demonic and flawed reason, we approach their lofty pride which is exalted against the knowledge of God; . . . and we can tear them all down . . . with weapons that are spiritual.

Yes, we must preach the gospel. Of course, we must pray. This battle, however, is not only spiritual—it is *natural. Real babies shed real blood, not spiritual blood! Their physical bodies need our physical protection.*

Final Observations

A Call to Courage

The bottom line is that there are no cheap solutions. This is going to be a long, drawn out battle. We will need rescues, lobbying, and intense prayer; we will need strong apologetics, courageous statesmen, and much, much more. Christians will need backbones with steel and foreheads of flint. We will need the courage and the ability to rise up and press on after being knocked to the canvas. We will need nothing short of providential miracles. Our needs are so great! God help us!

Principles Above Lives. Those who argue against rescues are like the Pharisees who wouldn't permit Jesus to heal a man on the Sabbath because it was against the law. Jesus said, "Is it lawful on the Sabbath to do good, or to do harm, to save life, or to destroy it?" (see Luke 6: 6–11 and Mark 3: 1–6). Our Lord also said, "The Sabbath was made for man [the rest principle] and not man for the Sabbath" (Mark 2: 27). Likewise, the authorities of Romans 13 (the authority principle) were made for man and his protection, not man for Romans 13.

Avoiding the Victim. The preceding arguments show little compassion for the children about to be murdered. They rarely mention babies or murder. They do not reveal the horror of child-killing; the dismemberment, burning, poisoning, or Caesarean section abortions where viable children (children old enough to live outside the womb) are removed and suffocated, injected with a deadly narcotic, or just left to die. This is a holocaust.

Guilty by Association. By beating and beating the drum of civil disobedience and comparing us to the revolutionaries or radical movements of the sixties, each paints a distorted image of this movement which elicits a negative knee-jerk reaction. Most conservative evangelical ministers over forty years old have a very bad taste about the sixties (and well they should in many respects).

To even remotely compare peaceful, godly rescuers with radical feminists or anti-American protesters of the sixties is a gross distortion. Beyond that, to compare in any way rescuers with Robespierre and the French Revolution is to betray historical integrity and is simply dishonest.

The Fruit of Rescue. Our Lord said, "But wisdom is justified of her children" (Matthew 11:19, NKJV).

I have had numerous pastors and countless lay people approach me saying that their own spiritual life and their church have been radically enriched by their involvement in the Rescue Movement. They are experiencing revival as they respond to God's call to repent and sacrifice.

During our times in jail (which have been few), we have experienced the greatest prayer meetings and preaching services which many of us have ever attended. The praise is vibrant; the presence of God is real; and through our witness, many inmates have been won to Christ.

Beside these blessings, there are the miraculous stories of mothers being helped and of children whose lives are saved. Hundreds of children are alive today who would otherwise be dead if not for the obedience and sacrifice of the rescuers. Would the detractors of the rescue say that these children should be dead because they were saved in an un-Biblical manner?

If this were not a move of God, it is doubtful that God would visit us with such evident and abundant blessing.

Showing Partiality to the Wicked. "God takes His stand in His own congregation; He judges in the midst of the rulers. How long will you judge unjustly and show partiality to the wicked? Vindicate the weak and fatherless; do justice to the afflicted and destitute. Rescue the weak and needy; deliver them out of the hand of the wicked" (Psalm 82:1–4). Each of these men and others who argue against rescuing children have shown partiality to their murderers. What an awful indictment.

Finally, those in the church, especially ones in leadership, who remain unsure of the moral uprightness of rescues, please, I beseech you, take Gamaliel's advice. Hold your peace for a time. Do you really want to be on record as opposing what *might* be a move of God?

13

WE ARE THE ENEMY: NO TIME FOR PRIDE

I hope this book has aroused your anger. I sincerely desire to do so. Lest, however, our denunciation of all these accessories to murder becomes too self-righteous, we must face our own horrific guilt in this holocaust. The flow of these children's blood can easily be traced to our churches, our jobs, and our homes. In short, the blood is on our hands.

We either directly support the killing industry, or we quietly ignore it, giving our silent amen to the trade in human flesh. As Scripture says, "When you spread out your hands in prayer, I will hide My eyes from you . . . Your hands are covered with blood" (Isaiah 1:15).

If we hope to ever defeat child-killing, we have to repent of our complicity with this bloodshed. That repentance must take concrete forms. First, let's expose some of the sin in our camp.

We pay taxes—federal, state, county, city—which find their way into the pockets of the largest child-killer in America, a group dedicated to the destruction of the family and the poisoning of the minds and lives of our youth. Often we pay these taxes without a peep. We fail to work to defund Planned Parenthood from the local level up. City and county governments are very vulnerable and sensitive to the desires and concerns of local citizens. If local politicians were properly educated and pressured, Planned Parenthood's funding would probably be cut. If these politicians refuse to defund the murderers at Planned Parenthood, then we must labor to elect officials who will.

Some of us carelessly give money to the United Way, who in turn gives a portion of that money to Planned Parenthood. We still use AT&T, who gives money to the National Organization for Women. We don't fight the school-based sex clinics which Planned Parenthood has sought to establish nationwide or work to prohibit their materials from reaching children in public schools. We meekly coexist with one of the most vile and hateful organizations on the face of the earth.

NOW and Feminism

We've let the anti-child, career-first, bigger houses rather than bigger families attitude creep into our churches and families. Christian homes have two working parents when only one is necessary. We deliberately limit the size of our families, viewing children as intrusions and burdens rather than as the most precious gift on earth short of salvation. We cite the justifications of money, time, and work—all the reasons the feminists have! We need to repent of the anti-child attitude in our churches and in our homes and again adopt the Biblical view of children—"Blessed is the man whose quiver is full of them!" (Psalm 127:5)

American Civil Liberties Union

We know that the ACLU is a wicked, perverse organization working for the destruction of the Judeo-Christian influence upon society in the name of freedom and justice, but we don't help their counterparts such as the Rutherford Institute or CASE (Christian Advocates Serving Evangelism), who are struggling against the bigotry and hatred of the ACLU in the courts. Unlike the ACLU, the Rutherford Institute, CASE, and other Christian law firms are drastically underfunded. If we knew how critical they were to preserving and restoring our quickly dwindling freedoms, I think we'd find a way to help them financially, especially through our churches.

Gynecologists

It always bewilders me when I learn of a Christian woman who has a baby-killer for an obstetrician-gynecologist. What in the world are we thinking? Tell him to repent and that as long as he is a murderer, he will not touch you or your babies! We let these butchers have nice, respectable practices, where child-killing is not the main source of income, right in our own neighborhoods. We need to hound these doctors, exposing them to the community until they quit child-killing. When we begin regularly arriving at the offices of Obstetrician-Gynecologists with a handful of picketers and signs reading "Smith Kills Children," "Blood money earned here," "Doctors should deliver babies, not kill them," many of these part-time killers will quit murdering children immediately.

We also use hospitals where children are butchered. Perhaps while we're having our heart checked, a baby is having its heart forever silenced down the hall or on another floor. This is gruesome reality. Boycott hospitals where children are killed! Picket them. Pressure them at board meetings and with press conferences. In this hour of crisis in hospital funding and profitability, a serious boycott may provide the financial incentive (since some serve money more than people) necessary for them to stop allowing their premises to be used for dismembering babies.

Additionally, many of us are paying for child-killing through our monthly health insurance premiums. We must thoroughly investigate our insurance companies. If so-called elective abortions are covered, if possible, we ought to drop that carrier and switch to another one that understands the value of human life.

ABC, NBC, CBS, et al.

We so often believe their lies! We're so gullible! We watch their character assassinations of religious and political leaders whom they despise, and we foolishly believe their deception. Even when we recognize their lies and distortions of the truth, we fail to call or write to complain. We don't hold them accountable for their betrayal of the babies and of truth.

Moreover, many of us continue to fill ourselves with the moral and artistic slop they feed us night after night. We let our children's minds be poisoned by this garbage, naively believing, "Oh, this is only entertainment." We ought not ignore the voices in the wilderness working to clean up this mess. Thank God for such men as Don Wildmon.

Print Media

As with the television media, we fail to properly hold newspapers accountable for their coverup of the killing. We subscribe to godless papers and believe their distortions. We actually base our opinions of godly men on the verbal character-assassinations written by these enemies of the gospel! Let's stop being so gullible!

I have been interviewed by *USA Today*, the *New York Times*, the *Washington Post*, and dozens of other papers, and I have seen firsthand how a reporter (or editor) can twist and distort the truth. I've seen facts (i.e., how many rescuers were arrested; how many pro-aborts present) so blatantly disregarded that I've wondered if this was the same event I was present at. Don't be gullible! Some of these reporters and many of their editorial boards have an agenda—keep the killing-centers open. To lie or distort in order to prop up the killing industry is a very small thing.

Courts

We allow tyrant judges and district attorneys to tyrannize people. We fail to use the First Amendment right of redress of grievances when they run roughshod over our brothers and sisters who rescue. We need to hold them accountable to God for their action and call for their resignation when they betray their trust.

We fail to investigate the views of judges and prosecutors before they are elected to office, and we fail to oppose the appointment of godless judges. By the way, conservative judges will allow you to be sued for RICO and send you to jail for trespass just as fast as liberal ones. We need judges and district attorneys who fear God.

The same applies to police chiefs and police officers. We don't take the time to confront them; we don't rock the boat; we think there's nothing we can do. We can hold their feet to the fire so they discipline unruly members. *I've seen it happen more than once, and I've seen police back off their brutal tactics.* In many cities where brutality has continued, the Christian community simply has not led the entire citizenry in a voice of outrage against the police state tactics.

These various officials need to hear from us via telephone, mail, personal visits, press conferences, picketts or prayer vigils at their office or home, and finally, at the ballot. Remember, if we tolerate the oppression of the few, we pave the way for the oppression of the many.

RCAR, et al.

The church—the mystical body of Christ—has grown afraid to denounce heretics. Only one Christian position on child-killing exists: it is murder. Anything else is damnable heresy. Yet those who hold to orthodoxy on this life-and-death issue tolerate those who believe in and promote child-killing. We remain afraid to publicly and vigorously denounce those who claim to follow Christ yet promote infant sacrifice. Our own internal weakness is a dangerous enemy.

It's time to clean house. When *Time* and *Newsweek* can quote reverends and bishops of various denominations who insist that Christianity accepts or permits child-killing—or homosexuality or adultery—without a hue and cry from the Christian community, what kind of religious wimps have we become? Why doesn't the hierarchy of these denominations attempt to excommunicate such heretics? Bishop Maher in California had the courage to deny Lucy Killea communion because of her outspoken pro-death stance. He did the right thing and encouraged many hearts by his action.

And what of those hierarchies that doctrinally support child-killing? Well, obviously they are accursed and have denied the faith. But a bigger question is, why do orthodox clergy stay in those denominations? Why do orthodox Christians and clergy remain in churches and denominations where the official church stand is pro-death? Why do we pay tithes and offerings to churches or denominations who will then use that money to actively promote the killing that we are trying so hard to stop? Is it confusion? Cowardice? Lack of spiritual clarity? A false hope that we can change the system?

Some truly well meaning Christians and clergy will clamor that this is divisive. It is. But there are some principles that demand dividing over. "Can two walk together, unless they are agreed?" (Amos 3:3, NKJV).

Would you go to a church where the pastor publicly stood for slavery or called for fidelity to Adolf Hitler and the Third Reich?

Then how can we continue in churches where the pastor is pro-death, or the denomination's official position endorses child-killing? Is it any wonder we have so little strength when we have so little conviction? If we ever hope to bury the child-killing industry, we have to first confront our own compromises and covenants with the death-merchants.

Reeds in the Wind

Numerous pastors and other Christian leaders have told me that this move of God (the Rescue Movement) is the most important spiritual move in their own lives and in the heart of the church in America in many years. Anyone who has experientially been touched by the deep calls to repentance and the picking up the cross that are at the heart of this movement can attest to the verity of these statements.

Still, a few very prominent Christian leaders have openly withstood the Rescue Movement. When well-known leaders actually denounce us for saving babies through rescues, leaders who esteem *Roe v. Wade* above the law of God, leaders who discuss whether it is appropriate to rescue slaves from slavery or whether it would be right to hide a fleeing pastor from Stalin, is it any wonder the moral fiber of the church is like worn-out cardboard? With pillars of jello as our respected elders, how can we contend with a movement in league with hell, whose leaders are in deadly earnest to promote death and to tear the heart out of Christianity in America?

We need to mourn and pray for the state of the spiritual leadership in America. Many shepherds have covenanted with death by their refusal to stop the killing or by denouncing those who do try to stop the killing. This is undoubtedly paving the way for further oppression of the church and Christian families. The tragedy is that while many shepherds have led Christians astray in America, those Christians will still bear the brunt of God's judgment, as well as the shepherds who deceived them (see Jeremiah 23:1–5). God will not excuse us because we allowed some deceived or deceiving minister to tickle our itching ears.

Christian Media

We need more guts, more raw courage. We must not squander our resources out of fear. Those in the visual media must continue to show the carnage—the decimated bodies of the children—regardless of whom it offends!

Moreover, we must stop worrying about offending the powers that be by telling them the truth. If they are godless enemies of Christ, let us say so. If they have compromised and made covenants with death, we must say so. For example, when a pro-life president campaigns for promoters of murder to maintain unity in his party, he reveals the shallowness of his convictions. Those of us in Christian media must say so and call on him to repent of his betrayal of the children. When Lee Atwater says, "The Republican Party is big enough for people on both sides of this issue," we need to denounce such folly. He reveals not only the shallowness of his pro-life commitment but also the weakness of his leadership. The committed core of the Republican Party is die-hard pro-life. He is jeopardizing his whole party, and we need to let him know.

The Problem Is with Us!

We have rejected, or at least forgotten, Biblical Christianity, which has a cross for all to bear. We have exchanged it for a crossless and self-serving Christianity. God has called us to be the salt of the earth; but having lost our savor, we're now being trampled under the foot of men.

Yes, we've traded an aggressive, storm-the-gates-of-hell Christianity for a passive, cowardly, let's-make-a-deal-with-the-enemy religion. Like the men of Jabesh-Gilead, we're willing to sell our children into slavery rather than sacrifice and fight. We accommodate those whom we should withstand to the teeth. We confuse love your enemy with roll-over-and-play-dead. Most tragically, we're trading our children's future freedoms and welfare for our current comfort and ease.

We've loved and coveted material blessings more than self-sacrifice and pleasing God. We've become undisciplined, unholy, selfish, prayerless, Sunday morning pot-luck Christians, who have stood by while our culture has slid into hell.

If this description doesn't fit you—if you're one who sighs and cries for our abomination and has sacrificed to stop the flow of wickedness, I trust you won't be mad. "For God is not unjust so as to forget your work and the love which you have shown toward His name, in having ministered and still ministering to the saints" (Hebrews 6:10). He who has seen what you have done in secret will reward you openly.

If this description does fit you, I hope you do get mad—at yourself and the devil. It is not enough that you pay your tithes and keep from theft or adultery. Do you sigh and cry over the abominations that fill our nation? (see Ezekiel 9:4). Do you grieve over the ruin of Joseph (see Amos 6:6)? What have you done to rescue this nation from the path of destruction it is on? What have you done to rescue even one child from murder?

Conclusion

We must know our enemies. We must identify and work against those who hate God and love death. We must stop those bent on silencing the church before they succeed.

We must do all this, but first we must repent. We must cry out to God for His mercy and forgiveness for the horrendous ways we have betrayed Him and His Word, made agreements with our enemies, and allowed godless philosophies to dominate our homes and churches. We've got to stop holding the hands that wield the murderer's knife. We've got to privately and publicly clean house concerning ministers, churches, and denominations that support child-killing. We need to face the hard truth that, in our current state of apathy and compromise, we are the enemy.

PART FIVE

THE ALTERNATIVE

14

THE CHRISTIAN MEDIA

O peration Rescue's first major activity in Cherry Hill, New Jersey, our pilot run, was bearing down on us. We approached Thanksgiving weekend in 1987 rushing about, making phone calls, checking last minute details, estimating how many rescuers would participate, and contacting Christian media.

The Christian news outlet that I believed was most critical to reach was *The 700 Club*. After numerous press releases and several phone calls, we learned that they had committed to send a camera crew to cover the event. We were elated. Only now do I realize truly how critical their presence and the press coverage of several other Christian periodicals was to the growth of the Rescue Movement. If the Christian media had not covered Cherry Hill and then New York, most of the body of Christ in America would not have even known Operation Rescue existed, because the secular press did all they could to ignore us. For example, on the same day that nearly three hundred pro-lifers blocked Cherry Hill's Women's Center in the largest rescue up until that time with over two hundred arrested, a GI Joe plant was picketed by an anti-war group. A national secular radio outlet covered the GI Joe picket but chose to blatantly ignore the arrests of hundreds of pro-lifers. That was typical in those days.

Showing the Truth

The Christian media, including television, periodicals, and radio stations, have been the only news source with the integrity to consistently expose the abortion holocaust. While Dan Rather and the *New York Times* have steadfastly refused to show the American public the truth about child-killing, the Christian media have been a beacon of truth with the guts and integrity to show the victims of abortion.

Many Christians received their first exposure to the bloody and vicious reality of child-killing through photographs in a religious periodical, film footage on a Christian television program, or gruesome descriptions on Christian radio. We must thank God for the Christian media who have shown and told the truth to the American public.

To be sure, some feared offending constituents with the graphic nature of the subject and watered down their coverage. Nevertheless, without the Christian media, the plight of the children and the exploitation of mothers would be far more ignored and distorted than it is now.

This holds true with news on other issues as well. Many of us know the value of Marlin Maddoux's "Point of View," the USA Radio Network, Family News in Focus, and other Christian outlets in presenting the whole truth through a Christian perspective.

Showing the Rescues

Not only have the Christian media informed the Christian community about the Rescue Movement; their continued coverage is vital to the health, life, and growth of the Movement. As *millions of Christians* have watched this growing movement and heard the message of repentance and judgment we face because of our shedding of innocent blood, thousands have joined the ranks of those risking arrest for the children. Moreover, *tens of thousands* have been freshly invigorated or newly involved in pro-life activism in other arenas such as picketing, sidewalk counseling, crisis pregnancy centers, and the political process. *Hundreds of pastors* and *thousands of believers* have testified of revival in their lives—of a new depth and meaning to their Christianity. Obviously, all of this cannot be attributed solely to Christian media; but God knows how crucial Christian media have been to resounding the Word of the Lord in this hour. I shudder to think how much worse our nation would be without them.

Exposed Injustice

We've seen how the secular media have systematically ignored or distorted the police brutality and courtroom injustices faced by the rescuers. In contrast, most elements of the Christian media have sought to expose this tyranny. For example, had Christian media not exposed and raised a voice of outrage against the sexual harassment and molestation of Christian women in Pittsburgh's jail, the whole incident may have quietly been forgotten or, at least, ignored by the authorities.

Likewise, the Christian media played a key role in our release from custody in Los Angeles in March 1989. Because of the Los Angeles Police Department's injustice, we had already spent the entire Easter weekend in jail. The Christian television and radio stations, however, began reporting on the injustices we were suffering and releasing the phone numbers of the appropriate authorities. The Christian community then exercised their right to redress of grievances and demanded our release. It worked. We were all released without posting bail; false felony charges against four of us were dropped; and everyone without identification was released. Many such incidences have occurred in the past two years.

The money you spend in subscriptions and donations to the Christian media who have told the truth, exposed this holocaust, and covered pro-life activism is well spent.

A Pro-Life Media Tragedy

In stark contrast to the upright news coverage given the Rescue Movement by the Christian media stands the National Right to Life's publication, *NRL News*. They champion this periodical as the pro-life journal of record, yet they have blacked-out all Rescue activities. The evident problem manifested itself during Joan Andrew's incarceration in Florida. *NRL News* never once mentioned her incarceration and the accompanying injustices.

Since the dawn of Operation Rescue, our name and activities have graced the pages of *NRL News* only once. Dr. Jack Wilke used his editorial column to attack us and to argue that the man-hours invested in O.R. were ill spent—that we should be working to elect George Bush. (We were working to elect Bush. It is our contention that O.R.'s activities in 1988 did more to hurt Dukakis on child-killing and help Bush than anything else we could have done.)

Frankly, it is more than a disgrace; it is a tragedy that *NRL News* reports only NRLC news. (This wouldn't be so bad if they didn't call themselves the pro-life paper of record.) They have lifted a faint voice of protest, saying that they fear RICO lawsuits. Reporting news, however, is not endorsement or conspiracy. No other news organizations—secular or religious—has been sued for simply reporting O.R. activities. The reasons go far deeper than that.

Room for Improvement

With all the praise I have given Christian media, I would be amiss if I didn't mention a few areas where improvements could be made.

Cover Child-killing More

Many Christian media outlets have at times slid back to covering child-killing a few times a year or even just once a year, usually around January 22, the anniversary of the Roe v. Wade decision. This is sad. Isn't it news that over four thousand babies were murdered today—and yesterday? It shows how calloused we have become to the murdered children, having lived alongside this holocaust for so long.

For example, if four hundred or forty or even four children were killed every day in a schoolyard by some lunatic, wouldn't this constitute a newsworthy story every day?

There's little doubt that it would. Well, not only four or forty or four hundred but over four thousand children die every day at the hands of ruthless, hired murderers. Isn't this newsworthy? We must keep reporting and denouncing the daily murder of children, even if it is only a small portion of the news. The Christian community must perpetually be reminded of this holocaust; we owe it to the children to remember their death (and our shame).

Moreover, we need to show the victims of this holocaust more often. It struck me over a year ago that O.R. was a pro-life organization, yet publications regularly left our office that did not show the victims. I then made a commitment that every mailing sent from our office would show a victim of abortion. That's why we're here—to stop babies from being murdered and to expose the crimes against them.

A few will complain that such pictures are gruesome (which they are) and should therefore not be shown. But that is a head-in-the-sand mentality that helps us forget the offensive reality in which we are entrenched—dead babies. Some publishers and editors may be afraid of offending a few of their constituents. Take warning. Do not placate a few complainers at the cost of ignoring innocent children. We must be confronted with what is happening in order to provoke our hardened hearts and lives to action. When Eisenhower liberated concentration camps, he instructed the media to film the atrocities which they discovered and to broadcast the footage back in the United States. He understood the necessity of graphically confronting individuals with the reality of man's own inhumanity to man.

Be Bolder

Here's another challenge. Don't worry so much about offending the powers that be. For example, if a pro-life president (or any politician) such as Ronald Reagan or George Bush campaigns for a pro-death politician (as both have), we must speak out loudly against their hypocrisy and betrayal of the children. If they don't like it—too bad—they should not be campaigning for those who promote the murder of innocent children.

Likewise, when Lee Atwater-types publicly comment, "The Republican Party has room for people with both views [pro-life and pro-death]," our editorials and broadcasts should expose and denounce the wickedness of such compromise. Those who are registered Republicans should make it clear that they are committed to principle, not party, and that such compromise with death will lead only to large-scale defections of the voting electorate from the Republican Party.

Protecting Pro-Lifers

Even though the Christian media has been a blessing in exposing and speaking out against injustice, oppression, and tyranny toward rescuers, the trend is moving away from this. At first a cry went up if we spent two days in jail—and justifiably so. It is an outrage that someone would spend one minute in jail for trying to stop murder. However, as the stakes have gone up from two days to two weeks to two months to two years, the outcry against this tyranny has actually diminished rather than increased. This is suicidal.

Could it be that the same hardening of hearts that has happened toward the babies is occurring towards those who rescue babies? Could it be that it's just not "news" anymore? I'm not sure, but I'm terrified of the long-range danger this hardening poses to the whole church and to our children.

Take warning. To quietly tolerate the oppression of the few is to prepare the way for the oppression of the many. Yes, if we silently stand by while our brethren are being tortured, we prepare the way for our own torture. The Christian media must not become an unwitting partner in the coming oppression of the many because it ceased to protest the oppression of the few. Please, brethren, whether you have a newsletter with a circulation of five hundred or a television show that reaches five million, heed Paul's admonition, "Remember those in chains—as if mistreated with them" (Hebrews 13:3).

Moreover, cry out against the tyranny of police brutality and the imprisonment of Christians for trying to stop murder. Cry out against these unjust, crippling lawsuits. Cry out in your editorials. Release the phone numbers and addresses of the guilty government officials and encourage people to call, write, or picket in opposition to these injustices. Mobilize people to action.

We sit and marvel as we watch "people power" in the Philippines and in Eastern Europe. We rejoice over Romania's deliverance. Do *we* have to endure four decades of hell before we rise up to stop tyranny at home? We certainly possess the media resources required to mobilize opposition to the oppression in our own land. We just have to use them!

If we fail to act, however, we will train the church to harden their hearts to their imprisoned brethren. Then, when home-schoolers, Christian school principals, and pastors are imprisoned for their obedience to other Biblical beliefs, who will cry out? We will have become accustomed to our own oppression and set ourselves up for disaster. Then, when the oppressors silence you, who will speak out?

THE RESCUE MOVEMENT

S moke filled the air, and blaring rock music filled my ears; a dim light filtered through the bars of the nicotine-stained windows and lit the dingy cell block. My emotions went the gammut: at times I felt like a caged animal; other times I felt like a triumphant warrior for the truth. Those are some of the most memorable times in my life—sharing Christ with hurting inmates, reading my Bible, praying, and thinking, thinking, *thinking.* It was March 1986.

During one of those moments of noisy solitude, a single verse leapt off the page: Judges 5:2. Then the entire chapter followed. My imagination raced excitedly. Peering through those verses in my mind's eye, I envisioned a mass movement springing into existence seemingly from nowhere. I saw clergy leading courageously by example; there were thousands of Christians and other pro-lifers joining the fray, filling the streets, rescuing children. The target year was 1988.

In that hour, Operation Rescue was conceived in my heart. Many thanks are due to Judge Hillis, who sentenced me to thirty days in jail after I refused to pay a sixty-dollar fine. Some may ask, what exactly are Operation Rescue and the much broader Rescue Movement? Is this simply civil disobedience as some claim?[1] Is it a Marxist tactic, as others insist?[2]

No. This is a life-saving, repentance-based move of God. Let me give a brief history of rescue missions.

History of Direct Action

Long before Operation Rescue, courageous people were peacefully blocking access to killing centers with their bodies in order to rescue the innocent. Joan Andrews, John Ryan, Tom Herlihy, George Grant, John Cavanaugh-O'Keefe, and many others were involved as early as 1970.

These rescues were called sit-ins, interventions, nonviolent direct action, and finally rescue missions. The primary emphases of the direct action movement were

- Rescuing children from murder;

- Preventing mothers from being exploited; and

- Adding political clout and credibility to our rhetoric. Abortion is murder.

These emphases are critical, and those who sacrificed their freedom and reputation long before Operation Rescue are to be applauded for their courage. God knows the example they have been to me.

Operation Rescue and what is now referred to as the Rescue Movement have added three more emphases to those already mentioned, thus differentiating itself from the Direct Action Movement.[3] I believe that these emphases are the driving forces behind the incredible growth of this movement. They are:

- Repentance and obedience to God;

- The determined involvement of clergy, and

- The vested interest of the rescuer.

From my perspective, the immediate motivation to rescue and the long-term goals of the Rescue Movement are derived from these six emphases and a firm foundation of repentance. So, let's examine each of them individually.

Saving Children

This is the immediate reason for a rescue mission: a fellow human being, made in the image of God, is about to be murdered. As we have seen, those who ignore the child know nothing of the Rescue

Movement. When we block access to a killing center, we are neither protesting nor practicing civil disobedience; we are protecting defenseless human beings.

We understand (better than most) that ultimately we are buying time for the child by preventing the mother from fulfilling her death wish. Tragically, many, if not most, of those children scheduled to die on the day of a rescue are executed in an abortion at a later date. Nevertheless, the lives of many children are spared because of the time we bought for their mothers.

Our sidewalk counselors plead for the child's life with every pregnant mother arriving at the abortion mill to have her baby killed. They may take her to a restaurant or a pro-life counseling center to offer her whatever assistance she may need—medical, housing, adoption alternatives, and so forth. In this manner hundreds of women have changed their minds and given birth to beautiful children. We recently received a note from a woman who was thus spared the nightmare of a dead baby.

> To All at Operation Rescue,
>
> There are really no words to express how I feel. "Thank You" is, well—it just doesn't seem to be enough. I will never be able to repay you. . . . How can I? The gift of life is priceless! I want to say one very important thing—Please—don't ever give up. What you are doing has saved at least 1 unborn child; this I know for a fact. Her name is Nicole, she is five months old. I know that it is because of your efforts she is here. How do I know? You see—I am her mother, a very proud one at that. I love being a mother—thanks to you I now have the chance to say that.

In addition to those who have talked to our counselors, many others have come to the abortuary, seen the hundreds of rescuers and dozens of police officers, and returned home without discussing their situation with anyone. Then in the recesses of their own hearts, they decided to let their child live and never returned to the mill. Thank God!

We grieve for those children who die despite our efforts. At times, I feel like we are firemen who rush into a burning building full of children trapped inside. We're able to rescue some, but many others perish in the fire. We're thankful for the ones we saved, but we mourn for the loss of the others.

The Mother

Under the current state of law, the mother is in many ways a second victim. She is pressured by her boyfriend or family into killing the child. She is lied to by abortion mill employees and told "it's not a baby but a blob of tissue." The procedure is described as "a gentle suctioning" with little or no side affects.[4] These women, many young and vulnerable, are wantonly deceived.

The fruit of these lies is evident. Women are experiencing the living hell of nightmares, depression, guilt, and self-hatred, which has come to be known as "post-abortion syndrome"[5] in addition to physical complications including infections, hemorrhages, lacerated and perforated uteri, miscarriages, premature births, infertility, hysterectomies, and even death. God only knows how many hundreds have committed suicide to escape the haunting guilt.

Even the abortionists' literature confesses to these complications (in the fine print, of course). Most killing centers actually require mothers to sign a waiver before she is allowed to go under the killer's knife. The waiver clears the abortionist of any wrongdoing should the woman experience a perforated uterus, require an emergency hysterectomy or even die. The killers know that legal child-killing does not mean safe child-killing. Our rescue efforts, therefore, are also efforts to protect women from being exploited.[6]

Political Clout

For so many years, those in the pro-life movement had been saying abortion is murder and then writing a letter or carrying a sign once a year at a march. If you were about to be murdered, I'm sure you would want me to do more than write your congressman! We were thus suffering a serious credibility crisis. So, direct action and, in particular, the Rescue Movement of the late eighties and early nineties has added tremendous political clout to the entire pro-life movement. We are acting, to some degree, as if abortion is really murder. The logical response to murder is to physically intervene on behalf of the victim.

Politicians have therefore taken notice; they understand that we mean business. Someone wisely said, "Politicians don't see the light until after they feel the heat." The Rescue Movement is causing many to feel that heat now.

Repentance

At its heart, the message of Operation Rescue is very simple: repent, repent, repent. We must repent of the apathy that has allowed child-killing to flourish; of the selfishness so deep that we have stood idly by while babies have been slaughtered; of our dead religion. We must repent of exalting the laws of men above the laws of God and, finally, for our refusal to pick up our cross and to follow Jesus.

The holocaust is our fault as well as the abortionist's. Child-killing is still here because we *let* it remain. We've failed to be the salt of the earth and the light of the world. We must repent of hiding in our churches while babies have been butchered, of basking in our comfort zones while children need our help in the danger zone. We share in the guilt of their blood for we stood idly by while we knew they were being killed.

Most individuals who have spoken out against rescues have never attended a rescue or a pre-rescue rally. If they had done so, they would have heard a stirring call to repentance. They would have seen the hundreds and hundreds of Christians crying out to God, asking for His forgiveness for our sins of apathy and selfishness and pleading with Him for mercy on our nation. They would hear Christians acknowledging that the blood is on our hands (see Isaiah 1:15). In fact, the church in America has so little power and so little authority because of the blood-guilt under which we live and labor.[7]

The Clergy

"As goes the shepherd, so go the sheep." This is simple reality and Biblical truth. Pastors (Protestant, Roman Catholic and Orthodox) have a God-ordained responsibility to guard the flock and to lead by example.

I believe that failure of the pro-life movement in many of its objectives is due to a failure by many pro-lifers to honor (or even understand) the pastoral office. Many pro-lifers acknowledge the *tactical* need for clergy; they can recruit many new troops, but fail to understand the *spiritual authority* and, hence, responsibility God has given them. Pastors hesitate to lead their flocks into unchartered waters, and rightly so. They need to know if the cause is of God and if the leaders (local, state, and national) are godly men and women. Beyond this, a thousand different programs clamor for their attention, seek their blessing, and insist on their participation. It's all too easy for a pastor to set aside requests from unknown organizations and people or from those whom he believes are merely trying to use him and his influence.

A primary contributor to the Rescue Movement's rapid growth has been the deliberate and determined efforts of Operation Rescue and other such groups to honor pastoral authority and to integrate pastoral leadership at every level. In fact, in many cities the key leaders *are pastors*. Thank God. They are not just giving tacit approval but are wholeheartedly leading the way. This helps invoke and secures the blessing of God. "That the leaders led in Israel, that the people volunteered, bless the Lord."[8] For the most part, however, the pastoral community has miserably failed in its divine duty to defend the defenseless and to protect the fatherless (see Psalm 82:1–4).

One main reason is the faulty heritage we have received. Many clergy have been trained, explicitly and implicitly, to ignore social issues and to focus on spiritual needs. James reveals the fallacy of this training: "This is pure and undefiled religion in the sight of our God and Father, to visit orphans and widows in their distress, and to keep oneself unstained by the world" (James 1:27). If we fail to help the helpless, we are betraying our spiritual duties. Furthermore, in a desire to build a safe and comfortable congregation, many clergy are taught to avoid controversial issues—as if following a Man who claimed to be God wasn't controversial!

Thus, the call for clergy to repent has rung loud and clear in the house of the Lord and, thankfully, has borne much fruit. Hundreds of pastors have rescued and been arrested; and scores have been jailed for days and even weeks. This is arguably the most ardent street-level activism from the clergy since the Abolitionist Movement and, perhaps, since the American Revolution.

If the church is to awaken and repent, if America is to be restored and saved from the annihilation of God's judgment, an even greater move of God must occur among the clergy. By God's grace, though, we have good beginnings; and the prophet challenges us, "Do not despise this small beginning" (Zechariah 4:10, TLB).

The Vested Interest of the Rescuer

While many of us rescue as the fruit of our repentance and to save the lives of innocent children, many of us also possess a righteously selfish motivation. *We're acting on behalf of our own children and their futures.* We understand the imminent danger we face as a nation. God could at any time severely chasten us because of the blood that cries from the ground for vengeance.

If God brings calamities upon our economy or in our military defense, we and our children surely will suffer. Moreover, if the United States continues her plunge into cruelty and moral anarchy, where will it end? Pro-lifers have already endured severe police brutality, sexual molestation, lengthy prison sentences, harassing lawsuits; what's next? Our children may have to stand for truth and justice at the cost of their blood. As frightening as it is, we are one bullet chamber away from a Tienanmen Square here in America. We don't want our children coming home to us in a coffin in ten or twenty years, so we continue to sacrifice and to stand for righteousness *now*.

The Rescue Movement Defined

The Rescue Movement goes far beyond saving children and even beyond ending child-killing altogether. Our extended goals include

- Rescuing our very nation from self-destruction;
- Giving God a reason to remember mercy in the midst of judgment;
- Rescuing the future for our children; and
- Being part of revival in the church and reformation in our culture.

The defeat of child-killing will be the first victory in a series of victories.

If we can crush legalized child-killing, we could have the momentum and manpower to restore uprightness and integrity to our government, to wipe out child-pornography and deglorify other sexual perversions, to reform our public education system, to reform our prison and judicial systems, and to clean up television and the entertainment industry. Some changes will occur legislatively, others by popular consensus. In whatever manner it occurs, this reformation will cause America to better reflect Judeo-Christian ethics in her laws and cultural norms—a reflection she possessed as recently as the 1950s.

The Catalyst

Child-killing is the flashpoint, the main battle front to which the divine trumpet is calling. (There are many critical battle fronts on which we must fight; but this is the most critical at this juncture because of the principle of shed innocent blood.)[9] Those placing their bodies on the line are the front-line troops. They are indispensable. We cannot win the war without them. But they are not enough. To crush the abortion holocaust (and ultimately reform our culture) we need an all-out assault on child-killing from every angle. Thus, child-killing cannot be ended by rescues alone; but it could never be stopped without them.

Moreover, the Rescue Movement has provided the dedication, sacrifice, excitement, and stoutness of heart that motivates people to fight for change. Countless pastors and laypeople can testify to their revival and the life-changing experiences they've experienced as they stood for the innocent. They can recount the incredible experience of blocking the gates of hell, singing and praying. They tell of their awesome times behind bars: the incredible prayer meetings and anointed preaching which followed their arrests and jailings for trying to stop murder.

The real-life battle experiences of rescue have transformed thousands of pew-sitting, comfortable, and often self-centered Christians into individuals ready to lay down their lives for the King of Kings, for His truth and justice. I've watched pro-lifers go into jail for a few days soft and flabby in their hearts and come out with fire in their eyes and a forehead of flint. The Rescue Movement has been an incredible spiritual boot camp. It's no wonder the death industry is terrified of rescuers; they are a truly frightening unit of troops!

Our enemies, however, are not going to give up without a serious fight. They recognize far better than our own constituents that this is a fight to the finish. We intend to annihilate child-killing from our culture. No exceptions, no compromise. They want to continue slaying children on the altar of self-determination, to crush the Rescue Movement beneath the heel of judicial tyranny, and to stamp out virtually every vestige of Christianity from our laws, morals, institutions, and, ultimately, our families. Child-killing is not just another issue. It is the fiercest battle in a war of ideologies and allegiances. Who is Lord—Caeser or Christ? Will God's or man's law prevail on the earth? Will life be honored as sacred or discarded as trash? In this great conflict for our nation's soul, there will only be one winner.

The Choices

Either America will continue its plunge into cruelty and moral and legal anarchy, bringing forth the continued slaughter of millions of children, the effectual silencing of the church, and the divine judgment of our culture; or we will rise up with stout hearts and wills and turn back the enemy right now, before it's too late.

Winston Churchill spoke these profound prophetic words:

> Still, if you will not fight for the right when you can easily win without bloodshed; if you will not fight when your victory will be sure and not too costly; you may come to the moment when you will have to fight with all the odds against you and only a precarious chance of survival. There may even be a worse case. You may have to fight when there is no hope of victory, because it is better to perish than live as slaves.[10]

16

TURNING THE TIDE OF INJUSTICE

The Rescue Movement has brought Christians into direct contact (and often confrontation) with several categories of "public servants" whose primary duty is to uphold justice and to protect the well-being of America:

- prosecutors,

- police departments,

- judges,

- prison officials, and

- politicians (mayors, city councilmen, governors, and state assemblymen).

Many of these officials (but not all, thank God) have shown themselves to be ardent protectors of child-killers and the death industry. We have exposed the corruption and injustice that resides in these various offices. Or as a dear friend of mine has said, "we've brought the dragon out of its lair." How are they going to lead this country in uprightness and justice if they are determined to preserve the child-killing industry?

I believe God has given us an opportunity to beat a familiar path to the door of these officials that will help bring justice in other areas at a later time. It should be standard procedure for us to hold judges and prosecutors accountable. We should be accustomed to demanding uprightness and justice from politicians. Now that our brethren are being mistreated by these elements, we have a strong motivation and responsibility to confront these officials with their defense of child-killers and persecution of believers.

Once we begin to regularly hold them accountable in this area, we will naturally do so in other critical areas as well, such as pornography, sex offenses, drugs, government corruption, and "homosexual rights." This is critical if we ever hope to reform this culture. Leaders must have a healthy respect and indeed a fear of the people of God. Presently, they view us as a paper tiger, as a tolerated annoyance at best and as a joke at worst. Unfortunately, we have given them ample justification to hold that opinion.

That, however, could change quickly if, like Saul, we became so enraged at the oppression of God's people that we fought to throw off this yoke. Abuse against fellow Christians should awaken the Church to the dangers we all face and motivate us to action.

It is a tragedy and a sign of horrible callousness that much of the Church has grown accustomed to child-killing. We don't like it; we may even hate it; but we tolerate it. We have lived alongside this gruesome crime for so long that we have hardened our hearts against fighting to end it. This is a grievous sin—the height of selfishness—and we must repent.

There is hope. The images of fellow Christians suffering brutality at the hands of godless police and the reports of prison abuses and lengthy jail sentences have sparked new flames of anger and motivation. I believe this is providential. If we tolerate the oppression of the few, we pave the way for the oppression of the many. If the Church stands idly by while some of its members are victims of tyranny, she is preparing the way for her own demise.

The Front Lines

Many in the church have had kind words for the Rescue Movement, especially those being arrested and jailed. Many have said we are fighting on the front lines.

If this is true—if we are truly the front-liners, the shock troops of the church—than the whole church had better awaken and be forewarned.

An enemy army treats those captured on the front lines just as it intends to treat the whole army. If the godless and corrupted men of this nation (some undoubtedly demonically inspired) have treated the front-liners of the church with such brazen injustice, what do you think awaits the rest of the church? Jesus said, "If men do these things when the tree is green, what will happen when it is dry?" (Luke 23:31, NIV). If you have stood mute while babies have been murdered, and then as our brethren have been brutalized, arrested, and jailed in their defense, who will speak up for you when you are hunted?

Most of us know the quote from Martin Niemoller, but I don't believe we grasp what a terrifying epitaph of defeat it is.

> In Germany, they came first for the Communists, and I didn't speak up because I wasn't a Communist. Then they came for the Jews, and I didn't speak up because I wasn't a Jew. Then they came for the trade unionists, and I didn't speak up because I wasn't a trade unionist. Then they came for the Catholics, and I didn't speak up because I was a Protestant. Then they came for me and by that time no one was left to speak up.

The leopard is at our throats. When will we awake?

> For death has come up through our windows;
> It has entered our palaces
> To cut off the children from the streets,
> The young men from the town squares. (Jeremiah 9:21)

The demonic and human enemies of God are bent on death and will not stop with unborn children. History teaches us that they will not stop anywhere until they are stopped by force.

The Covenant of Silence. During Hitler's regime and later in eastern European nations under Stalin's thumb, many pastors knew that innocent people—often their brethren—were being oppressed, but they chose to ignore the tyranny. They had made a "covenant of silence" with their oppressors in the hope that they would be spared: "You can brutalize my brethren; and I won't try to stop you or speak out against you." Their cowardice and compromise did not squelch the injustice; it paved the way for their own demise and the death and oppression of millions of people. I fear we, especially the clergy, are making the same mistake.

The poisonous axiom of life—"If it doesn't affect me and mine, I don't want to know"—will be our undoing. By the time it does affect you and yours, it will be too late. We must speak up now!

Being a Prisoner for Christ. Being a prisoner for a faith in Christ is undoubtedly a great blessing, both for the prisoner and for the body of Christ.

Concerning the body, Paul commented, ". . . and that most of the brethren, trusting in the Lord because of my imprisonment, have far more courage to speak the word of God without fear" (Philippians 1:14). He told the Ephesians, "Therefore I ask you not to lose heart at my tribulations on your behalf, for they are your glory" (Ephesians 3:13). To the Colossians he wrote, "Now I rejoice in my sufferings for your sake, and in my flesh I do my share on behalf of His body (which is the church) in filling up that which is lacking in Christ's afflictions" (Colossians 1:24).

Finally, Paul admonished Timothy,

> Remember Jesus Christ, risen from the dead, descendant of David, according to my gospel, for which I suffer hardship even to imprisonment as a criminal; but the word of God is not imprisoned. For this reason I endure all things for the sake of those who are chosen, that they also may obtain the salvation which is in Christ Jesus and with it eternal glory. (2 Timothy 2:8–10)

When Christians are arrested and jailed for Christ, it releases heavenly virtue for the rest of the body. It emboldens believers and keeps the body in fellowship with the sufferings of Christ. We all want to know the power of the Resurrection, but we must also know the fellowship of his sufferings (see Philippians 3:9). For some of us, that means incarceration. Prisoners can also experience great blessings as they witness for God to the inmates and guards (see Philippians 1:13, Ephesians 6:20) and offer up many prayers, which undoubtedly take on a fragrance of their own in the heavenlies.

In addition, the lonely hours produce tear-filled prayers for family. The challenge to love our captors and other inmates and to always honor God leads one to deep soul searching and healthy introspection with intense prayers for God to purge us from unrighteous anger, hatred, and all that is unlike Him.

The Scriptures come alive as God graciously opens our hungry hearts to receive His eternal truth. Sections dealing with imprisonment and protection from danger finally make sense. I have always loved the psalms, but some of them have exploded with meaning for me during my incarceration. Times of prayer are animated with the presence of God; and His comfort in deep, heartaching hours is a precious, priceless experience (which, of course, can be experienced out of jail, as well).

What Prisoners Hope For

The desires of prisoners are simple and few. They pray and hope that their families are well and taken care of and that they will be there for them when they get out. They want friends to visit them, and they yearn for letters and cards through the mail. They hope the basic needs of their prison lives will be met. Most of all, *they want to be out of jail with their families* and earnestly desire for people to work to get them out. They don't want to be *forgotten*.

Thus, the solemn duty of the Church is to obey God's command, "Remember the Christian prisoners—as if mistreated with them." Let me go over some of the practical and Biblical ways in which we must remember them.

We Must Pray for Them. Pray for their safety, for boldness to preach the Gospel, and for their release (see Ephesians 6:18–20, Philemon 22, Philippians 1:19–26).

We Must Visit Them. Christ views this as visiting Him (see Matthew 25:36–40). Likewise He views not visiting them as abandoning Him (see Matthew 25:43–45). (Be sure to check visiting schedules so that you do not interrupt a visit of a husband or a wife.) One cannot imagine the joy of seeing a Christian minister or layman after being locked away, often with men or women who don't love God.

Scripture says that, after Paul landed in Italy and began his journey to Rome, "the brethren. . . came. . . as far as Appii Forum and Three Inns. When Paul saw them, he thanked God and took courage" (Acts 28:15, NKJV). I can imagine Paul's situation. He was lonely, perhaps a little discouraged, and troubled about his upcoming trial. He then saw the brethren and rejoiced, bowing his head in earnest thanks to God and praying, "Thank you, Lord Jesus. You knew I needed this. Thank you." Paul then received fresh courage from their fellowship.

We Must Provide for the Prisoners' Needs. When Paul received the gift from the Philippians, he said,

> But I rejoiced . . . greatly, that now at last your care for me has flourished again. . . . [Y]ou have done well that you shared in my distress . . . Indeed I have all and abound. I am full, having received from Epaphroditus the things sent from you, a sweet-smelling aroma, an acceptable sacrifice, well pleasing to God. (Philippians 4:10, 14, 18)

Their gifts to him in prison were seen as sacred acts of worship to God. During his second imprisonment, he wrote Timothy, "The Lord grant mercy to the house of Onesiphorus for he often refreshed me, and was not ashamed of my chains; but when he was in Rome, he eagerly searched for me and found me" (2 Timothy 1:17). He later said, "Bring the cloak that I left at Troas with Carpus, and the books, especially the parchments" (2 Timothy 4:13). I know from experience how invaluable the Scriptures and Christian books are in jail, as well as the blessing of proper clothing ("the cloak"). Gifts of such everyday items as socks, underwear, simple toiletries or, perhaps, a tape player can be tremendously encouraging. (During this imprisonment, a "walkman" tape player has blessed me greatly, drowning out the yelling of my fellow inmates and the noise of the television and even helping me to write this book!)

This principle of providing for prisoners in jail extends to their families. Many American Christian prisoners (as well as tens of thousands overseas) have lost their jobs as a result of their imprisonment for Christ. The body of Christ has the burden (and privilege) of providing for them and their families in the interim. This responsibility falls primarily on the local churches in that area. Collectively, we have a duty to help the families of overseas prisoners. Many children have starved to death or died from exposure while daddy was in prison because of laws prohibiting assistance to the families of "political prisoners."

We Must Pray for Their Release; but We Must Also Work for Their Release. Believe me, if you were in jail for any length of time, you would want to be released. Joseph fervently sought his own release, pleading with Pharoah's cupbearer to remember him and get him out. Although it took two years, it was ultimately the cupbearer who got Joseph out (see Genesis 40:14, 15; 41:9–14). Jeremiah likewise spoke up for himself and warned his captors of God's judgment (see Jeremiah 26:14, 15). When a mob rose up to kill him, he petitioned the king not to be returned to Jonathan's prison house, "lest I die there." The king granted his request, and he was held in the court of the prison (see Jeremiah 37:18–20).

We see in the Scriptures that "insiders" helped alter the sentences of "righteous criminals." By "insiders" I mean those in the same sphere of influence with the ruling powers. Jonathan delivered David from death at the hand of his father, Saul (see 1 Samuel 19:1–7). As I already pointed out, Joseph's release was secured by an attendant closest to Pharoah. When Jeremiah was facing death at the hand of an angry mob, the elders of the people rose to his defense and delivered him (see Jeremiah 26:1–19, 24). Furthermore, when Jeremiah was lowered into a mud pit and faced death again, Ebed-Melech the Ethiopian went to the king on his behalf and had him placed in the court of the prison (again!) (see Jeremiah 38:4–13). Similarly, when the Pharisees discussed killing the apostles, Gamiliel, himself a Pharisee, dissuaded them; the apostles were instead only beaten and released (see Acts 5:33–40).

Lest, however, you think you're off the hook if you're not an insider, think again! Scripture teaches of the importunate widow who, though she had no influence and though her judge feared neither God nor men, prevailed in her request for justice simply because she persisted (see Luke 18:1–5). When the temple guards arrested the apostles they did so with the utmost professionalism, afraid that the people would stone them in defense of the apostles (see Acts 5:26). When Saul intended to have Jonathan killed because he had broken a royal edict, the people rose up and delivered Jonathan, again; and the sentence was altered (see 1 Samuel 14:24–30, 43–45).

I have seen this principle again and again with imprisoned rescuers in American jails. When "insiders" or the "general public" spoke up in defense of the Christians, they were released from custody, pending trials, or their sentences were reduced.

This type of public outcry against police brutality in Atlanta in October 1988 forced the police to act professionally. If locals around the country would cry out against police brutality in their own cities, undoubtedly there would be less police violence. If Christians would cry out against the lengthy jail sentences and tyrannical lawsuits, they would cease or be greatly curtailed.

We must understand clearly—it is our solemn duty to stand in solidarity *with* Christians facing government harassment, and to stand *against* those officials who have set themselves up against Christians. Give them no rest, in the First Amendment sense, utilize your constitutional right of "redress at grievance" to the fullest. Send a resounding message to the tyrants in government: If you mess with a few of us, you will deal with a lot of us! Then seek to remove them from office.

Do it for the sake of the preborn. Do it for the sake of justice. Do it for your fellow Christian. *Do it for the sake of your children.*

17

GRASSROOTS REFORMATION

W ho would have believed that Abraham Lincoln, a poor boy from Illinois who failed in two businesses and lost three elections, could have become President of the United States and led our nation through a civil war? Who would have thought that the work of a poor English girl, Amy Carmichael, could have led to the outlawing of child prostitution in India? Who would have thought that a ragtag army of five thousand could defeat the strongest military force in the world and secure the independence of the thirteen colonies? Who in their right mind would have dared to believe that a band of twelve Jewish men, from fishermen to tax-gatherers, followers of a crucified carpenter whom they insisted was still alive, could have literally changed the world *forever. Be real—would you have turned over such an awesome responsibility to Peter and his friends?*

Yet history is replete with stories of the improbable individual performing the impossible. I certainly would not have picked a teenage shepherd to be the king of Israel. Let's face it. We wouldn't have chosen a poor young Jewish girl to give birth to God incarnate or a simple carpenter to rear Him; we wouldn't have chosen a wild-eyed man clothed in camel's hair and subsisting on bugs to herald the Savior's coming.

But God did, and God still does choose the "foolish things of the world to shame the wise" (1 Corinthians 1:27).

Despite the abundant testimony of Scripture and the witness of history, we still long for the elite to take the reins of change. We desire the well-bred to lead the revolutions, the educated to rectify our social injustices, and the well-dressed and articulate to perform the impossible.

This naive hope is sadly helping to further the demise of our civilization. Local politicians look to state politicians; state governments beg at the feet of the federal bureaucracy. Congregations expect their pastors to correct all their ills while pastors, in turn, look to their bishops to save them! We've grown dangerously out of balance in our top-down mentality.

There is an appropriate place for authority in our society and in our churches. We cannot have renegades and rebels forever doing what is right in their own eyes. We don't want anarchy. We need authority; therefore, we need leaders. I am not speaking of eliminating authority and submission; rather, I am addressing the allocation of resources and the need for action.

I have become so sick and tired of television reporters looking to Washington to solve our problems, as if the federal government were our savior. Whether the concern is the war on drugs, education policy, public housing, teenage pregnancy, or any other issue, the media and our nation's politicos are forever begging the Administration for more funds or blaming it for a program's failure (or both).

When Will We Wake Up?

Skyscrapers are not built from the top down but from the bottom up. Similarly, healthy societies are not built from the top down. Top down societies such as China and the Soviet Union are oppressive and tyrannical. The political regimes control every area of an individual's life; they even seek to control one's very thoughts. The answers and solutions provided by a centralized power inevitably result in the loss of freedom. Moreover, centralized authority structures simply fail to perform. Governments that seek to solve all of a society's ills and meet all of its needs are unmitigated disasters.

Strong families and self-government remain the bedrock of healthy societies. Even they, however, are not the entire building. Many Christians have strong families. The husband and wife share a great mutual love and respect and stand as godly examples of uprightness. They deliberately train their children in the ways of the Lord by word and deed, and their children are obedient and disciplined. In short, there are many strong, self-governed Christian families.

Tens of thousands of such families, however, fail to participate in the development of society at large. They are, in fact, completely ignorant of their elected officials and the electoral process. Over half of them are not even registered to vote. This is *disgraceful.*

Political Apathy

The political arena in America is in such a chaotic state because we've let it become that way! The Scripture says, "When a wicked man rules, the people groan" (Proverbs 29:2). It earlier admonishes, "When the wicked rise, men hide themselves" (Proverbs 28:28). We, however, have only ourselves to blame. We've been called to be the salt of the earth and the light of the world; but, concerning our nation's government, we have hid our light under a bushel. Is it any reason that homosexuals such as Barney Frank are still in office?

Tom Minnery of *Citizen* magazine recently pointed out that to be a good citizen (according to Romans 13) means to fulfill our duties and responsibilities as they relate to civil governments. If we fail to work to elect upright officials or, at least, vote intelligently, then we are disobeying the direct injunction of Romans 13. (Please note that there is more to acting as a godly citizen than simply voting.) Moreover, we are squandering the precious privilege which God has given us to decide who our leaders will be.

Do you realize that most elections are decided by 15 to 18 percent of the eligible voting electorate? In some races this percentage is even lower. What a tragedy! Yet, it is also an opportunity. It's a tragedy because it reveals the apathetic state of our society. It is an opportunity because it reveals that even a small Christian community could determine their areas' political future. How much more of a difference could eighty million Evangelicals and Roman Catholics make in the destiny of our nation? Only slightly more than forty million elected George Bush in 1988. If we could vote as a bloc, on the child-killing issue alone we could remove every servant of death in politics. Tragically, however, millions of pro-lifers are not even registered and many who are registered don't vote. Worse yet, many of us who are registered vote for pro-death politicians.

For example, millions of Evangelicals and Roman Catholics voted for Michael Dukakis for the presidency in 1988. This is inconceivable to me. Here is a man who ardently, without reservation, supported child-killing (as well as the homosexual agenda) and favored the use of federal funds—your tax-dollars—to pay for the brutal murder of innocent children. Yet, millions of individuals who profess to love God went to the polls and pulled the lever for Michael Dukakis! This is *deplorable*.

Now, for those who are incensed that I would declare the obvious, hear me out. I realize that there were other issues in the campaign—the economy, defense, Central America, poverty programs. These issues certainly are important; but none, however, remotely compares to the over twenty-six million children already murdered and the nearly five thousand who die daily.

Suppose you agreed with a candidate on nuclear arms, loan guarantees for Eastern Europe, a proper China policy, an overall trade policy with Japan, SDI, Social Security reform, tax cuts, and our support of the various freedom fighters; but there was one glitch—he was a Nazi. What if he supported importing Peruvian peasants as indentured servants—or as slaves? Would you vote for him? Absolutely not, right? Then why would you vote for a candidate who believes in dismembering or burning innocent children to death? It is a horrible compromise.

The bottom line is this: We could remove every pro-death politician in the next six years if we really wanted to. We could then impeach every godless, pro-death judge. But the question remains, do we possess the necessary desire, discipline, and courage to do what is right? May God change our hearts and actions! Thomas Jefferson scribed these words in our Declaration of Independence, "The government derives its just powers from the consent of the governed." (Only a partially true statement.) When we repent of our selfishness and apathy and resolve that we will no longer consent to legalized child-killing, this holocaust will be shortly over. We need to heed the lessons of Eastern Europe *now*. We must now set our faces like flint against the growing oppression in our own land before we have to endure forty years or more of a terroristic state.

Should We Really Separate Church and State?

Grassroots activism obviously encompasses far more than political involvement. I shall address some of these arenas momentarily, but first let me share more about the political arena.

Ultimately, there are three primary institutions which God has given authority to: the family, the church, and the government. All three are answerable to Him and, at times, answerable to each other. Every Christian in America recognizes the need for us to exercise leadership and authority according to the principles of God's Word in our families and in our churches. What, however, of the government?

Is the government accountable to those same standards? Should Christians "leaven" the political arena for righteousness sake? Does the Bible contain the principles by which men ought to exercise civil law and authority? Or are governments autonomous, exempt from the precepts of God or not answerable to God and His Word?

If governments are accountable to God and His Word and we are to be the salt and leaven of those institutions, then why do so many Christians neglect or even eschew their responsibility in this arena? Worse yet, why do some Christians (and a few Christian leaders) insist that we *not* demand the Lordship of Jesus Christ in the political arena? Is Jesus Lord of all or not?

Furthermore, why do we spend so much time teaching and training our people to lead and exercise authority in our families and the church but then teach them (by word or deed) to *ignore* the institution that has the power to wreak havoc in the family and the church? Remember, it is the *government* in the Soviet Union that closes churches and imprisons pastors. It is the *government* in China that breaks up families, removing children from Christian parents and forcing Christian women to kill their children.

As we foolishly surrender the crown rights of King Jesus in civil government at every level, our enemies who insist on the separation of God and government are secretly, and now even openly, working to extinguish the practice of Biblical Christianity in our families and in our churches. They care little what you *think* and *believe*. They *do* care how you rear your children and what you teach about child-killing and homosexuality in your Christian school and in your church. They do want you to hire homosexuals in your church and teach homosexuality as an alternate lifestyle in your Christian school. They do hate the truth that there is a hell for those who reject the Triune Godhead. They despise the claims of Jesus Christ. Yet we seek to make compromises and covenants with those who seek to silence us.

Why not exert the same level of enthusiastic training for leadership and authority in civil government as we do in our families and churches? Why not declare the black and white claims of God's authority over the nation—not only in a safe, hidden prayer meeting in which we rebuke demons but also in the bright light of the public arena where we rebuke godless men and women? When will we stop allowing our enemies to define the agenda and the scope of our responsibility and authority?

If we continue to play the ostrich in politics or to treat God's Word as just another voice among equals (i.e., Socialism, Communism), then we will continue to get our butts kicked; and God only knows what terrors our children and grandchildren will face because of our foolishness and compromise. It's time to quit playing games, to stop trying to appease our enemies by toning down God and His Word, and to begin holding up the truths of God as the righteous and sure cornerstone of civil government. For anyone who doubts, it is a trustworthy statement that a society based on the transcendent law of God is far better off (even for the heathens) than one shifting upon the ever-changing quicksand of humanism.

Other Areas of Grassroots Activism

What are some other areas of grassroots activism? Whatever you decide to do to make a difference for righteousness.

Discussing politics in this way leads to a critical choice which many will soon face. We will be forced to choose between speaking the whole mind and will of God and maintaining our tax-exempt, tax-deductible status.

Our tax-exempt, tax-deductible status has definitely been a blessing for churches and other religious organizations, including many Christian media outlets. We have been able to raise money more easily, and the donors have had the benefit of not being taxed on their gifts to such groups. (This is definitely a blessing in an hour when some people pay forty to fifty cents or more in taxes on every dollar they earn.)

However, like so many programs in our government and society, what began as a benefit has been perverted into a curse. More and more frequently, the IRS and federal and state officials are using the tax-deductible status to tell men of God and religious organizations what they can and cannot say. This puts us in a very precarious position. We cannot allow the government to tell us what we can preach, write, promote, or denounce. If we do so merely for the financial benefit accruing to us or our donors, we are in jeopardy of selling our birthright, of selling out our anointing for tax-deductions.

Please hear me out. If we submit even once to a government official who threatens to remove our tax status if we refuse to bridle our message, we have opened the door to complete government censorship and, ultimately, control of our Christian message. When the government, the IRS, declares what is the gospel ("You can be saved!") and what is political ("Governor so-and-so is in sin for promoting child-killing and no professing Christian in good conscience could vote for a man who promotes rebellion to God's command to not murder, or homosexuality is an abomination to God and should never be taught or promoted in our public schools."), we are in great danger. Churches, in fact, have already been taken to court for their stands on these two issues. Where will it end? The tax-exempt status is quickly becoming an evil means by which wicked government officials can bully churches into silence over Biblical truth that these tyrants find offensive (oops—I mean political).

There is a simple solution. We ought to abandon our tax-deductible status. I know this may seem radical to some today. Ten or fifteen years from now, however, it may be normal. Frankly, as I have shared this thought with many Christian leaders, I have heard only one consistent opposing argument: "How will we raise money if we're not tax-deductible?" This prompts some other questions:

- Is God your provider or not?

- Is He limited by your tax-deductible status?

- Do people give to your work because they love God and believe in your ministry, or solely because it's tax-deductible? (With many, I'm sure it's both.)

I am speaking from experience. Project Life, a pro-life group I began in 1983, was tax-deductible. In 1986 we surrendered our tax-deductible status and started Operation Rescue. I can testify to God's ability to provide and to His people's generosity. Our income went up over ten-fold in the ensuing two years. I'm not saying that it is *because* we aren't tax-deductible. I'm just saying that if you are doing God's will and God's people believe in your ministry, they will give to the work. In fact, such sacrifice makes their gift all the more meaningful to them because they are giving solely to bless the work of God. By the way, God forbid that we should fall into the trap of letting the *government* define God's work. We will surely be cursed and doomed if that happens. This is what China, Russia, and other oppressive regimes have done. They decide what the church is and what the church does. The fruit is obvious and terrifying.

What then are churches and ministries if not for the tax exempt status of "501 (c)(3)?" A number of options exist: DBA's (Sole proprietorships with "Doing Business As" for name), Ad Hoc committees, sole incorporations, incorporations, trusts, and unincorporated associations, to name a few. All of these have positive and negative points. You should discuss these options with your attorney to determine which would be best.

Let me reiterate my main point. 501 (c)(3)s are being increasingly used by the government to repress and control the message of the church. The sooner we wake up to this fact and get out of the yoke with those who hate God, the safer we and our children will be. Don't worry. God's people will give to God's work. Let God deal with the few who won't.

The war against child-killing offers many alternatives—rescue missions, sidewalk counseling, picketing at killing centers and the homes of killers and mill directors; writing letters, making phone calls, attending marches, rallies, and prayer vigils; actively working in the campaign of a pro-life politician, lobbying other politicians on pro-life legislation, laboring to defund Planned Parenthood, both locally and nationally; financially supporting pro-life ministries, stuffing envelopes for their mailings; boycotting products and services whose manufacturers and providers support Planned Parenthood or NOW and informing them why you're doing so; calling up radio talk shows and letting the truth be heard. The list is endless.[1] Why not create your own niche in pro-life activism! You must, however, *do something!*

Let me state this in practical terms. What are you doing on Saturday morning that is so important that you cannot (or won't?) commit yourself to picketing at your local killing center every other week or two? What television show is so important that you can't attend an evening prayer vigil at a jail in which your brother and sister Christians are being incarcerated to pray for them and to encourage their hearts? Why can't you sacrifice a night or two a week during campaign season to help elect a godly public official?

There is much talk of grassroots work, but few really understand what it means. Those who have led and participated in grassroots work, however, know that it means just that—*work. Hard work.*

But oh the blessedness of such work! Those who have participated in pro-life, pro-family, or Christian activism of any ilk can testify to the friendships and comraderie, the laughter and the tears, and the memorable corporate prayer times. I have personally witnessed a particularly deep commitment to one another among those in the Rescue Movement. This, I can assure you: if you have never been involved in an activist project with fellow Christians, you're missing a precious experience.

The Family

"What about my family?" some may ask. "If I go head over heels into pro-life work, I'll never have enough time for my family." First of all, there must be a balance. If you give every free moment to your involvement in a cause and rarely see your wife and children, you're just looking for trouble, perhaps even a disaster. We have a covenant commitment before God as fathers and mothers to shepherd our families.

Again, we must maintain balance. One who is away for seven days a week, month after month, for the sake of ministry is definitely in danger and may be arguably in sin. (I am not referring to those in military service or involved in a short-term mission project in a foreign nation. I am addressing the reckless neglect of our familial responsibilities and duties.) The other extreme, however, is also dangerous and quite destructive.

If you stay at home every night, week after week, what are you doing? Watching television? Playing games? Is that the way to disciple your children to be servants of Christ, the leaders of the next generation? Perhaps you're not watching the television but rather are reading good Christian literature to your family; you're even home schooling your children. This is great; but still, if you never lead them out to *do* something for God's kingdom, you may be developing a cloistered, spiritually-selfish mentality in your children. Jesus said, "Go ye into all the world!" (Matthew 28:20, KJV) not "Stay ye at home!"

If one sets aside one or two nights a week and an occasional Saturday to become involved in some godly endeavor, it will not harm your children. Rather, you will teach them *by your example* about servanthood, hard work, Christian fellowship and comraderie. Further-more, *involving* your children in Christian activism is excellent training for their own development. I love to see a table full of children of all ages, stuffing envelopes side by side with their parents, hearing the adults tell their war stories. Sometimes the smaller ones tire quickly and are off to romp around; but so what? Their civic duty and obliga-tion to work for the extension of God's kingdom won't be some ab-stract concept in a textbook lesson but an experienced reality.

We and many of our friends regularly bring our children with us to picket. We take children to rescues to watch and to pray. We in-clude them as much as possible in our activism. After all, sooner or later they will have to confront the crises of this nation. These chil-dren activists may be the ones who eventually lead America out of this moral swampland.

This may be familiar to some of you, but the majority of mission-aries on the mission field were reared in missionary families. They grew up on the mission field watching their mothers and fathers con-tinually laying down their lives for those they sought to reach and teach for Christ. They saw their commitment and dedication, and they chose to follow in their footsteps. Godly missionaries reproduce godly missionaries. Godly activists will reproduce godly activists. Self-centered, lazy Christians will, at best, reproduce the same level selfish-ness and apathy in their children. At worst, their children's sloth will exceed theirs.

It is my observation that children who are reared in lukewarm, selfish, and aimless Christian homes often turn away from the faith as young adults. None of us want that for our children. I am not arguing that activism alone will produce godly children and later adults. The fervent love for God and people, however, that motivates much Chris-tian activism can only be a positive force and a godly example in the development of our children's own dedication to God.

Single?

For those of you who may be single and without children, your read-ing has not been wasted. Just store this advice in your memory banks in case you get married and have children.

Meanwhile, however, *what are you doing!* I must be honest with you. I am more frustrated with single, childless Christians than any other believers. You are usually the most free of heavy responsibility— a wife or husband, children, a career, mortgage payments; and yet, singles are often the most self-centered and apathetic Christians in our churches. (Most of the heavy sacrifice has come from married men and women in their late twenties through early forties with small children. Their involvement is greatly motivated by their fears for their children's futures.)

What are *you* doing that is so important that you cannot take off for six months or even a year to devote yourself full-time to rescue? If you're arrested, you are in a far better position to risk a few weeks or months in jail. Or why can't you put your belongings in storage, sell your late model car, move to an appropriate city and volunteer to help godly pro-life officials get elected? When I was single, I was able to spend nearly two-and-a-half months on the mission field in Haiti, Costa Rica, Honduras, and Mexico. I may never have that opportunity again because of my current responsibilities (and calling). Nevertheless. I am eternally thankful to God that I went while I could.

Can't you devote a year of your life to reforming America? Can't you work to ensure that America will even *be* here twenty or thirty years from now? Are your comfortable apartment, new car, and fancy stereo so important in the eternal scheme that you cannot lay them down—even for a season—for the kingdom of God? Please, do your part! Alleviate some of the stress on married couples with small children. Join the fray. Take risks. Be courageous. Remember, courage is not the absence of fear but the will to do what is right despite our fears.

In Closing

America is in chaos, and rough times lie ahead. I believe that certain calamity awaits our nation. There is one critical question which must yet be answered—who will lead us out of the rubble? Will it be a tyrannical and godless regime or godly Christian men and women? Will we as Christians show the courage and prudence *now* necessary to win the confidence of the citizenry and to lead this nation out of insanity? Or will the church be considered an irrelevant sideshow that was uninvolved and unconcerned for our nation's well-being even as it collapsed into chaos?

The answer lies with us. Will we *now*, while there remains a window of opportunity, launch into and expand our grassroots activism?

Will we train our children to be salt, light, and godly leaven by our example? Will we infiltrate and reclaim the institution which we have abandoned—our government—for its righteous king, the Lord Jesus? Or will we continue wandering in our religious wilderness, irrelevant to and ignored by those around us? Will we squander away our children's future freedom and security for our current comfort and ease? God forbid! May he embolden us and enable us to do all we can to rescue this nation from the hands of godless men and demonic hosts. Prayer and action can prevail!

THE INEVITABLE?

W e must understand that America is not static. The ideas and ideologies of our nation are slowly changing. We must also understand that these ideas and ideologies have consequences. The question remains, what further consequences will the prevalent godless ideas and ideologies have on our families, our churches, our governments, and, in sum, our entire culture? How will they alter (or pervert) the life of our nation and determine its destiny?

We Do Not Live in a Vacuum

We do not live in a vacuum. There is a God in heaven who reigns and who judges men and nations, holding them accountable for their deeds. We can no more change this fact than we can alter the law of gravity. The cup of our nation's wickedness and depravity is running over. The cup of God's wrath is about to run over as well. When it does, we will all experience its fury.

As a nation, we are drenched in the blood of innocent children. This barbaric crime will not go unpunished *in this life*. America will pay for this bloodshed as surely as we breathe. The *severity* and *length* of God's coming judgment, however, remains an open question whose answer will, in part, be determined by our prayers, repentance, and ensuing actions.

Judgment Is Here. One fact is clear: *we are already under the judgment of God.* The rampant degradation and searing of our national conscience is the beginning of judgment. Romans 1 teaches that when a people have the truth but suppress it in ungodliness, when they know of the true God but refuse to be thankful to Him and worship Him, then God will give them over to corruption and a debased, depraved mind.

God gives them their own way until they grow sick of it. The ultimate stages of their depravity are listed in the final verses of Romans 1. Granted, these sins have been committed by men at all times in history. They are now, however, performed en masse, often with little or no guilt. Many of these atrocities are now being extolled as good and desirable. That is frightening. That is the beginning of the judgment of God.

> And just as they did not see fit to acknowledge God any longer, God gave them over to a depraved mind, to do those things which are not proper, being filled with all unrighteousness, wickedness, greed, evil; full of envy, murder, strife, deceit, malice; they are gossips, slanderers, haters of God, insolent, arrogant, boastful, inventors of evil, disobedient to parents, without understanding, untrustworthy, unloving, unmerciful; and, although they know the ordinance of God, that those who practice such things are worthy of death, they not only do the same, but also give hearty approval to those who practice them (Romans 1: 28–32).

Not the Great Tribulation. Many kind people sent me letters of encouragement as I have sat here in jail. Many have written that my incarceration and the betrayal of justice on so many fronts are signs of the times, that the end is near (for the world), and that the Lord must be coming any day.

One Christian wrote, "I don't know if you believe Jesus is coming soon, but I do, and I'm praying for it. This world is getting so wicked. Just in the last ten years, it is so incredible how awful it has gotten. I want out of this place so badly."

Another wrote, "I'm so looking forward to Christ's return. This world is getting so rotten." These believers have been converts one and a half years and one year, respectively, so they are only parroting what they've heard in the church.

For both the unbelieving reader and the Christian, let me leave no room for doubt. The coming calamities I'm about to speak of are not because of the Second Coming. I am not talking about the Great Tribulation, the end times, or the last days. (According to the Apostle

Peter, we've been in the last days since the day of Pentecost. See Acts 2:17 and Joel 2:28.) I am not talking about Armageddon.

I am talking about the judgment of God being poured out on America, about His chastisement falling on the church in the same way that He has judged nations and His people since the birth of His church and since the beginning of time.

Many letters I receive betray an attitude of arrogance and poison in the American church, a confidence that we will not go through tribulation, judgment, and suffering. They believe *de facto* that Americans, or at least American Christians, are somehow exempt from God's judgment. This attitude is so deep in some Christians that the only tribulation they can ever imagine America enduring is The Great Tribulation. Therefore, if America is collapsing, being severely judged, or being threatened by tribulation, it must mean that the end is near and that the Lord is about to return. Therefore, we won't suffer because He will rapture us out. But what if He doesn't return for another ten, or hundred or thousand years? What if America's collapse isn't because of what's written in Matthew chapter 24, but Matthew chapter 5, because we've failed in our holy duty to be God's witnesses, His salt and light, discipling the nation in His commandments?

If you have a hard time swallowing this pill, just think of our brethren in China. They are even now being tortured and martyred for the cause of Christ. They probably still are in the Soviet Union without our knowledge. What difference does it make to them if they are so persecuted for the testimony of Jesus by the communists or the anti-Christ? What difference does it make to them if they are killed because they won't denounce the Lord or because they won't take a mark on their forehead or their right hand?

We simply expose our American arrogance when we imagine that the atrocities which have happened to Christians in Russia, China, and other nations over the last two thousand years won't happen in the United States. We are foolish to think that the onset of such suffering and tribulation in our nation could *only* be the Great Tribulation and could *only* signify the end of the age. Like covenant Israel, however, many of us believe the false prophets who say "We will not see sword or famine. . . ." (Jeremiah 5:12)

Hence, we have little strength for the inner trials, persecutions, and sufferings that are coming. We just wander along in our self-deception that God won't let His people experience such torments. Tell that to Watchman Nee or Aleksandr Solzhenitsyn! If we continue to believe such deception, we are not going to be ready when the curtain goes up.

God Judges Heathen Nations. Some may question whether or not God judges heathen nations. Well, He does. More specifically, He judges nations and peoples who are not in covenant with Him and fail to believe and obey His Word. Some Christians believe that God relates only with individuals and not with nations. They consider Israel, God's covenant nation, to be the only nation with which He has ever dealt. This is folly.

God's Word clearly records that He *judges* not only individuals but entire nations. God judged Moab, "for he magnified himself against the Lord," causing them to be plundered and destroyed (Jeremiah 48:26, NKJV).

> Put yourselves in array against Babylon all around, all you who bend the bow; shoot at her; spare no arrows, for she has sinned against the Lord. Shout against her all around; she has given her hand; her foundations have fallen, her walls are thrown down, for it is the vengeance of the Lord (Jeremiah 50:14, 15, NKJV; also see entire chapter).

He said He would "avenge Himself on His adversaries" in Egypt (Jeremiah 46:10, NKJV). The Lord also declared prophetically that He would overthrow Philistia, that "The Fathers will not look back for their children, lacking courage" (47:3), and that He would cause to be heard the "alarm of war." Philistia was to be a "desolate mound" and "her villages [shall be] burned with fire" (49:2). Against Kedar He said, "I will bring their calamity from all its sides . . ." (49:32). And it goes on and on. And lest anyone think proclaimed destruction is limited to Jeremiah, read Isaiah, Ezekiel, Amos, Jonah, Obadiah, Exodus, Numbers, and Joshua.

Signs of the Times

Before I describe the possible scenarios of judgment against our nation and the church, let me make one thing clear: I have not had a vision nor have I had a dream about what I'm going to share.

Rather, I am basing my comments strictly on what I see in the Scriptures, which I trust shall prove "a more sure word of prophecy" (2 Peter 1:19, KJV). We have the *foresight* of *hindsight*. We can look back over time and see in the Scriptures how God destroyed nations and judged His people, knowing that His Word never changes. He is the same yesterday, today and forever; and there is no shadow of turning in Him.

Lest anyone get self-righteously excited about the sword that hangs over America's head, let's remember that judgment begins at the house of God (see 1 Peter 4:17).

> And it will come about at that time that I will search Jerusalem with lamps, and I will punish the men who are stagnant in spirit, who say in their hearts, 'The Lord will not do good or evil!' Moreover, their wealth will become plunder, and their houses desolate; yes, they will build houses but not inhabit them, and plant vineyards but not drink their wine. (Zephaniah 1:12,13)

Financial Collapse. A person or nation can prosper financially for a season and that this is not necessarily a sign of God's blessing (see Psalm 73:3, 12; Psalm 37). Those people and their finances are doomed to be lost in the judgment of God (see Psalm 37: 7–10, 35, 36; Jeremiah 17:11). Even God's people can increase in wealth while they ignore the plight of the needy and the fatherless (see Jeremiah 5:26–29). Amos preached a coming destruction at the zenith of Israel's wealth, and that destruction surely came. Thus, the wealth of our nation and the wealth in some churches are at best poor indicators of God's blessing. Indeed, at worst, such riches can convey false confidence to us and the wicked as we imagine our wealth an unscaleable wall (see Proverbs 18:11).

America's economy is hanging precariously over a cliff and realistically, it wouldn't take much to push it over the edge. There are two preeminent crises: our own national debt and that of Third World countries. Our own debt is such that the annual interest, not even touching the principle, amounts to over $600 for every man, woman, and child in the country! What is truly frightening is the complete refusal of our government officials to deal intelligently with the crisis. They keep spending what they do not have.

Drought and Famine. God—not the devil, not mother nature—controls the rain. As Jeremiah stated, "When He utters His voice, there is a tumult of waters in the heavens, And He causes the clouds to ascend from the end of the earth; He makes lightening for the rain, And brings out the wind from his storehouses" (Jeremiah 10:13;

see also Jeremiah 5:24, 14:22, 51:16; Job 5:8–10, 36:26–33; Deuteronomy 11:14, 28:12).

The lack of rain is a judgment from God, ". . . the heavens are shut up and there is no rain, because they have sinned against Thee. . . ." (1 Kings 8:35; see also Jeremiah 3:2, 3; Deuteronomy 11:17, 28:22–24). Obviously a lack of rain will cause the staff of bread to be broken. No crops will grow; famine will ensue (see Jeremiah 14:2–6; Ezekiel 5:15–16). Ezekiel prophesied,

> They shall fling their silver into the streets, and their gold shall become an abhorrent thing; their silver and their gold shall not be able to deliver them in the day of the wrath of the Lord. They cannot satisfy their appetite, nor can they fill their stomachs, for their iniquity has become an occasion of stumbling. (Ezekiel 7:19)

In recent years we have seen a small portion of what long-term drought would be like. At different times rain levels have been very low. We've watched millions of acres of forest burn out of control. We've seen crops fail in the South and in the Midwest and watched farmers rally to one another's help providing feed for cattle. We have also seen many cattle diseased and dead and many farms close due to the drought. Imagine the panic of a one-, two-, or three-year full-scale drought!

If drought and famine occur in even moderate proportions, can you imagine the looting and the marauding bands searching for food and water? Can you imagine the terror in the cities? God only knows what terrors could follow.

Plagues and Pestilences. The Scriptures plainly teach that at times God smites a people with sickness as a chastisement. He smote the Egyptians with boils (see Exodus 9:8–11) and then killed the first born of every family (see Exodus 11:4–5). When the Philistines harbored the Ark of the Covenant, the Lord struck them with hemorroids (see 1 Samuel 5). After David sinned by numbering Israel, the angel of the Lord struck down 70,000 Israelites with a plague (see 2 Samuel 24). When the children of Israel murmured and spoke against Moses and Aaron, prior to the intercession of Moses, God's intention was to destroy the entire nation with a plague (see Deuteronomy 14). God, through the prophet Jeremiah, later threatened the Israelites again with plagues (see Jeremiah 14:12).

Let me hasten to say that all sickness is *not* from God, sickness is not necessarily from sin, some afflictions are from Satan, and God still heals people. Indeed, we ought to pray earnestly that God would heal the afflicted, trusting in his divine providence and seeking that His will be done.

In light of the Scriptures showing plagues as a chastening, however, what should we think of venereal diseases and AIDS? Whether these sicknesses are the result of God *directly* judging us (active judgment) or whether they are the natural consequences of sin (passive judgment—as Romans 1:27 says, "receiving in themselves the penalty of their error which was due," NKJV)—both are forms of chastening.

The Locust. Another form of God's chastening is the sudden appearance of deadly insects or animals. He smote the Egyptians with locusts in abundance and destroyed all vegetation (Exodus 10); He brought lice upon the people and frogs into their homes (Exodus 8); He warned the Israelites that wild man-eating animals would increase and devour some of their number. In Solomon's prayer at the dedication, he acknowledged that the "locusts or grasshoppers" could be the judgment of God (2 Chronicles 6:28).

Simply stated, God could send a swarm of insects to devour our fruit and vegetable crops. If this happened on a large scale, the results for our nation would be catastrophic. Beyond insects, God could increase and incite wild animals to be a scourge to our people (see Jeremiah 15:3).

The Sword. Again and again, God threatened His people with the judgment of "the sword" (see Isaiah 1:20; Jeremiah 12:12, 14:12, 15:12; Ezekiel 5:2). Moreover, He punishes heathen nations with the same. [See Jeremiah 46:10 (Egypt); Jeremiah 47:6 (Philistia); Jeremiah 48:2 (Moab).] These wars may be civil wars or against external enemies.

Oh that America could see the flashing sword that terrorized Jerusalem! Oh that the stubborn might hear the screams of women and children being slaughtered by a merciless invading enemy! Would to God that the rebellious might know what will be the ultimate cost of their rebellion! May God enable us to see the danger we are in, and to warn this rebellious nation with Jeremiah's fervor and agony.

> O my soul, my soul! I am pained in my very heart! My heart makes a noise in me, I cannot hold my peace, because you have heard, O my soul, the sound of the trumpet, the alarm of the war.

Destruction upon destruction is cried, for the whole land is plundered. Suddenly my tents are plundered, and my curtains in a moment.

How long will I see the standard, and hear the sound of the trumpet? (Jeremiah 4:19–21, NKJV)

What Lies Ahead

I believe there are two questions yet to be answered:

1. How severe will God's judgment against America be?

2. Who will lead us out of the coming crisis?

The answer to the first question depends upon our prayer, repentance, and ensuing actions. We will greatly determine how far America plunges into disaster by how effectively we are the salt of this nation, the preservative, and the priest-guardians of this culture. America's survival depends primarily on the church. George Grant writes succinctly, "The survival of any nation depends entirely on the fulfillment of the disciple's priestly duties. If the people of God fail to be salt, then the nation cannot be preserved from putrefaction, and it *will* fall into judgment."[1]

The answer to the second question—who will lead us out of the coming crisis—also depends in part on the wisdom, courage, and action we display *now*. Will we have credibility with the country because we forewarned it of the coming disaster and held forth Biblical answers for our nation's ills? Or will we be viewed as irrelevant escapists who hid in our Christian ghettos while the nation collapsed? Let me ask it this way—who will lead America out of the coming crisis—God-fearing men and women, or iron-fisted tyrants?

The coming judgment in America will inevitably produce great national convulsions. It is highly likely that America will be radically different than it is now—radically better or radically worse. The United States simply will not remain static—not because we're the United States but because of the nature of humanity and the judgment of Almighty God.

It is my sincere hope and prayer—it is my goal—that the Christian community will be prepared to face the coming catastrophes and that we are ready to serve the needy, bind the nation's wounds, and lead her out of the wilderness of her rebellion. May God grant it. Amen.

WHAT YOU SEE IS WHAT YOU GET

Have you ever felt that you were being manipulated when you read the news? Well, I want to confirm your intuition.

Just Words on a Page

Most of us understand that we cannot believe everything we read, especially regarding the pro-life issue. We know that the print media has generally taken a pro-death stance on their editorial pages; we also know that this editorial stance heavily influences their coverage of child-killing and related people and events. Having personally done hundreds of interviews with the media (printed press, radio, television) and having participated in scores of events that were covered by the media, I know this to be true.

Why it's true is obvious—the ones writing and editing the articles are committed to the death ethic. But the how is more difficult. Indeed, how can the press still limply claim to be fair and objective when their articles read so completely pro-death?

I recently came across the master's thesis of Kathryn I. Pyle, which she presented to the School of Journalism, College of Communication at Regent University (formerly CBNU). It is entitled, "Newspaper Coverage of Operation Rescue Activities in Atlanta, October 1988: A Case Study in Bias in Reporting." It was incredibly enlightening to me for two reasons:

- It documented the media bias of various newspapers concerning O.R. activities (seven newspapers were studied over an eight-day period).

- More importantly for this discussion, it showed how they implemented their bias.

My purpose here is not to discuss the content of her thesis in which she did a thorough, fantastic job. My purpose is to equip you to see how the print media distorts truth and virtually lies while purporting to present the truth. This is so that you will be "wise as serpents" when you read the press on any issue and, hopefully, better able to discern when the press is trying to pull the inky wool (or wooly ink) over your eyes.

Miss Pyle based her study of bias on the seven criteria used by Teun van Diik in his book, *News Analysis.* "The seven criteria for the analysis were inclusion (the number of stories in each newspaper), placement (location of the story within the newspaper), length, language, photographs, headlines and sources."[1]

She examined seven papers: the *New York Times,* the *Washington Post,* the *Washington Times,* the *Christian Science Monitor,* the *Richmond-Times Dispatch,* the *Virginian-Pilot,* and the *Atlanta Constitution.* The papers were covered from October 2nd through October 9th, 1988 during the height of O.R.'s activity in Atlanta.

Inclusion. The *New York Times* only covered the week's events once. By comparison, the *Washington Post* and the *Washington Times*—both non-local papers—covered the events four and five times, respectively. The *Richmond-Times Dispatch* covered the event seven times.

Perhaps the greatest power of the press (aside from aggressive character assassination via lies and distortion) is the ability to ignore valid news and to lie by omission. They decide what is news, what will be printed, and therefore what people will think about. Events critical to the church, our families' freedoms, and the very nation are regularly ignored.

Placement. The *Atlanta Constitution* had seven front-page stories. That is to be expected because the events occurred in Atlanta. The *Richmond Times,* the *Virginia-Pilot,* and the *Washington Times* all had one front page story. The others had none. This is a second manner in which papers can demonstrate bias and project what they consider to be important. Is the story on the front page, the second page, or buried somewhere in the paper below a mattress ad?

Length. The length of the story sends a clear message as to importance and therefore is heavily influenced by the bias of the press. Is the story ten paragraphs? fifteen? five? Is it just a news brief on the left-hand column? "Oh, yes, and by the way, 591 people were arrested in Philadelphia in an antiabortion protest. Molly Yard, a defender of women's rights, called the group, 'terrorists'." How can you properly encapsulate a five- or ten-hour event involving hundreds of people and dozens of police in a one-inch newsbrief?

Language. The language of a text can take two forms.

• The press writes as fact or commentary.

• Quotes are included from individuals who have been interviewed.

For example, in the *Atlanta Constitution*, we are quoted, calling ourselves "rescuers." Our enemies are quoted calling us "born-again bigots." The newspapers generally referred to us as antiabortion (almost never pro-life, which is more positive sounding). The *Atlanta Constitution* once actually referred to us as "self-proclaimed soldiers in God's army." We're supposed to believe we get fair coverage! Of seven papers, five printed names slurring us. The *Washington Times* (which has a generally pro-life stance) did not, and surprisingly neither did the *New York Times*.

I'll never forget the opening line of an A.P. report on the verdict in my Los Angeles trial: "Randall Terry and four of his followers in the militant anti-abortion group were acquitted of charges stemming from an illegal demonstration. . . ." First of all, the others were not my followers; in fact, two of them were leaders. Second, we don't consider ourselves (nor do we act) militant; but the press loves to paint us as extremists. Third, if the demonstration was illegal, why were we acquitted?

In contrast, of the seven papers studied by Miss Pyle, only two included direct references to the abortionists. These were, of course, quotes from us: "Baby-killers," "Killers," and "You kill babies." The other five papers contained not one disparaging word from us or themselves toward those who defend child-killing or the child-killers themselves.

Photographs. If a picture paints a thousand words, the *New York Times* was doing its best to guard the silence. It was the only paper without one picture. The other papers had a total of thirty photographs among them. That week's activities were marred (both physically and photographically) by police brutality. Of the many pictures taken which showed the brutality, however, two newspapers chose pictures which portrayed the police in a neutral light but which made Operation Rescue participants look bad.[2] Apparently, it's proper to make those who try to stop child-killing look worse than the police who brutalize them. (Again, much of the press remains enslaved to ideology.) I have seen so many pictures printed of individuals (myself included) with their eyes half-closed, licking their lips (which looks bizarre when caught in a picture) or with some mean-looking scowl. Just be aware that pictures are sometimes chosen (or ignored) in order to manipulate the reader.

Headlines. The headlines studied by Miss Pyle were all fairly neutral in content, except for the titles of a few editorials in the *Atlanta Constitution* chastening police for their brutality. (We were thankful that the *Constitution* spoke up.). This, however, does not mean headlines are always neutral. Look for variance in:

- Size (in height)
- Length (in words)
- Content—is there a subtle or aggressive slur, distortion, etc.

A perfect example of the latter is demonstrated by two headlines from the *Boston Globe* and the *Boston Herald* from December 19, 1989. The *Globe* headline read, "GOP's Pierce: I'd limit abortions, might even seek ban." In contrast, the *Herald* headline reported, "Pierce softens stance on abortion issue." It appears as if two completely contrary statements were made. This is exactly what I mean.

Sources. This is critical to the press in building a story and often in manipulating one. A typical way to build a story is "A.B.A.B.CCC." Quotations are taken from the warring parties (ABAB), and then an expert is quoted who is supposed to set things straight and to tell the confused reader which side was right.[3] What often happens is that the "expert" quoted is ardently pro-abortion and defends whatever side the paper favors. (The latter applies to other issues as well.) Furthermore, the A (proabort) quote is usually smooth and loaded with rhetoric, while the B (pro-life) quote is often halting or rather bland and void of content.

In Miss Pyle's study, the number of sources quoted was clearly (and unusually) in favor of Operation Rescue. Also, one paper deleted derogatory quotes from a NARAL spokesperson in a story but left the O.R. quotes. She reasons that more sources from O.R. were used because of the newness and novelty of the activities to the press. Hence, they were preoccupied discovering why people would subject themselves to arrest, police brutality, and imprisonment. It also must be remembered that, although more O.R. sources were quoted than pro-death, the quotes against O.R. were far more derogatory and inflammatory in content.

What to Look Out for in Broadcast News

Manipulating the masses through television broadcasts is a high-tech art. Keep in mind these few truths as you watch the news:

- You don't know what got left on the editing room floor. Often a ten or twenty minute interview will yield an eight to ten second sound bite.

- The footage shown (and any quotes contained herein) could have been taken out of context.

- The media wants you to feel as if you are independently forming an opinion about the issue being covered, but they are sure to select the evidence and structure of the debate in a manner that leads you to their desired conclusions.

- The media can take a fumbling statement and make a person appear inept and foolish. Doing a ten to twenty minute interview without stumbling is very difficult, especially for one not accustomed to being interviewed.

- A reporter may ask a question again and again until he gets the answer he wants or until he thoroughly agitates the interviewee.

Radio, Radio

Secular radio in some ways is a hybrid between television and the printed press. Many radio reporters get their stories from the *Associated Press* or *United Press International* wires which supply many of the biased stories in the printed press. Like television, they also tape interviews—usually over the phone—and then extract "sound bites" from wherever they want.

The radio cannot be accused of visually "hiding the truth" of child-killing from people, but they do continue to obfuscate the hideous reality of murdered children through their choice of rhetoric. As long as the debate is framed by "women's reproductive freedom" and "safe and legal abortions," the radio media acts in complicity with the killers.

The radio does have one redeeming feature—the call-in talk show. These shows are very popular in cities all over America and, unlike television and newspapers, give the average citizen the opportunity to share his mind with the community without being edited (unless one uses profanity). They are a tremendous avenue to educate people on the horrors of abortion and can be used to expose and denounce the present police brutality and rampant courtroom tyranny.

NOTES

Chapter 1: A Letter from Jail

1. Obviously, Edwin Allred is not a murderer in the eyes of our society or in a legal sense. However, the term should be understood here and following from a Biblical perspective. In God's court, he is guilty of murder.

Chapter 2: The Blessing of Anger

1. James Strong, et al, *Strong's Exhaustive Concordance of the Bible* (Nashville, TN: Abingdon Press, 1978).

2. Praise the Lord for Pastor Skip Robokoff—a rescue leader in Fort Lee, NJ—who has rebuked such "ministers"; once in the midst of an ordination service being held for several homosexuals.

3. See chapter 8, "Their Blood Cries Out!," in *Operation Rescue* (Springdale, PA: Whitaker House, 1988) for a discussion of the importance of the shedding of innocent blood.

Chapter 3: Planned Parenthood

1. Margaret Sanger, *Birth Control Review*, May 1919, 2.

2. Sanger, *Pivot of Civilization* (New York: Brentano's, 1922).

3. This review of Margaret Sanger's life is distilled from George Grant, *Grand Illusions* (Brentwood, TN: Wolgemuth & Hyatt, 1988), 41–61, and Elasah Drogin, *Margaret Sanger, Father of Modern Society* (New Hope, KY: CUL Publications, 1986), 85–95.

4. Margaret Sanger, *Pivot of Civilization*, 279.

5. Ibid., 177.

6. Ibid., 105–23.

7. Ibid., 108.

8. Linda Gordon, *Woman's Body, Woman's Right: A Social History of Birth Control in America* (New York: Penguin Books, 1974), 333.

9. *Washington Times*, August 10, 1984.

10. Margaret Sanger, *Birth Control Review*, April 1932, 107.

11. *Birth Control Review*, May 1919, 12.

12. *Birth Control Review*, November 1921, 2.

13. Gordon, *Woman's Body*, 263, 278–79, quoting from Sanger's *Autobiography*.

14. Margaret Sanger, *Birth Control Review*, October 1926.

15. "Birth Rates in Fascist Countries," *Birth Control Review* (November 1939). Quoted in M.W. Perry, "The History of Planned Parenthood."

16. Planned Parenthood Association / Chicago Area. Text accompanied by cartoon caricatures of religious leaders, April 8, 1978.

17. *The Great Orgasm Robbery* (Denver, Colorado: Rocky Mountain Planned Parenthood, 1977).

18. *Ten Heavy Facts About Sex* (Syracuse, NY: Ed-U Press, 1975).

19. Excerpts taken from a taped presentation at Santa Maria High School, Santa Maria, CA. The lecture was given by the Director of Santa Barbara North County Planned Parenthood, Robert Webber, November 16, 1983.

20. Grant, *Illusions*, 106–7.

21. Quoted in Grant, *Illusions*, 112.

22. Ibid., 114.

23. Ibid., 116–7.

24. Robert Ruff, *Aborting Planned Parenthood* (Arlington, TX: New Vision Press, 1988), 45.

25. Alan Guttmacher Institute, "The Effects of Sex Education on Adolescent Behavior," *Family Planning Perspectives*, 18:4 (July/August 1986), 169.

26. Planned Parenthood Federation of America, *A Five-Year Plan: 1976–1980*.

27. Alfred Moran, Executive Vice-President, Planned Parenthood of New York, *Planned Parenthood News*, Summer 1979.

28. Planned Parenthood Federation of America, *1987 Annual Report*, 26–7.

29. Faye Wattleton, "Humanist of the Year" acceptance speech, *The Humanist*, July-August 1986.

30. Ibid.

31. See Grant, *Illusions*, 141–45; also Judie Brown, Robert G. Marshall, and Herbert Ratner, *Stop School Based Sex Clinics* (Stafford, VA: American Life League, 1987).

32. Grant, *Illusions*, 144.

33. Ibid.

34. Planned Parenthood Federation of America, *1987 Annual Report*, 29.

35. Ruff, *Aborting*, 14.

36. From a Planned Parenthood fundraising letter quoted in *Action Line* [Falls Church, VA: Christian Action Council], February 28, 1989.

Chapter 4: National Organization for Women and Other Hard-Core Feminists

1. Excerpts from Kalamazoo Area NOW Chapter Newsletter, June—July 1989.

2. Mary Pride, *The Way Home* (Westchester, IL: Crossway Books, 1985), 3. While I do not agree with every jot and tittle of this book, it nevertheless is must reading for husbands and wives who want to order their home according to Biblical patterns.

3. Early feminist literature includes: Mary Wollstonecraft, *A Vindication of the Rights of Woman* (1782); Cornelius Agrippa, *The Superior Excellence of Women Over Men* (16th century); Marie Le Jars de Gournay, *Egalite' des hommes et des femmes* (1622) and *Grief des dames* (1626); Poulain de la Barre, *D'elegalite des deux sexes* (1673). For a discussion of these works and an anthology of later American feminist writings, see Miriam Schneir, *Feminism: The Essential Historical Writings* (NY: Random House, 1972).

4. Betty Steele, *The Feminist Takeover* (Waite Park, NY: Park Press, Inc., 1987), 42.

5. Ibid., 43.

6. Ibid., 14.

7. Valerie Solanis, "SCUM Manifesto," in ed. Robin Morgan, *Sisterhood is Powerful* (New York: Vintage, 1970), 514—15, 519.

8. Pamela Kearan, "Man Hating," *Notes from the Second Year*, 1970.

9. Solanis, 516–7.

10. National Organization for Women, 1989 National Conference official program, 10–13.

11. Evans & Novak, "Eleanor Smeal: Housewife who heads feminists groups wants women to "raise hell," *Star*, Tarrytown, New York, September 3, 1985.

12. Mary O'Brien, *Feminism in Canada: From Pressure to Politics* (ed. Angela R. Miles, Geraldine Finn (Montreal: Black Rose Books, 1982), 261.

13. Steele, *Takeover*, 57.

14. Ibid., 53.

15. NOW 1989 National Conference official program, 12.

16. Garrett Hardin as quoted by James Webber in *Grow or Die!* (New Rochelle, NY: Arlington House Publishers, 1977), 184.

17. Pride, *Way Home*, 85.

18. Steele, *Takeover*, 59.

19. Ibid., 111.

20. Sheila Cronan, "Marriage," in ed. Koedt, *Radical Feminism* (New York: Quadrangle, 1973), 219–220.

21. Steele, *Takeover*, 53.

22. Ibid., 12.

23. "Oprah Winfrey," July 6, 1989.

24. People of Destiny, September/October 1984, 5.

25. "Oprah Winfrey", July 6, 1989.

26. Pride, *Way Home*, 58–63.

27. *The Wanderer*, August 10, 1989, 5.

28. NOW 1989 National Conference official program, 10.

29. Naomi Goldenberg, *Changing of the Gods: Feminism and the End of Traditional Religions* (Boston: Beacon Press, 1979), 92.

30. Pride, *Way Home*, 7.

31. Goldenberg, *Changing of the Gods*, 4.

Chapter 5: What Is the ACLU?

1. *ACLU Annual Report*, 1984-1985, pp. 8-16.

2. Although the ACLU was not chartered in its present form until January 1920, it had existed in various other guises ever since Roger Nash Baldwin came to New York and established the Bureau for Conscientious Objectors for the American Union Against Militarism in 1917. See Chapter Four for further details.

3. *ACLU Annual Report*, 1986-1987, p. 18.

4. Compared with the supporting memberships of Phyllis Schlafley's Eagle Forum, Beverly LaHaye's Concerned Women for America, Jerry Nim's Moral Majority, Jerry Falwell's Liberty Federation, Don Wildmon's American Family Federation, Randall Terry's Operation Rescue, James Dobson's Focus on the Family, Pat Robertson's 700 Club, D. James Kennedy's Coral Ridge Ministries, and John Whitehead's Rutherford Institute, the ACLU membership is miniscule at best.

5. *ACLU Annual Report*, 1986-87, pp. 16-18.

6. *Insight Magazine*, March 21, 1988, p. 15.

7. *The New York Times*, October 2, 1988.

8. Quoted in a fund raising letter from Barry Steinhardt, Executive Director, ACLU of Pennsylvania, Spring 1986.

9. As an example of this kind of influence see the case examples in Chapter One.

10. Nat Hentoff, "The Enemy Within the ACLU," *Sweet Land of Liberty*, n.d.

11. *ACLU Annual Report*, 1986-1987, p. 10.

12. William A. Donohue, *The Politics of the American Civil Liberties Union* (New Brunswick, NJ: Transaction Books, 1985), p. 36.

13. Ibid.

14. *Civil Liberty: A Statement defining the Position of the ACLU on the issues in the United States Today*, July 1920.

15. Ibid, 39.

16. Ibid, 94.

17. See *The Washington Times*, October 29, 1982; and Norman Dorsen, ed., *Our Endangered Rights: The ACLU Report on Civil Liberties Today* (New York: Pantheon Boks, 1984).

18. *The Wall Street Journal*, October 20, 1988.

19. *The New York Times*, October 2, 1988.

20. *ACLU Briefing Paper*, no. 1, 1987, p. 1.

21. Ibid.

22. Quoted in Peggy Lamson, *Roger Baldwin: Founder of the American Civil Liberties Union* (Boston: Houghton Mifflin, 1976), p. 192.

23. *Policy Guide of the American Civil Liberties Union*, 1986, pp. 222-232.

24. Ibid, 242-244.

25. Ibid, 434.

26. *Insight Magazine*, March 21, 1988.

27. *San Francisco Chronicle*, October 5, 1973.

28. *The Boston Globe*, February 27, 1984.

29. *Insight Magazine*, March 21, 1988.

30. Donohue, p. 5.

31. Ibid.

32. Ibid, 4.

33. *The New York Times*, October 2, 1988.

34. *ACLU Annual Report*, 1984-1985, p. 1.

35. Donohue, p. 49.

36. Ibid.

37. Ibid, 51.

38. *Policy Guide*, p. 95.

39. *ACLU Annual Report*, 1984-1985, p. 6.

40. It has often sided with those who wish to "prohibit the free exercise" of the Christian faith. See *The Washington Times*, October 29, 1982.

41. In the Watergate impeachment case, the ACLU proposed that President Nixon waive his right to refrain from incriminating testimony and that President Ford be stripped of his pardoning powers. See *The Boston Globe*, September 12, 1974.

42. *The Butler Eagle*, September 28, 1970.

43. *Operation Rescue News Brief*, March 1989.

44. *Policy Guide*, pp. 98-99.

45. Ibid, 100-101.

46. *ACLU Annual Report*, 1986-1987, p. 6.

47. Ibid, 9.

48. Ibid.

49. *Policy Guide*, pp. 334-361.

50. Ibid.

51. Ibid.

52. Donohue, pp. 102-103.

53. *Crossbow Magazine*, Spring 1978.

54. *Insight Magazine*, March 21, 1988.

55. *Conservative Digest*, December 1988.

56. *Operation Rescue Newsbrief*, March 1989.

57. *The Boston Herald*, April 6, 1988.

58. Janet Benshoof, et al, *Preserving the Right to Choose: How to Cope with Violence and Disruption at Abortion Clinics* (New York: ACLU Reproductive Freedom Project, 1986), pp. 34-35; and Janet Benshoof, et al, *Parental Notice Laws: Their Catastrophic Impact on Teenagers' Right to Abortion* (New York: ACLU Reproductive Freedom Project, 1986), pp. 8-9.

59. *Pittsburgh Post-Gazette*, September 22, 1981.

60. *The New York Times Magazine*, June 19, 1966.

61. *ACLU Briefing Paper*, no. 1, 1987.

62. *The Wall Street Journal*, March 29, 1965.

63. *Civil Liberties*, May 1961.

64. *World Magazine*, November 21, 1988.

65. *Accuracy in Media Report*, November 1988.

66. Lamson, 191.

67. Janet Benshoof, et al, *Preserving the Right to Choose* (New York: ACLU Reproductive Freedom Project, 1986).

68. *ACLU Annual Report*, 1986-1987, p. 27.

69. Ibid.

70. *ACLU Policy Guide*, p. 345.

71. Benshoof, pp. 13-14; *ACLU Policy Guide*, p. 87.

72. Quotes taken from Hugo Adam Bedau, *The Case Against the Death Penalty* (New York: ACLU, 1984), p. 2.

73. Ibid, 3.

74. Ibid, 3-4.

75. Ibid, 4.

76. *ACLU Policy Guide*, pp. 345-348; Benshoof, pp. 3-50; and Lynn Paltrow, et al, *Parental Notice Laws* (New York: ACLU Reproductive Freedom Project, 1986), pp. 1-28.

77. Benshoof, pp. 5, 18-22; and *ACLU Policy Guide*, p. 87.

78. Benshoof, pp. 11, 13, 16-17; and *ACLU Policy Guide*, pp. 334-342.

79. *Butler Eagle*, September 28, 1970; and *Operation Rescue News Briefs*, March 1989.

Chapter 6: Hired Assassins and Their Blood-Bought Prophets

1. See William Brennan, *The Abortion Holocaust* (St. Louis: Landmark Press, 1983).

2. Judith Areen, Patricia A. King, Steven Goldberg and Alexander Morgan Capron, *Law, Science and Medicine* (Mineola, NY: The Foundation Press, Inc.), 273.

3. Ibid., 275–6.

4. Bernard Nathanson, speech on March 22, 1989, Anaheim, California.

5. Bernard Nathanson, *The Abortion Papers* (New York: Frederick Fell Publishers, Inc., 1983), 164.

6. Ibid.

7. Marvin Olasky, *The Press and Abortion: 1838–1988* (Hillsdale, NJ: Lawrence Ehrlbaum Associates, 1988), 29.

8. Nathanson, *Papers*, 165.

9. Ibid., 166.

10. Ibid., 3.

11. Ibid., 167.

12. It is interesting to note that the AMA at its annual meeting on December 6, 1989 asserted that the "early termination of pregnancy [read: murder of an unborn child] is a medical matter . . . subject to the patient's informed consent."

13. Nathanson, *Papers*, 170.

14. Ibid., 15.

15. *New York Times*, January 8, 1990, A1.

16. Nathanson, *Papers*, 41.

17. Ibid., 41–2.

18. Herbert Ratner, "A Public Health Physician Views Abortion," *Child and Family* 7 (Winter 1968), 3.

19. Mary S. Calderone, "Illegal Abortion as a Public Health Problem, " *American Journal of Public Health* 50 (July 1960), 948–54.

20. Nathanson, *Papers*, 42.

21 Ibid., 40.

22. Ibid.

23. Ibid., 184.

24. Ibid., 185.

25. Ibid.

26. Ibid., 177.

27. Ibid., 178–9.

28. Ibid., 191.

Chapter 7: ABC, NBC, CBS: Ministries of Propaganda

1. Marvin Olasky, *The Prodigal Press* (Westchester, IL: Crossway Books, 1988), 116.

2. *Between the Lines*, July 1988.

3. *America*, May 5, 1962.

4. *New York Times*, April 6, 1965.

5. Ibid.

6. *New York Times*, April 7, 1965.

7. *New York Times*, June 6, 1969.

8. Quoted in Marvin Olasky, *The Prodigal Press*, 59.

9. Ibid.

10 Ibid.

11. *MediaWatch*, May 1989.

12. Ibid.

13. *Adweek,* March 6, 1989.

14. *New York Daily News,* May 22, 1989.

15 *Boston Globe,* January 31, 1985.

16. *All About Issues,* June/July 1989.

17. *MediaWatch,* November 1989.

18. Ibid.

19. "Media Hanky-Blanky," *National Right to Life News,* November 2, 1989, 2.

20. *MediaWatch,* November 1989.

21. In fact, Representative Courter has now become a full-fledged traitor to the children. Yes, he's pro-death. *The Washington Post,* dated February 15, 1990, quotes Rep. Courter, "[I have] ultimately conclude[d] that freedom to choose was not only correct, but more consistent with my overall philosophy of individual liberty and freedom; a philosophy that heralds the power and freedom of the individual conscience, a conscience free from intrusive government regulation."

22. *Citizen,* Focus on the Family, December 1989.

23. *CWA News Digest,* February 1990.

24. *RSC Bulletin,* Republican Study Committee, October 13, 1989.

25. *Action Line,* Christian Action Council, September 19, 1989.

26. *RSC Bulletin.*

27. *ALL News,* October 5, 1989.

28. *MediaWatch,* April 1989.

29. *New York Times,* March 25, 1978, 37.

30 Ibid.

31. *American Family Association Journal,* July 1989.

32. See *MediaWatch:* July 1988, January 1989, May 1989, January 1990.

Chapter 8: The Print Media: The Lapdogs of the Death Peddlers

1. Marvin Olasky, *The Press and Abortion: 1838–1988,* 26.

2. Ibid., 25.

3. Ibid., 29.

4. Ibid., 37.

5. Ibid., 37–8.

6. Ibid., 25.

7. Ibid., 41.

8. Marvin Olasky, *The Press and Abortion: 1838–1988,* 34–5.

9. Ibid., 39.

10. See Marvin Olasky, *Prodigal Press,* Chapter 6.

11. Mary S. Calderone, *American Journal of Public Health,* 949.

12. *New York Times,* July 4, 1989.

13. Marvin Olasky, *Prodigal Press,* 118.

14. Ibid., 134.

15. Ibid.

16. Ibid.

17. Ibid., 135. Note that these series of articles led pro-death legislators in Illinois to work for the passage of strict medical regulations for abortion mills—the same regulations which later were challenged by abortionists (with widespread pro-death support) and recently gutted when Turnock v. Ragsdale was settled out of court prior to its Supreme Court hearing.

18. Dr. & Mrs. J. C. Wilke, *Abortion Questions & Answers* (Cincinnati, OH: Hayes Publishing Company, Inc., 1988), 76.

19. William Brennan, *The Abortion Holocaust: Today's Final Solution* (St. Louis: Landmark Press, 1983), 63–65.

20. Marvin Olasky, *Prodigal Press,* 128.

21. Ibid.

22. *MediaWatch,* May 1989.

23. "Pro-lifer 'show' uses fetuses—and the media," *Chicago Sun-Times,* May 7, 1987, 7.

24. Linda Greenhouse, *New York Times Magazine,* June 28, 1970, 7.

25. *Between the Lines,* July 1989.

26. *New York Times,* April 26, 1978, II: 10.

27. *MediaWatch,* May 1989.

28. *Washington Post,* April 9, 1989.

29. *Between the Lines,* May 1989.

30. *MediaWatch,* May 1989.

31. Charles Paul Freund, *Washington Post,* April 25, 1989.

32. *Wall Street Journal,* December 8, 1988.

33. Getting arrested is never the objective; rescuing children is. This is why we speak of risking arrest.

34. An excellent overview of the current media bias is contained in David Shaw's four-part series in the *Los Angelos Times,* July 1—4, 1990.

Chapter 9: The Courts: A New Breed of Tyrants

1. The memo from Potter Stewart to Harry Blackmun, dated December 14, 1972, was contained in William O. Douglas's confidential Supreme Court papers.

2. *Roe v. Wade*, 410 U.S. 113, 222 (1973) (White, J., dissenting).

3. Speech by Justice Charles E. Hughes at Elmira, NY, on May 7, 1907.

4. Justice Oliver Wendell Holmes, *Harvard Law Review*, XL (1918) quoted in Francis Schaeffer, *A Christian Manifesto* (Westchester, IL: Crossway Books, 1982), 27.

5. Quoted in *The Citizen's Handbook*, Grapevine Publications.

6. *New York Journal*, Spring 1788.

7 *Northeast Women's Center, Inc. v. Michael McMonagle, et. al.*, E. D. Penn., Civil Action No. 85-4845.

8. Chief Justice William Rehnquist, "Get Rico Cases Out of My Courtroom," *Wall Street Journal*, May 19, 1989, A14.

9. *New York Times*, October 11, 1989.

10. Several senators and congressmen are working to revise the RICO statutes so that they cannot be abused in this fashion, but the process has been torturously slow.

11. "RICO, First Blood?," *Wall Street Journal*, November 11, 1989, A26.

12. My own thinking has evolved considerably on this issue, with many thanks to Michael McMonagle. I used to speak of "civil disobedience"; but now I am convinced that we are not breaking any laws, because "trespassing" to save a life (or put out a fire!) does not constitute a crime.

13. 88 Civ. 3071 (R.J.W.), October 7, 1988.

14. Judge Hekman has also written a book on this topic, *Justice for the Unborn* (Servant Books, Ann Arbor, 1984).

15. *In the matter of Jane Roe*, Kent County Probate Court, Grand Rapids, MI, October 25, 1982.

16. St. Louis Circuit Court, St. Louis County, MO, August 16, 1989.

17. Missouri State Circuit Court, August 24, 1989.

18. *Charlotte Observer*, May 23, 1989.

19. *Charlotte Observer*, June 11, 1989.

Chapter 10: Police, Prisons Guards, and Pain

1. The names of certain of the victims in this chapter have been changed to protect them from future reprisals. Their stories remain frightening and enraging.

2. *New York Times*, "Incident at Selma," March 9, 1965.

3. According to Michael McMonagle who has had a working relationship with Sergeant Leskowski for several years.

4. *FBI Law Enforcement Bulletin*, "Policing Demonstrations," August 1989.

5. See *Operation Rescue*, chapter 5.

6. Ibid., 234–5.

7. Statement by Reverend Joseph Foreman.

8. *Atlanta Journal-Constitution*, October 2, 1988, 1C.

9. Videotaped interview with victim, CDR Communications, Inc., September 8, 1989.

10. *Atlanta Journal-Constitution*, October 7, 1988, 1A.

11. "20/20," October 28, 1988.

12. Ibid.

13. *Gwinnett Daily News*, October 6, 1989, 1A.

14. *Atlanta Journal-Constitution*, October 7, 1988, 1A.

15. Phone conversation with victim, February 3, 1989.

16. See chapter 1, "Letter from Los Angeles Jail, " for more details.

17. *Los Angeles Times*, August 29, 1989, II-3.

18. *Los Angeles Times*, March 11, 1989, II-3.

19. Videotaped interview, CDR Communications, Inc.

20. The quote is from Captain McKinley's sworn statement.

21. *Los Angeles Times*, March 26, 1989, I-3.

22. *Orange County Register*, March 26, 1989, 24.

23. The quote is from Captain McKinley's sworn statement. The statement does not indicate a causal relationship. This is a conclusion drawn by the author.

24. Videotaped interview with Samuel B. Casey, CDR Communications, Inc., August 7, 1989.

25. Videotaped interview with Joseph Foreman, CDR Communications, Inc., September 8, 1989.

26. Videotaped interview with victim, CDR Communications, Inc., August 7, 1989.

27. Videotaped interview with victim, CDR Communications, Inc., August 22, 1989.

28. Videotaped interview with victim, CDR Communications, Inc., August 22, 1989.

29. Videotaped interview with victim, CDR Communications, Inc., August 21, 1989.

30. Videotaped interview with victim, CDR Communications, Inc., August 21, 1989.

31. Videotaped interview with lawyer, CDR Communications, Inc., August 21, 1989.

32. Videotaped interview with victim, CDR Communications, Inc., August 21, 1989.

33. Ibid.

34. William F. Buckley, *Newark Star-Ledger*, July 23, 1989.

35. Videotaped interview with victim, CDR Communications, Inc., August 21, 1989.

36. Videotaped interview with victim, CDR Communications, Inc., August 22, 1989.

37. Videotaped interview with victim, CDR Communications, Inc., August 21, 1989.

38. Videotaped interview with lawyer, CDR Communications, Inc.

39. Ibid.

40. *Hartford Courant*, June 18, 1989.

41. Videotaped interview with victim, CDR Communications, Inc., August 21, 1989.

42. *Staten Island Advance*, June 20, 1989.

43. *West Hartford News*, June 22, 1989.

44. Nat Hentoff, "The Painful Education of a Schoolteacher," *Washington Post*, September 2, 1989, A25.

45. *Herald* (New Britain, CT), June 20, 1989.

46. *West Hartford News*, June 22, 1989.

47. West Hartford Town Council Resolution adopted unanimously at Council meeting June 27, 1989.

48. *West Hartford News*, June 19, 1989.

49. Videotaped interview with victim, CDR Communications, Inc.

50. Phone interview with Reverend Tucci, February 9, 1990.

51 Sworn affidavit by victim.

52 Civil Action 85-411, U.S. District Court in Western District of Pennsylvania; fined $5,000.00.

53. Videotaped interview with Rosanna Weissart, CDR Communications, Inc., July 25, 1989.

54. Videotaped interview with friend of victim, CDR Communications, Inc., July 25, 1989.

55. Sworn affidavit by victim.

56. Sworn affidavit by victim.

57. Sworn affidavit by victim.

58. Sworn affidavit by victim.

59. Sworn affidavit by victim.

60. Sworn affidavit by victim.

61. Sworn affidavit by victim.

62. Sworn affidavit by victim.

63. Sworn affidavit by victim.

64. Sworn affidavit by victim.

65. Sworn affidavit by victim.

66. Sworn affidavit by victim.

67. Sworn affidavit by victim.

68. Videotaped interview with victim, CDR Communications, Inc., July 25, 1989.

69. Videotaped interview with victim, CDR Communications, Inc., July 25, 1989.

70. *Wall Street Journal*, August 18, 1989, A-6.

71. Ibid.

72. *Congressional Quarterly*, October 21, 1989, 2793.

73. William F. Buckley, *Newark Star Ledger*, July 23, 1989.

74. *Congressional Quarterly*, October 21, 1989, 2795.

75. Don Feder, *Boston Herald*, June 29, 1989.

76. Letter dated June 27, 1989.

77. *The Congressional Record* - House, H4011, July 20, 1989.

78. *The Congressional Record* - Senate, S11357, September 19, 1989.

79. Ibid.

80. Hentoff, "Schoolteacher"

81 "Anti-Abortion Protest Groups Win Help From Congress," *Congressional Quarterly*, October 21, 1989, 2794.

82. *Wall Street Journal*, August 18, 1989, A-6.

Chapter 11: Wolves in Sheep's Clothing

1. George Grant, *Grand Illusions* (Brentwood, TN: Wolgemuth & Hyatt, 1989), 190–1.

2. Ibid., 195.

3. *RCAR Fact Sheet* (Washington, DC: Religious Coalition for Abortion Rights).

4. Dr. Paul D. Simmons, *Personhood, the Bible & the Abortion Debate* (Washington, DC: Religious Coalition for Abortion Rights, 1987), 8.

5. Ibid., 17.

6. Ibid.

7. Ibid., 4.

8. *Religious Freedom and the Abortion Controversy* (Washington, DC: Religious Coalition for Abortion Rights).

9. *RCAR Fact Sheet.*

10. *Social Principles* (Washington, DC: The General Board for Church and Society), 9.

11. Ibid.

12. *Religious Freedom and the Abortion Controversy* (Washington, DC: Religious Coalition for Abortion Rights).

13. *Special Report #61* (Gaithersburg, MD: Human Life International), 6.

Chapter 12: Reeds in the Wind

1. In this context, to engage in "civil disobedience" is simply to disobey civil laws.

2. Robespierre', the leader of the French Revolution, was a godless reprobate who violently overthrew the French monarchy and sought to destroy any remnant of Christianity.

3. *The Matthew Henry Commentary* (Grand Rapids, MI: Zondervan, 1961), 134.

Chapter 15: The Rescue Movement

1. See chapter 12, "Reeds in the Wind," especially the rebuttal of Bill Gothard's arguments.

2. Joseph Morecraft has referred to our tactics as "Marxist and Hegelian." See *The Council of Chalcedon* (December 1988), 15.

3. There is, however, much overlap in ideology and personnel.

4. *Facts about Abortion,* provided by Southern Tier Women's Services (Vestal, NY).

5. David C. Reardon, *Aborted Women: Silent No More* (Westchester, IL: Crossway Books, 1987).

6. If someone you know has been injured in an abortion, she can still sue for damages regardless of the waiver. Suing abortionists is one means to "inspire" them to quit killing children.

7. See *Operation Rescue*, chapter 8, "Their Blood Cries Out".

8. See *Operation Rescue*, chapter 10, "A Remnant—That's All We Need".

9. See *Operation Rescue*, chapter 8.

10. *The Gathering Storm*, vol. 1 *The Second World War* (Boston, MA: Cooperation Publishing Company, Houghton Mifflin, 1948), 348.

Chapter 16: Turning the Tide of Injustice

1. See Merton L. Dillon, *The Abolitionists* (Dekalb, IL: Northern University Press, 1974).

2. Financial assistance for the families of Christians imprisoned in communist nations for their faith may be directed to: Christian Missions to the Communist World, PO Box 938, Middleburg, IN 46540.

3. Richard Wurmbrand, *Tortured for Christ* (Glendale, CA: Diane Books, 1967), 50.

Chapter 17: Grassroots Reformation

1. See Joseph Scheidler, *Closed: 99 Ways to Stop Abortion* (Chicago: Regnery Books, 1985).

Epilogue: The Inevitable?

1. George Grant, *The Changing of the Guard* (Tyler, TX: Dominion Press, 1987), 39.

Appendix: What You See Is What You Get

1. Kathryn I. Pyle, "Newspaper Coverage of Operation Rescue Activities in Atlanta, October 1988: A Case Study in Bias in Reporting," (Master's Thesis: Regents University), May, 1989, 52.

2. Ibid, 69, 97.

3. Marvin Olasky, *The Press and Abortion: 1838–1988*, 114.

ABOUT THE AUTHOR

R andall A. Terry was born on April 25, 1959. He graduated from Elim Bible Institute in Lima, New York. Randall Terry is the founder and executive director of Operation Rescue National.

Mr. Terry has been arrested thirty-five times in nine cities, and he has spent seven months in jail. Four of those months were at a prison work camp. While jailed for his pro-life activism, Randall has written two books, *Operation Rescue* and *Accessory to Murder*. He has also written several articles and a manual on pro-life activism entitled *To Rescue the Children*.

Mr. Terry has appeared on ABC's "Nightline," CBN's "700 Club," "Straight Talk," the "Oprah Winfrey Show," the "Morton Downey Jr. Show," CNN's "Crossfire," "20/20," "48 Hours," and PBS has broadcast news documentaries featuring Mr. Terry. He has also had time on radio programs such as Dr. James Dobson's *Focus on the Family* and the *On the Line* show.

The typeface for the text of this book is *Baskerville*. Its creator, John Baskerville (1706–1775), broke with tradition to reflect in his type the rounder, yet more sharply cut lettering of eighteenth-century stone inscriptions and copy books. The type foreshadows modern design in such novel characteristics as the increase in contrast between thick and thin strokes and the shifting of stress from the diagonal to the vertical strokes. Realizing that this new style of letter would be most effective if cleanly printed on smooth paper with genuinely black ink, he built his own presses, developed a method of hot pressing the printed sheet to a smooth, glossy finish, and experimented with special inks. However, Baskerville did not enter into general commercial use in England until 1923.

Substantive Editing:
Michael S. Hyatt

Copy Editing:
Peggy Moon

Cover Design:
Steve Diggs & Friends
Nashville, Tennessee

Page Composition:
Xerox Ventura Publisher
Printware 720 IQ Laser Printer

Printing and Binding:
Maple-Vail Book Manufacturing Group
York, Pennsylvania

Cover Printing:
Strine Printing
York, Pennsylvania